P9-DGW-569

Alaska

John Murray
Photography by Don Pitcher

Additional writing and photography
by Nick Jans

COMPASS AMERICAN GUIDES
An imprint of Fodor's Travel Publications

Compass American Guides: Alaska

Editor: Kristin Moehlmann, Jennifer Paull
Designer: Tina R. Malaney
Compass Editorial Director: Paul Eisenberg
Compass Creative Director: Fabrizio La Rocca
Photo Editor and Archival Researcher: Melanie Marin
Map Design: Mark Stroud, Moon Street Cartography

Cover photo: Don Pitcher

Copyright © 2008 Fodor's Travel, a division of Random House, Inc.
Maps copyright © 2008 Fodor's Travel, a division of Random House, Inc.

Compass American Guides and colophon are registered trademarks of Random House, Inc.
Fodor's Travel is a division of Random House, Inc.

All rights reserved. Published in the United States by Fodor's Travel, a division of Random House, Inc., and simultaneously in Canada by Random House of Canada Limited, Toronto. Distributed by Random House, Inc., New York.

No maps, illustrations, or other portions of this book may be reproduced in any form without written permission from the publisher.

Fifth Edition
ISBN 978–1–4000–0736–3
ISSN 1558–0601

The details in this book are based on information supplied to us at press time, but changes occur all the time, and the publisher cannot accept responsibility for facts that become outdated or for inadvertent errors or omissions.

Compass American Guides, 1745 Broadway, New York, NY 10019
PRINTED IN CHINA BY TWIN AGE LIMITED

10 9 8 7 6 5 4 3 2 1

Dedicated to four great Alaskans:
Joe Firmin, Lynn Castle, Billy Campbell, and Michio Hoshino

C O N T E N T S

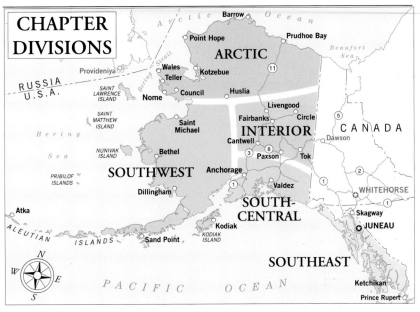

CHAPTER DIVISIONS

Arctic Ocean · Barrow · Point Hope · Prudhoe Bay · *Beaufort Sea*

ARCTIC

Provideniya · Wales · Teller · Kotzebue · Council · Huslia · Livengood · Fairbanks · Circle · Dawson

RUSSIA / U.S.A.

SAINT LAWRENCE ISLAND · Nome · Saint Michael · **INTERIOR** · Cantwell · Paxson · Tok · CANADA

SAINT MATTHEW ISLAND

Bering Sea

NUNIVAK ISLAND · Bethel

PRIBILOF ISLANDS · **SOUTHWEST** · Anchorage · Valdez · WHITEHORSE

Atka · Dillingham · **SOUTH-CENTRAL** · Skagway · JUNEAU

ALEUTIAN ISLANDS · Sand Point · Kodiak · KODIAK ISLAND

SOUTHEAST

PACIFIC OCEAN · Ketchikan · Prince Rupert

N W E S

Literary Extracts

Topical Essays and Sidebars

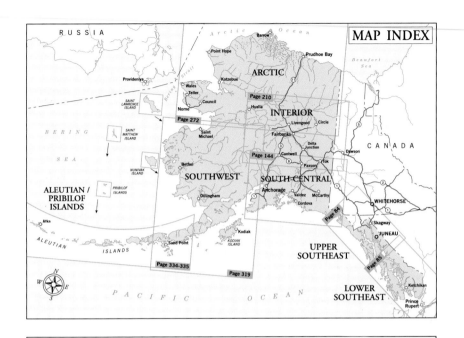

Maps

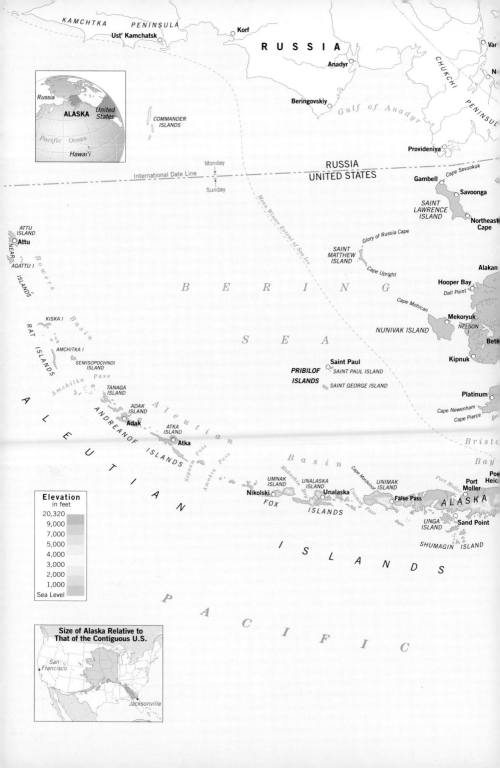

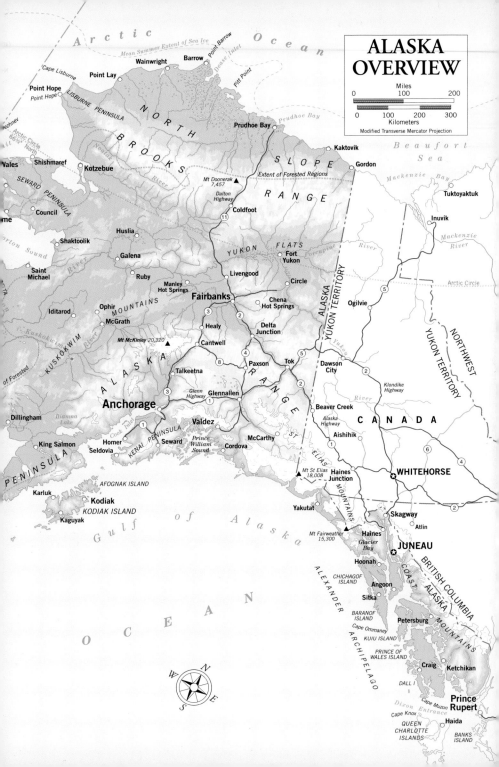

O V E R V I E W

A subcontinent that links Asia and North America, Alaska is larger than Texas, California, and Montana combined. At its center are the 20,320-foot Mount McKinley and the mighty Yukon River. Alaska is an outdoor lover's dream—an immense wilderness, where a visitor may travel as much by floatplane and boat as by car. Bears are at home here, as are caribou, moose, and an abundance of other creatures that dwell on land, sea, or sky. Cities and towns dot the wilderness, but even in urban Anchorage, an unspoiled landscape is always close at hand.

■ **SOUTHEAST AND THE INSIDE PASSAGE** *pages 82–139*
Along Alaska's southeastern Panhandle lie thousands of forest-draped islands and small towns set on emerald-green bays. Ferries and cruise ships ply the Inside Passage, passing islands and fjords where whales breach and bears can be seen fishing in coastal waters. Nearby small towns offer fishing tours and "flightseeing," and galleries sell Eskimo and Tlingit art. Juneau, the only state capital in the continental United States that cannot be reached by road, arguably enjoys the most spectacular setting of any American city. At the northern extremity of the Panhandle is magnificent Glacier Bay.

■ **SOUTH-CENTRAL** *pages 140–207*
With a population of more than 260,000, Anchorage is a bustling metropolis with good restaurants and modern accommodations. Alaska's largest city, it serves as a jumping-off point for excursions to Denali National Park and Preserve, the beautiful Kenai Peninsula, and Prince William Sound.

■ **INTERIOR** *pages 208–269*
Embracing mountain and taiga, the heartland is dominated by magnificent Mount McKinley (Denali), the highest mountain in North America. The surrounding national park is the habitat of grizzlies and brown bears, wolves, caribou, moose, and Dall sheep. Fairbanks is the Interior's only sizeable city. The area's most famous sport is mushing, or dogsledding; its most popular sports are salmon fishing and big-game hunting, both of which are as close as the nearest bush pilot's plane.

THE GREAT GIFT

My prayer is that Alaska will not lose the heart-nourishing friendliness of her youth—that her people will always care for one another, her towns remain friendly and not completely ruled by the dollar—and that her great wild places will remain great, and wild, and free, where wolf and caribou, wolverine and grizzly bear, and all the Arctic blossoms may live on in the delicate balance which supported them long before impetuous man appeared in the North. This is the great gift Alaska can give to the harassed world.

–Margaret Murie, *Two in the Far North, 1962*

■ **THE ARCTIC** *pages 270–315*

Tundra stretches in a great arc along the Arctic Ocean from the Bering land bridge—where hunters of the Asian steppe crossed into North America as early as 30,000 years ago—to Barrow, where the sun doesn't set 83 days of the year. Home to Inupiat (Eskimo) culture, as well as to enormous herds of caribou, and polar bears who live on the ice floes, this vast and empty space has undeniable magic for those who experience its wildness. Remote villages, national parks, and wilderness lodges in this area are reached via the Dalton Highway or bush plane.

■ **SOUTHWEST** *pages 316–347*

This enormous expanse of land remains pristine and remote. Here are active volcanoes, vast areas of tundra, the Aleutian Islands inhabited by millions of seabirds, and seas crowded with walrus, seal, and whale. Kodiak Island, thought by early explorers to resemble Ireland, is home to the enormous Alaskan brown bear.

An iceberg in Tracy Arm Fjord, one of the most popular day-trip destinations from Juneau.

INTRODUCTION

Alaska represents one of the last unspoiled wildernesses on earth, a vignette of the primordial world. Imagine tens of thousands of caribou streaming through mountain passes, dozens of brown bears fishing rivers thick with salmon, or flocks of mountain goats grazing above a glacier larger than Rhode Island. As volcanoes vent ash and smoke, the ghostly green northern lights dance among the stars. In Alaska you will see North America in its morning freshness, when the rivers had no dams and the trees had yet to feel the ax, and not one animal had ever heard a human voice. You may feel that you've gone back in time, that you're seeing the world as you did as a child—when everything was still new, and wonderful, and incredibly big.

Everything in Alaska is off the scale. The state sprawls across 21 degrees of latitude and 43 degrees of longitude. Consider that for a moment: it is more than 2,400 miles across and 1,400 miles from north to south! From the Alaskan island of Little Diomede, the nearest Russian territory is less than three miles away. Portions of Alaska lie almost 1,000 miles west of the Hawaiian Islands. And yet, in its southern extremity, Alaska is only an hour's flight from Seattle, Washington. If the state were to be superimposed on the Lower 48, the southeast tip would rest along the Georgia coast and the Aleutians would extend past Los Angeles into the Pacific Ocean.

In Alaska are the largest bears in the world, the biggest salmon in the world, the largest national parks, forests, and wildlife refuges in the world, the largest gatherings of bald eagles in the world. And so on. Alaska is not so much a continental peninsula as it is a massive sub-continent. It extends far into the Pacific, nearly to Asia, and, in terms of fauna, flora, and geography, is sometimes more Siberian than North American. Yet, myriad ecosystems can be found in the state, from shadowy rain forest to dry frigid tundra, from apocalyptic volcanic wasteland to bird-filled salt marsh, from spectacular glacial fjord to rolling subarctic taiga.

The purpose of this book is to guide you through a state that overwhelms even lifelong residents. Because the state is so large and the recreational opportunities so diverse, this book is, of necessity, selective rather than comprehensive. What I have

The Alaska Range stretches across a vast area of interior Alaska.

tried to do is give you the benefit of my half-dozen years in Alaska, a period during which I traveled from the frosty arctic coast to the forested tip of the Kenai Peninsula, from the wind-swept Canadian border across the interior wilderness, from a nameless mountain in the Arctic National Wildlife Refuge to the crowded streets of Anchorage.

Although travel in Alaska is accomplished quite simply via the road system, I would encourage visitors also to leave the roads and hike in the backcountry, or take an hour-long flightseeing trip, or float a river, or hire a fishing boat at one of the many seaside villages. In this way you will see the "true Alaska," a timeless, beautiful realm beyond the reach of civilization, a realm where you may watch two bull moose lock antlers in the twilight, or catch a glimpse of a wolf pack patrolling its home territory, or spot a humpback whale breaching in a remote bay.

"The spell of Alaska," Ella Higginson wrote in 1908, "falls upon every lover of beauty who has voyaged along these far northern snow-pearled shores . . . or who has drifted down the mighty rivers of the interior which flow, bell-toned and lonely, to the sea . . . . No writer has ever described Alaska; no one writer ever will; but each must do his share, according to the spell that the country casts upon him." This book has been written in the spirit of Higginson's eloquent passage. Alaska is a place that will change you forever, if you let it, and each person must, as Higginson suggests, experience that change in a different way. For me, the joy of Alaska has always been in the small things—picking wild blueberries on the tundra domes around Fairbanks in the fall, feeling the sharp tug of a salmon while fishing the Kenai, spotting a bald eagle as it glides through the clouds, watching the delicate auroras play against the January constellations, listening to a wolf serenade the moon in the Alaska Range. Such memories return, reminding me of the rare abundance and innocence that are wild Alaska. Come with me, and let's roam this incredible state, which is as much a state of mind as it is a state of the Union.

Skunk cabbage growing near Ketchikan, in the rain forest of Southeast Alaska.

H I S T O R Y

My islands, you are my islands. The sky over them in the morning today is joyous. Just so is the morning of today. If I shall live henceforth, let them be just so in memory.

—*Lines from an Aleut song, 1840*

Imagine a summer day 40,000 years ago. You are standing on the low grassy hills north of Mount McKinley. A cold wind is blowing from the west. The sun is high in the sky. The scenery appears much as it does today. But take a closer look. What are those animals feeding along the river? How could there be elephants in the subarctic? You climb a knoll, close the distance. Yes, they are definitely a form of elephant, quietly browsing the fresh green willow and birch leaves. But these odd pachyderms are covered with shaggy brown fur. And their ivory tusks are different. They curve upward and then inward, and finally cross at the tips. The leader, the old gray female, has taken notice of you. Her tattered ears are flared, her flexible trunk raised warily. She is listening closely, taking your scent, assessing your intentions. Her eyes may be small but they see far. In that high-domed skull is the well-developed brain of a woolly mammoth. Don't step too close. Keep walking.

What else do you see in the McKinley Valley, part of a corridor leading through glaciers toward warmer land to the south? A steppe bison with the headgear of a Texas longhorn and a thick coat like a musk ox? A yak? A herd of wild Asiatic horses? A family of animals that resemble camels? A trio of lions? A curmudgeonly cave bear? A pack of dire wolves patrolling the riverbanks? Perhaps you'll notice a saber-toothed cat and her young ones devouring a ground sloth, a pair of giant condors circling on a thermal, a stag-moose with vast palmate antlers, or a beaver the size of a black bear.

This fantastic bestiary did exist in Alaska, and not very long ago in terms of geologic time. This was during the last ice age, the period in which human beings came out of Africa and spread through Europe and Asia to become the dominant species on earth. Even today, the arctic ice preserves some of these ancient animal bodies intact. More than once in recent history, modern scientists have had the chance to gaze upon a frozen, well-preserved mammoth.

■ HUNTERS CROSS THE LAND BRIDGE

Perhaps 10,000 years after that summer day near Denali, a small band of lean, sturdy folk walked about 60 miles over a narrow stretch of tundra, crossing from Asia into North America. The climate had recently grown colder—locking up more water in ice, lowering the ocean's water level, and leaving a dry passageway between the two continents. The emigrants were Asiatic people, and they carried all they owned with them. Alert, wolfish-looking animals, distant ancestors of the modern dog, patrolled ahead of the clan. The leaders were no doubt pleased with the widening valley between the glaciers that they found to the east. For one thing, the land forms, fauna, and flora were the same as those in northeastern Siberia. For another, there were no other people around to hunt the game.

These hunters were only one of successive waves of nomadic people who crossed into the New World. Though no exact dates will ever be certain, some

This painting of a Siberian Koryuk village, done in 1892 by artist George A. Frost, shows nomadic tribespeople and their reindeer, which are domesticated caribou. Alaska's early inhabitants migrated from Siberia, as did the caribou the Eskimos and Indians hunt today.

John Webber, the shipboard artist with Capt. James Cook's expedition in 1778, created this portrait of a man from Nootka Sound, in present-day British Columbia.

A few months later, on the same expedition, Webber drew this portrait of a woman from Unalaska, in the Aleutian Islands.

scientists place the first migration as early as 30,000 years ago. There were perhaps five or six great waves of arrivals, each with very different tribal groups bringing different traditions and different languages. Each new invasion of outsiders may have spurred others to move east or south. Some turned inland, crossing the broad rivers by boat in summer and by sleds across the ice in winter. Some no doubt used ocean-going kayaks or long boats to move south along the coast of Canada and the Pacific Northwest. They explored mountains, penetrated forests, discovered valleys, formed alliances, fought battles, settled in new homelands, celebrated marriages, had children, buried the dead, told stories, repeated histories, invented myths.

Much of their culture was perishable, and so we have only such artifacts as skulls, bones, flint points, arrowheads, grinding stones, and scattered ornaments to form the basis of our speculations about it. We know that those first hunters must have been infused with the bravery that was necessary to human survival during the Pleistocene epoch: picture a group of hungry men with stone-tipped spears facing a wounded woolly mammoth on the vast rolling steppes of prehistoric Alaska. Now *that* was big-game hunting. We also know that about 11,000 years ago, as glaciers retreated from North America, the great mammals of the Pleistocene began to die out, to be replaced by the fauna we know now in North America. Alaskans began to apply that bravery to hunting whales in skin boats on the open seas, and farther south, to hunting bear with arrows and lances.

From the first hardy pioneers—through epic migrations southward into the Americas—came such very different and vibrant cultures as the Uto-Aztecan people, town-dwellers and agriculturists who spread into the American Southwest and Mexico; the Algonquin people, who successfully destroyed the Norse settlements along the eastern shores of the continent only to fall prey to the English and French; and the Na-Déne group, or Athabaskans, among the last to migrate from Asia, some staying in Alaska, others

This ivory needlecase, carved in the shape of a human figure, was found near St. Michael on the Bering Sea and is thought to be about 500 years old.

moving south, cultural anthropologists surmise, to become the Navajos and Apaches. Pocahontas, Sitting Bull, Geronimo, and the last king of Aztec Mexico, Montezuma, all may have traced their ancestry to hunters who crossed during the great migrations between Asia and Alaska. The most recent group to migrate were the Eskimo peoples (known to ethnographers collectively as Inuit), who remained in the north of Alaska and down the southwestern coast.

By the year 1700, Alaska's natives had become either people of the Interior or people of the coast. Some, such as the Aleuts and the Tlingit, preferred life near the Pacific, where the Japanese current warmed the maritime provinces. Most Eskimos stayed in the frozen north, where the Arctic Ocean provided a reliable bounty in the late summer and fall. The Athabaskan people settled among the hills, valleys, forests, and meadows that make up the immense heart of Alaska—a state of affairs that persisted for thousands of years. Remnants of their old camps can still be found along Dry Creek just north of Denali National Park, in the foothills of the Brooks Range, and along the cutbanks of the Yukon and Tanana rivers. For centuries they moved and breathed with the land, and their way of life changed little.

Tlingit medicine men, here adorned with Chilkat blankets, inhabited the southeastern coast of Alaska.

ALASKA HISTORY TIMELINE

30,000 years ago	Hunters cross an Ice Age land bridge between Asia and North America, in the first of many migrations.
4,000 years ago	Na-Déne (Athabaskans), from whom Apaches and Navajos are descended, cross the land bridge.
2,500 years ago	Eskimos arrive.
1700s	Kaigani Haida Indians migrate up the coast to Prince of Wales Island, driving out the resident Tlingit.
1728, 1741	Vitus Bering explores Bering Sea for Russia, resulting in Russia's claiming Alaska.
1778	British navigator Captain Cook explores the coast of Alaska and meets with Russian fur traders.
1799	Russian territorial governor Alexandr Baranov buys a parcel of land from the Tlingit and founds Sitka to use as a fort and trading post.
1816	Russian navigator Otto von Kotzebue visits the Eskimo village 30 miles north of the Arctic Circle that now carries his name.
1830s	American whalers arrive in the north Pacific and sail back to New England with ships full of whale oil, baleen, and walrus ivory.

A Webber scene showing "sea horses," actually walruses, being shot for their meat.

1867	U.S. Secretary of State William H. Seward buys Alaska for $7.2 million from the Russians.
1878	Salmon canneries open at Klawock and Old Sitka.
1880	Joe Juneau and Richard Harris find gold near the site of present-day Juneau.
1891	Rev. Sheldon Jackson introduces reindeer into Alaska.
1896–1898	Klondike gold strike in the Yukon. Prospectors travel to the placer districts via southeast Alaska.
1912	Katmai and Novarupta volcanoes erupt, turning the Katmai region from a land of tall grasses and scattered trees into a barren waste.
1913	First successful ascent of Denali, which U.S. settlers have renamed Mount McKinley.
1917	Mount McKinley (Denali) National Park established.
1925	Diphtheria epidemic breaks out in Nome and dog sledders race 674 miles in six days carrying anti-toxin serum to inoculate citizens. Now commemorated with the annual Iditarod dogsled race.
1942	Japanese bomb Dutch Harbor and occupy Attu and Kiska islands; all 42 native Aleutians are taken to Japan. Construction on the Alaska Highway begins, connecting Alaska to the Lower 48.
1957	Oil is discovered on the Kenai Peninsula.
1959	Alaska becomes 49th state.
1964	A 9.2 magnitude earthquake, the strongest ever recorded on the North American continent, hits Alaska on Good Friday.
1971	Alaska Native Claims Settlement gives Aleuts, Eskimos, and Indians title to 44 million acres of land.
1977	Trans-Alaska pipeline, 800 miles long, completed from Prudhoe Bay to Valdez. Oil begins to flow.
1988	Alaskans visit the Soviet city of Providenyia, opening up the border between the United States and the eastern Soviet Union.
1989	Exxon supertanker spills more than 240,000 barrels of Prudhoe Bay crude oil into Prince William Sound.

A Russian art poster depicts Vitus Bering being greeted by Alaskan natives. The map depicts the journeys of his two ships, the St. Peter *and* St. Paul.

■ RUSSIAN EXPLORERS AND TRADERS

Suddenly, about 250 years ago, the situation in Alaska was altered dramatically and forever. A group of explorers sailing under a Russian flag headed east from the Kamchatka Peninsula in June 1741, seeking to fill a blank space on the map. No one knew what lay between arctic Asia and the Americas. It was one of the last unexplored corners of the earth. Did a northern passage exist between the Pacific and the Atlantic? What sort of people inhabited the region? Could gold be found, and other treasures?

Captain-Commander Vitus Bering, an ambitious Dane in the service of the Russian navy, undertook to answer these important questions. It was his second voyage across the sea that now bears his name; the first, in 1728, had turned back in dense fog just short of the Alaska mainland. With only two small wooden vessels, the *St. Peter* and the *St. Paul,* he ventured into what for the Europeans was the unknown. This second voyage of discovery was something like a *Star Trek* episode.

French artist Louis Choris accompanied a Russian voyage of exploration in 1815 and recorded the enormous herds of seals in the Bering Sea islands. Beginning in 1834, Russian and American companies began hunting the animals for their fur and by 1911 only 110,000 remained of an original population of some four million animals.

VANCOUVER SEES PRINCE WILLIAM SOUND

Friday, May 16, 1794

The weather was delightfully serene and pleasant, and the morning of the 16th was ushered in by a sight we little expected in these seas. A numerous fleet of skin canoes [kayaks], each carrying two men only, were about the *Discovery,* and, with those that at the same time visited the *Chatham,* it was computed there could not be less than four hundred Indians present. These were almost all men grown, so that the tribe to which they belonged must consequently be a very considerable one. They instantly and very willingly entered into trade, and bartered away their hunting and fishing implements, lines and thread, extremely neat and well made from the sinews of animals; with bags ingeniously decorated with needle work, wrought on the thin membrane of the whales intestines; these articles, with some fish, constituted the articles of commerce with these people, as well as with our Indian friends in Cook's inlet. . . . These good people, like all the others we had lately seen, conducted themselves with great propriety. . . . The coast we sailed along this day is in most parts very mountainous, and descends rather quickly into the ocean. We could not avoid remarking, that the whole of this exterior coast seemed to wear a much more wintry aspect than the countries bordering on those more northern inland waters we had so recently quitted. . . . Many trees had been cut down since these regions had been first visited by Europeans; this was evident by the visible effects of the axe and saw. It was remarked that during the surveying excursions not a single sea otter, and but very few whales or seals had been seen; and that the wild fowl were not met with in that plenty during Mr. Whidbey's, as in Mr. Johnstone's [previous British explorers], expedition.

George Vancouver, *Voyage of Discovery to the North Pacific Ocean in the Years 1790–1792*

Everything that could go wrong did. Two landing boats full of men disappeared. A storm destroyed the *St. Peter,* and left the crew stranded for the winter. Scurvy killed many of the sailors. The Captain-Commander died. However, on the basis of Bering's ill-starred exploration, Russia claimed Alaska, and went on to solidify its holdings through further explorations and by establishing trading forts such as Sitka.

Among the survivors of the *St. Peter* was one of the most capable scientists of his time, George Wilhelm Steller—a brilliant botanist, zoologist, and geologist. One of the only reasons he survived and was able to return to Russia on a makeshift craft was that he insisted on eating native plants; unknown to him they contained vitamin C, and thus prevented scurvy. It was Steller who recorded for the first time many unusual plant and animal species of Alaska, including the Steller's jay, which still may be seen in campgrounds around Homer; the sea otter, which is still plentiful in areas such as the Kenai Fjords National Park; and the now-extinct Steller's sea cow, which was a gentle, shallow-water manatee of the North Pacific islands.

Following the ill-fated Bering reconnaissance, more Russian expeditions explored the region, as well as two historic British missions, the first led by Capt. James Cook in 1778, the second by Cook's former lieutenant, George Vancouver, in 1794.

Captain Cook conversed with Russian traders and observed Tlingit Indians along the coast. He was not enthusiastic about the latter, in whom he noted, "a dull, phlegmatic want of expression." He accurately identified the Eskimos as the same people he'd encountered sailing the coast of Greenland, recording in his logs their similar vocabularies and the facility of the Eskimo in all things technological. Cook sailed north of 63 degrees north latitude into the Bering Strait, a daring feat for the primitive vessels of that century. (Later that same year Cook was killed by Hawaiians in a dispute over stolen goods.) George Vancouver conducted an important survey of what is now Cook Inlet, the coast of the Kenai Peninsula, and Prince William Sound. Interestingly, Vancouver noted—and this was 1794—that "the

Paddling through Unakwik Inlet in Prince William Sound.

visible effects of the axe and saw" were already noticeable in the forests along the coast and that populations of sea otters, whales, and seals were rapidly being depleted by the Russians.

Indeed, during this period the Russians were obliterating the sea otters with incredible rapacity. Employing (more like coercing) the native Aleuts, who were skilled hunters and trappers, the Russians virtually laid waste to entire colonies of otters, moving southward year after year until they reached the Mendocino coast of California. As for the Aleuts, they themselves nearly disappeared due to diseases that came with the colonial explorers.

Within 50 years of Bering's 1741 voyage, the central geographic facts about Alaska were known to the world, and one error after another was corrected. The maps began to fill with fascinating details. There were enormous rivers, like the Yukon and Copper, and towering mountain ranges, including one massif—called by the natives "Denali"—that appeared as high as the great peaks of the South American Andes. Glaciers abounded, in appearance like those of Norway, only much larger. The animal life was far more abundant than in Europe: islands along the coast were populated with more brown bears than people. And there were hundreds of islands, ranging in size from a pile of rocks to something on the order of Hawaii's Big Island. Along the southern coast the cedar totem poles of the Haida and Tlingit towered over deep, cold bays, and in those bays swam millions of salmon. The Interior—the central part of Alaska—still remained a mystery.

■ SEWARD'S FOLLY

Eventually the fur trade collapsed, and the Russians, facing hard times after the Napoleonic and Crimean wars, approached that little-known real-estate magnate Abraham Lincoln about selling what was then known as "Russian-America." Lincoln was intrigued with the idea—it would constitute the last major land purchase for the United States—but he had a Civil War to fight. Two years after Lincoln was buried back in Illinois, his former Secretary of State, William Seward, concluded the negotiations begun by his mentor. After the usual rancorous Senate debate, the territory was sold to the United States for $7.2 million. Considering that Alaskan tourism currently represents a $2.4 billion annual business, Alaska has to be one of the best investments ever made by the people of the United States. At the time, however, it

Russian tradition, as represented by the town church of St. Nikolas, lives on in the village of Nikoaevsk on the Kenai Peninsula.

was referred to as "Seward's Folly," with the common perception being that the Russians had extracted all the valuables from the region before selling it.

Alaska's riches were nowhere near depleted, though, and in the years to come Americans learned about fur seals, whales, halibut, salmon, herring, and, in 1897, gold. At first it was Klondike gold, in a Yukon strike reached most easily from the Alaskan coastal settlement of Skagway. A depression-weary American public leapt at this opportunity for instant wealth, and within a matter of weeks more than 100,000 men (with a few women and children) rushed for their stake in America's last great frontier. Among them was the mayor of Seattle, who resigned and headed north. Indeed, the Klondike gold rush and opening of Alaska has been called North America's "Last Grand Adventure, the ultimate human saga in the conquest of North America," by author William Bronson, a chronicler of the event.

This was the momentous event that drew impressionable young writers Jack London *(The Call of the Wild)* and Robert Service *(The Cremation of Sam McGee*

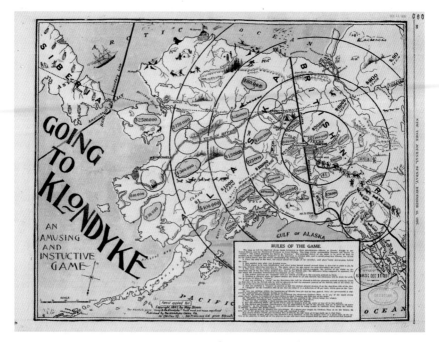

The object of this map game, published in 1897, was to score as many "claims" and "nuggets" as possible. The blindfolded players hoped to strike gold when they stuck their pins in it.

and *The Shooting of Dan McGrew)* into the northern country. Eventually gold was discovered in locations across Alaska, from Birch Creek near Circle City to the interior settlement that would one day become Fairbanks to the hills above Nome on the Seward Peninsula. Gold drew prospectors, and all the detritus that follows prospectors, into nearly every corner of the territory.

■ ALASKA'S NATURALISTS

Following the official expeditions of William Dall (1866) and Henry Allen (1885), a different sort of explorer, more tourist than government-sponsored geographer, began to venture north into Alaska. One of the first of these new private undertakings was led by Union Pacific magnate Edward Harriman, who in 1899 took naturalists John Muir and John Burroughs, along with photographer Edward Curtis, on a cruise trip north to Alaska. Muir had first visited the area in 1879 and was delighted for the opportunity to explore the "wonderland" again. It is interesting to note that the glacial ice observed by Muir clogging Glacier Bay in the 19th century has now all but vanished—a result, many scientists believe, of climate change, some of it manmade.

Perhaps the most significant event in Alaska's early 20th century was the formation of Mount McKinley National Park in 1917, largely as a result of the work of hunter-naturalist Charles Sheldon, author of *Wilderness of Denali*. National monument status was conferred on the Katmai area—"a valley of ten thousand smokes" following the massive 1912 eruption—in 1918, and on Glacier Bay in 1925. These would form an important precedent, and help shape public perceptions of the territory as a nature refuge as well as a treasure trove of natural riches.

■ JAPANESE INVADE ALASKA

The United States has experienced two foreign invasions since the War of 1812. The first was Pancho Villa's raid on Columbus, New Mexico, in 1916; the second was in June 1942, when a sizable Japanese naval force overwhelmed U.S. military installations on Kiska Island, in the Aleutians.

Within months Japanese Imperial forces controlled Attu, Shemya, and Amchitka islands. The Japanese generals and admirals were interested in Alaska for several reasons. First, Admiral Yamamoto was concerned about U.S. aircraft carriers that had escaped destruction at Pearl Harbor, and planned to lure them into the North Pacific, where they would be vulnerable to heavy land-based bombers.

Second, the Japanese high command needed a North American base from which to launch attacks against strategic targets on the U.S. West Coast, especially the Boeing aircraft plant in Seattle. And finally, this invasion would be a critical diversion from the Battle of Midway.

The key battle that restored American control over Alaska was fought in May 1943 at Attu Island, 1,700 miles west of Anchorage. More than 34,000 U.S. ground troops were involved in the operation. Enemy losses in the battle exceeded 2,000, including hundreds of young infantrymen who committed suicide in "Massacre Valley" rather than surrender. It was during the Attu battle that U.S. forces retrieved an intact Japanese Zero plane, designed by the skilled engineers of Mitsubishi. Study of this sophisticated aircraft helped the Allies better prosecute the air wars in Asia and Europe.

During this same period the Alaska Highway was built in order to move ground troops into Alaska in the event of a large-scale Japanese invasion. The road extended 1,500 miles from Dawson Creek in eastern British Columbia to Fairbanks in central Alaska. It was opened to the public in 1948 and, primitive though it was, it led to the first wave of post-war immigration into the Alaskan Territory.

A Japanese fighting plane shot down during the attack on the Aleutian Islands in June 1942.

■ STATEHOOD

Just as their ancestors had endured the travails of the Oregon Trail to reach the West Coast, a new generation of American homesteaders put up with axle-deep mud and jarring ruts to reach the wide open country of the Last Frontier. Here they encountered challenges and opportunities. First off, there was land: in a homesteading program that no longer exists, any person who lived on 160 acres for five years could have the land forever. There were jobs, too; along the Pacific Coast canneries were hiring, lumber mills were opening up, and gold mines were in need of workers. In 1954 the first pulp mills opened in Ketchikan, and in 1957 Atlantic Richfield discovered oil at Swanson River on the Kenai Peninsula.

Two years later, on January 3, 1959, Alaska was admitted to the Union as the 49th state. Almost immediately, and largely through the efforts of Supreme Court Justice William O. Douglas, a noted conservationist, the nine-million-acre Arctic National Wildlife Range was established in the extreme northeast corner of the state. This wildlife refuge is now more than 19 million acres in size—larger than the state of Maine.

The central business district of Anchorage was devastated by the 1964 earthquake.

Then, just as the fledgling state was preparing for a promising future, natural disaster struck. On March 27, 1964, Alaska was devastated by the most violent earthquake to hit North America since the New Madrid earthquake of 1812. Measuring 9.2 on the Richter Scale, the earthquake leveled parts of Anchorage and generated killer tidal waves that nearly destroyed the coastal towns of Kodiak, Valdez, and Seward. To this day survivors recount stories of great holes opening up in the earth and swallowing houses, and of 10-story waves thundering in from the sea to drown seaside villages.

■ MODERN ALASKA

The 1970s got off to a strange start when, in 1971, President Nixon ordered the detonation of an atomic bomb on the island of Amchitka, destroying a sea otter colony in the process. A more positive development was passage of the Alaska Native Claims Settlement Act, which allowed Native Alaskans to select more than 40 million acres of federal lands for village, tribal, and individual ownership. For the first time in U.S. history, native populations were given a settlement that recognized their thousands of years of tenure on the land.

In 1974, construction began on a pipeline designed to carry oil 800 miles from Prudhoe Bay on the Arctic Ocean south to Valdez on Prince William Sound. In order to send hot oil over the arctic permafrost without melting it, the three-foot-wide pipe had to be insulated and elevated above the ground. Construction crews scaled mountain ranges, crossed rivers, and battled the elements, until in August 1977 the first oil was sent down the pipeline to Prince William Sound, completing one of the most impressive engineering feats in history.

Three historic events marked the 1980s. The first was the Alaska National Interest Lands Conservation Act, signed into law by President Jimmy Carter on December 2, 1980. This bill—passed over the vehement protestations of the Alaskan congressional delegation—effectively doubled the lands administered by the National Park Service and tripled the size of the wilderness system. Many new parks—Gates of the Arctic, Kenai Fjords, and Wrangell–St. Elias, the largest park in the world—came into being at this time. The second development was the boom and bust in oil revenues; after an astonishing flood of money in the early 1980s, a crash in oil prices in 1985 sent Alaska's economy reeling. The third development was an unmitigated disaster—the grounding of the *Exxon Valdez* near Valdez on March 24, 1989, causing the worst oil spill in U.S. history. The spill

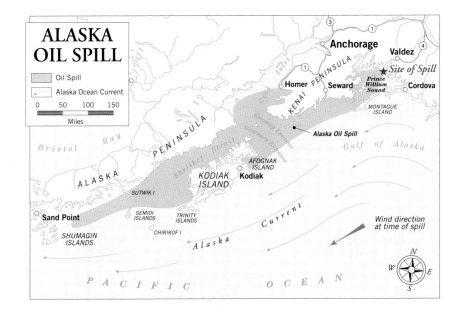

dumped more than 11 million gallons of crude oil into Prince William Sound, whose once-rich fisheries still have not fully recovered from the catastrophe.

The dawn of the 21st century has brought new variations on the old theme of boom and bust, with new voices both arguing for development and making the case for conservation. The biggest problems faced by Alaska continue to be in the area of natural resources—overfishing of the north Pacific, particularly by Asian factory fleets; overharvesting of timber in Southeast Alaska, which threatens to destroy historic salmon fisheries; the steady decline of the once-immense Prudhoe Bay oil field; and continued contentious debate about whether to open up the Arctic National Wildlife Refuge to oil drilling. A century from now, this will all be history. One hopes that the fisheries will still be there, and the forests, and all else that, since the beginning of time, has helped to define this remarkable place the natives proudly called Alyeska, the Great Land.

P E O P L E

As a university teacher in Alaska for half a dozen years, I came to know the people of the state. They were my students, my colleagues, the folks I saw in the stores and about town and in the bush every day. Alaskans are an incredibly diverse group, I came to learn, including Yupik and Inupiat Eskimos, Aleuts, Athabaskans, Tlingits, Tsimshians, and Haidas, as well as those of European, Asian, and African descent. In Fairbanks, as in the rest of the state, the bulk of the residents were of European descent, individuals whose reasons for living in Alaska were as diverse as their personal histories. We also had a sizable Korean-American community, many the children and grandchildren of pioneers who had originally come to work in coastal canneries. Near Fort Wainwright there was a large African-American community, consisting of military dependents as well as those who came to Alaska as active-duty personnel and liked it so much they stayed. The town also supported Native Alaskans who came to the university from all parts of the state to further their education and then return to home villages.

■ PERSONALITY AND SPIRIT

The chief quality of Alaskans is independence of spirit. They are a tough and self-reliant people, and freedom is in abundance here, as on any frontier. One of the state's political parties is the Alaska Independence Party, whose expressed purpose is to secede from the United States altogether.

The long, cold, and sunless winters create a variety of problems for Alaska's people. Many living in the higher latitudes are affected by Seasonal Affective Disorder, which results from the body being denied a proper amount of sunlight. The light of the sun stimulates melatonin production in the pineal gland, and melatonin is essential to the circadian rhythms that control sleeping, eating, and cognition. When there is a paucity of sunlight—in Fairbanks there are only three hours of "twilight" at the winter solstice, while in Barrow there is no light—melatonin production falls off precipitously. The results range from the nearly universal symptoms of insomnia and carbohydrate craving to chronic "blues."

A girl and her puppy in Ambler, Alaska, an Inupiat Eskimo village along the Kobuk River, north of the Arctic Circle.

Cabin fever is a related affliction familiar to all long-term denizens of the Far North. During prolonged periods of cold, people are trapped inside homes and offices for days, weeks, and months. Alcohol consumption is high.

And yet Alaska is a good place to live, particularly around Anchorage, where the warmer ocean waters moderate the effects of winter and direct flights to places like Honolulu and Cabo San Lucas are readily available. One distinct advantage of living in the state is that there is no state income tax. As a result of the Alaska Permanent Fund—state oil revenues invested in stocks, bonds, and real estate— each Alaska resident, regardless of age, receives an annual check. In recent years the dividend has ranged between $900 and nearly $2,000. Many parents use this to establish college educational funds for their children. Currently, the value of the Alaska Permanent Fund exceeds $27 billion and represents one of the largest investment portfolios in the world.

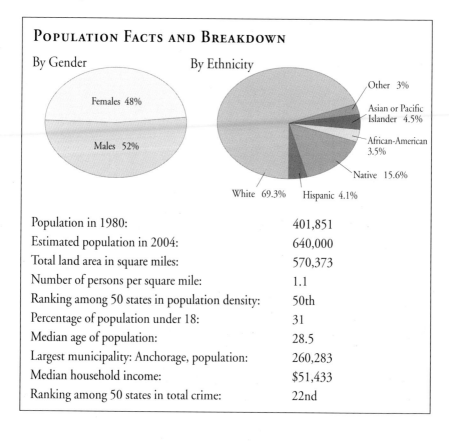

POPULATION FACTS AND BREAKDOWN

By Gender

Females 48%

Males 52%

By Ethnicity

Other 3%

Asian or Pacific Islander 4.5%

African-American 3.5%

Native 15.6%

White 69.3%   Hispanic 4.1%

Population in 1980:	401,851
Estimated population in 2004:	640,000
Total land area in square miles:	570,373
Number of persons per square mile:	1.1
Ranking among 50 states in population density:	50th
Percentage of population under 18:	31
Median age of population:	28.5
Largest municipality: Anchorage, population:	260,283
Median household income:	$51,433
Ranking among 50 states in total crime:	22nd

Trying to make the best of their close quarters, these cabin-bound miners enjoy a New Year's dinner.

At their best, the people of Alaska are optimistic and innovative. They approach hardship and adversity with humor and resourcefulness. To my way of thinking, the greatest resource of the state is not its fisheries, lumber, and minerals, but its people.

■ NATIVE ALASKANS

Native Alaskans fall into two groups—those who live by the sea and those who inhabit inland areas. Those who live by the sea include the Inupiat Eskimos, who reside along the northern and northwestern coasts; the Yupik Eskimos, who make their home along the Bering Sea coast and along the lower stretches of the major rivers (Yukon, Kuskokwim); the Aleuts (Alutiiq), who are found along the great island chain of the same name; the Tlingit, Eyak, Haida, and Tsimshian Indians, and the Chugach Eskimos, who inhabit the forested coastline from Prince William Sound to the Alaska Panhandle. These people traditionally had economies based on hunting and fishing for marine mammals, salmon, and waterfowl, but their world was dramatically changed by the arrival of modern culture. In 1971, the Alaska Native Claims Settlement Act provided Alaska's tribes with large land settlements, now owned and managed by Native corporations.

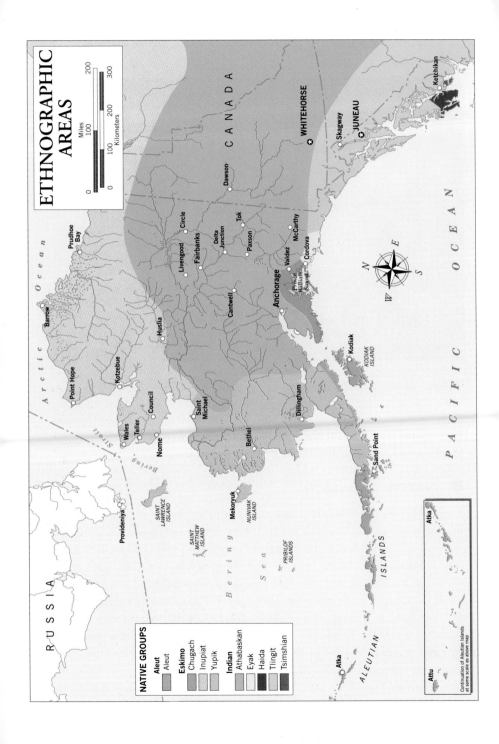

ETHNOGRAPHIC AREAS

Miles
0   100   200

Kilometers
0   100   200   300

RUSSIA

Arctic Ocean

CANADA

WHITEHORSE

Prudhoe
Bay

Barrow

Point Hope

Kotzebue

Wales
Teller
Nome

Council

Saint
Michael

Huslia

Livengood
Circle
Fairbanks
Delta
Junction
Tok
Cantwell
Paxson
McCarthy
Valdez
Cordova
Anchorage
Prince
William
Sound

Dawson

Skagway
JUNEAU
Ketchikan

Bethel

Dillingham

Kodiak
KODIAK
ISLAND

Sand Point

Mekoryuk

NUNIVAK
ISLAND

SAINT
LAWRENCE
ISLAND

SAINT
MATTHEW
ISLAND

PRIBILOF
ISLANDS

Provideniya

Bering
Strait

Bering
Sea

PACIFIC OCEAN

N
W   E
S

ALEUTIAN   ISLANDS

Attu

Atka

NATIVE GROUPS

Aleut
Aleut

Eskimo
Chugach
Inupiat
Yupik

Indian
Athabaskan
Eyak
Haida
Tlingit
Tsimshian

Atka

Continuation of Aleutian Islands
at same scale as above map

■ INUPIAT AND YUPIK ESKIMOS

The 40,000 Eskimo people of Alaska are related to the larger Eskimo populations of northern Canada, Siberia, and Greenland (collectively known as *Inuit).* In Alaska they have settled along the Bering Sea, the Arctic Ocean, and on remote islands such as St. Lawrence and Nunivak. In 1778, Captain Cook noted in his log:

> I have frequently mentioned how remarkably the natives of this
> northwest side of America resemble the Greenlanders and Eskimo in
> various particulars of person, dress, weapons, canoes, and the like. I
> was struck by the affinity which we found subsisting between the
> dialects of the Greenlander and Eskimo and those of Norton Sound
> and Unalaska. . . .

Alaska Eskimo culture and language fall into two groups: the Inupiat of the Far North and the Yupik on the Bering Sea coast. Long known collectively to outsiders as Eskimos—an Athabaskan term that means "raw meat eater"— many now proudly identify themselves by that name once given in ridicule; others prefer to be called by the more proper name of Inupiat or Yupik, which translates in either language as "The Real People." No offense is likely to be taken unless you commit the ultimate faux pas of calling an Eskimo an Indian, or vice versa—it's like calling an Irishman a Brit. Physically, Eskimos have an Asiatic look but are of a unique physical type; they are unrelated to American Indians. Note that the often-used term "Inuit," while not improper, is not used by Alaska Eskimos to describe themselves.

Eskimo culture changed dramatically during the last century,

Photographer Edward S. Curtis photographed this Nunivak Eskimo mother and child in 1928.

Eskimo residents of the Kotzebue Sound area in 1816, by Louis Choris, Russian explorer Otto von Kotzebue's official artist. After the expedition, Choris turned his sketches into a volume of hand-painted aquatints published in Paris in 1822.

Eskimo boys of Nunivak Island photographed by Edmund S. Curtis, ca. 1928.

especially in the 1980s and 1990s. No longer will you find people living in traditional dome- or Quonset-shaped sod homes—roofs supported by driftwood or whale bones and covered with insulating sod. (Igloos, or ice dwellings, were not used as regular dwellings by Alaska's Eskimos, but were built as temporary trail shelters.) Eskimos now live in prefabricated housing, and are centrally gathered in various communities and towns, some of which are quite large. Rarely will you find dogsleds used for anything other than racing—snowmobiles are the primary means of off-road transportation in winter.

Traditionally, the Eskimos pursued a semi-nomadic existence, moving with the caribou, fish, whale, and ringed-seal populations that provided much of their food. Today, in many cases, their income largely derives from oil and gas leasing, commercial fishing, outfitting and guiding hunters and fishermen, and activities related to the summer tourist season. Despite many changes, the northern Eskimo still seasonally hunt various marine mammals, such as seals and whales (and polar bears through special provisions in international endangered species accords). As a group they are among the world's toughest people, having lived successfully in the harshest environment of North America for at least 2,500 years.

■ ALEUTS (ALUTIIQ)

Racially and culturally related to Eskimos, the Aleuts, also known as the Alutiiq, historically lived on the barren Aleutian Islands, on the southwest coast of Alaska, and on Kodiak Island. They were among the first Native Alaskans to have contact with European civilization. Throughout the last 50 years of the 18th century, a variety of Russian and English explorers and traders encountered the Aleuts during expeditions along Alaska's southern coastline. Often these contacts were not friendly, and sometimes they degenerated into outright violence.

The natural world in which these people lived, though severe to the eye of the outsider, was rich in animal life that permitted their culture to thrive. Historically, the Aleuts harvested the salmon and the marine mammals that provided them with food and clothing, and they fashioned grass baskets so finely woven they would hold water. When the Russians appeared on the scene, they employed the Aleuts—usually in an involuntary fashion—as hunters for their otter fur industry.

Today, about 7,000 Aleuts live in Alaska, most on Kodiak Island. The Kodiak Aleuts are known as Koniag. In the mid-1990s, the Aleut people of Kodiak sold the U.S. Department of Interior a large tract of critical wildlife habitat on Kodiak Island, which they had earlier planned to commercially develop. It became part of the sprawling Kodiak National Wildlife Refuge, which protected the vital habitat of the fabled Kodiak bear. In this way, everyone came out a winner—the Aleuts, the American people, and the bears themselves.

Aleutian kayakers by Louis Choris.

■ ATHABASKANS

Life for the Athabaskans has always been a difficult proposition. Living as they do in the vast, austere wilderness between the Brooks Range on the north and the coastal mountain ranges on the south, they were always only a few weeks or months from starvation. A late winter, an early spring, a short summer—any of these minor climatic variations could spell death for an entire family, clan, or valley tribe. Anthropologists generally agree that sometime in the 16th century—perhaps prompted by environmental changes or wars with the Cree—many of the Athabaskans made a large-scale migration south into Arizona and New Mexico, where they became known as the Navajos and Apaches. Alaskan Athabaskans survived their harsh yearly cycle by hunting geese, cranes, and ducks that returned to lakes and ponds in spring. By late June and early July the sea-run salmon would begin to reach their headwater streams, and the Athabaskans caught and dried

Interior of a Tlingit chief's house, Chilkat, Alaska, ca. 1898.

large numbers of these fish. August was a good time to begin gathering wood, and September through early winter found men out in the marshes hunting moose and small game with bows and arrows. Women and children gathered forest and tundra berries, especially blueberries. Winter was spent fur-trapping and living more quietly indoors, particularly during the brutal cold spells of January. March was traditionally a time for visiting relatives in the region, before the snow began to melt and travel became quite difficult for several weeks.

Athabaskans are a diverse group, primarily united by language. This group includes the Kutchin of the upper Yukon Valley, the Koyukon of the Koyukuk River Country, the Tanana of the Tanana Valley, and the Tanacross of the Upper Tanana Valley. And this is only a partial list. Most live near rivers in small villages readily accessible by boat in summer and by dog sled or snowmobiles in winter. In many parts of Alaska—Huslia, Fort Yukon—these villages can be visited by outsiders in the summer, a trip I would highly encourage.

Today, Athabaskans also live in Fairbanks, as well as in more remote bush locations, notably along the upper Yukon and Koyukuk rivers. Others live near Cook Inlet and along the Cooper River near Cordova.

■ TLINGIT

The Tlingit (pronounced *klink*-it) Indians have long inhabited Southeast Alaska, and in the 18th century fought fiercely against incursions by the Russians. Tlingits are known for their carved and painted totem poles, which record clan figures and histories on cedar logs. Like the Aleuts, the Tlingits have been historically a seafaring people who traveled through the coastal waters in kayaks and huge ocean-going canoes carved from tree trunks. They built large houses near good fishing grounds and fished for salmon, hunted deer, and trapped important fur-bearers such as the sea otter. Traditionally a slave-holding people, they established social status by sponsoring enormous feasts, called potlatches, during which the host family gave guests lavish gifts, setting up an obligation of reciprocity.

Today, the Tlingits still live in both the villages and the cities of Southeast Alaska. At such places as Sitka and Hoonah, they still perform their traditional dances, and their artifacts can be viewed at museums in Sitka and Juneau.

ESKIMO ARTISTRY

INUPIAT MASK

For the Inupiat Eskimos in northwest Alaska, masks represented the spirits of animals and deities. They were made by shamans, or by carvers working under their direction, and were usually used for ceremonial dances. The shaman also wore the mask while working his power for good hunting, weather, or health.

ESKIMO PARKA

Patterned after the traditional Inupiat style, this Eskimo parka is made of muskrat, wolverine, beaver, and wolf furs, with calf-skin trim representing three mountains. Typically, parkas were worn by women in the village and considered among their most elegant articles of clothing. This parka was made by Esther Norton of Kotzebue.

COILED GRASS BASKET

Eskimo grass baskets are made mainly in southwest Alaska and are woven from very fine grass harvested in fall. Traditionally, seal gut colored with the dye of berries is interwoven into the baskets. The basket pictured here was woven by Lucy Post, a Yupik Eskimo weaver from Tununk village.

INK ON SEAL SKIN

Walrus on Ice Floe by Florence Malewotkuk tells the story of her people, the Eskimos of Saint Lawrence Island, and the animals on whom they depended for subsistence. Malewotkuk (1906–1971) was one of the most notable artists in the Bering Sea region and her work is widely available throughout the state.

IVORY GOOSE

Walrus ivory has always been the primary material used by Eskimo carvers, and Alaska seabirds a typical subject for coastal and island artists. This carving was done by Ted Mayac, Sr., from King Island Village. He is especially noted for his attention to detail and his careful coloring.

SEA MONSTER BOWL

This wooden bowl from Nunivak Island features a mythological creature, a favorite motif of Bering Sea artists. Yupik Eskimos painted bowls and other wooden objects for ceremonies such as the bladder festival, the messenger feast, and the launching of a new kayak. Circa 1945; artist unknown.

W I L D L I F E

Alaska offers some of the finest wildlife viewing opportunities in the world. Following is basic information about some of Alaska's more impressive animals and tips to increase your chances of observing them. Because local conditions and game populations vary both seasonally and annually, it is always prudent to check with the State of Alaska Department of Fish and Game for the latest information.

■ BLACK BEARS

Black bears are forest-dwelling animals. Largely vegetarian, the black bear *(Ursus americanus)* is more retiring than the grizzly bear, which prefers more open country. Black bears also exploit more habitats than grizzlies, and they have a higher reproductive rate. For these reasons, they are more plentiful. In fact, black bears outnumber all other types of bears found in Alaska, and there are more here than anywhere else in the United States. Areas of greatest black bear density in Alaska include the Kenai Peninsula, the perimeter of Prince William Sound, and Prince of Wales Island. In these areas there can be as many as 70 black bears per 100 square miles. The overall black bear population in Alaska exceeds 100,000—and may be twice that.

Anan Creek Wildlife Observatory, Tongass National Forest *map site: 2*
Black bears, and occasionally brown bears, fish for salmon in Anan Creek and can be observed at close range from the viewing platform and along a maintained trail. *35 miles southeast of Wrangell in Tongass National Forest, accessible only by boat or floatplane from Ketchikan or Wrangell. For more information contact the U.S. Forest Service, Wrangell Ranger District, 907-874-2323. See the "Southeast" chapter.*

Chena River State Recreation Area *map site: 23*
Bear sign is often encountered along the Chena River. Probably your best bet for viewing black bears is to hike the Chena Dome Trail into the uplands north of the river, find a good vantage point, and use binoculars. This is a particularly effective technique from early August until the snows fall, as black bears feed on the blueberries widely available across the tundra. *A short drive northeast of Fairbanks on Chena Hot Springs Road. See the "Interior" chapter.*

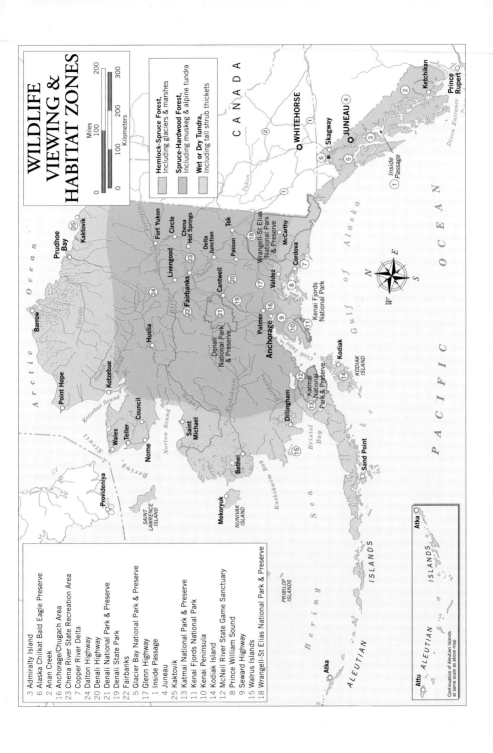

WILDLIFE VIEWING & HABITAT ZONES

Miles
0   100   200

Kilometers
0   100   200   300

Hemlock-Spruce Forest,
Including glaciers & marshes

Spruce-Hardwood Forest,
Including muskeg & alpine tundra

Wet or Dry Tundra,
Including tall shrub thickets

3 Admiralty Island
6 Alaska Chilkat Bald Eagle Preserve
2 Anan Creek
16 Anchorage/Chugach Area
23 Chena River State Recreation Area
7 Copper River Delta
24 Dalton Highway
20 Denali Highway
21 Denali National Park & Preserve
19 Denali State Park
22 Fairbanks
5 Glacier Bay National Park & Preserve
17 Glenn Highway
1 Inside Passage
4 Juneau
25 Kaktovik
13 Katmai National Park & Preserve
11 Kenai Fjords National Park
10 Kenai Peninsula
14 Kodiak Island
12 McNeil River State Game Sanctuary
8 Prince William Sound
9 Seward Highway
15 Walrus Islands
18 Wrangell-St Elias National Park & Preserve

Continuation of Aleutian Islands
at same scale as above map

Chugach State Park *map site: 16*
In early spring black bears can be seen foraging for grass and horsetail along most of the major drainages. Later in the season they migrate into the uplands, where grizzly bears can also be observed. This large state park is due east and south of Anchorage. *Access is via Eklutna Lake Road and Eagle River Road. There is also a good trail from the Ski Bowl Road. Chugach State Park office: 907-345-5014. See the "South-Central" chapter.*

Prince William Sound Area *map site: 8*
If you take a boat charter in the Sound, study snowslide areas for bears; also look at beaches and intertidal areas. Because of their striking color, black bears often are visible at great distance in the green vegetation of summer, or in the golds and reds of autumn foliage. *Board boat or ferry at Valdez. See the "South-Central" chapter.*

■ BROWN AND GRIZZLY BEARS

No other animals as powerfully evoke the North American wilderness as do the grizzly and brown bears of Alaska. The sight of a heavy silvertip grizzly lumbering over the tundra, or of a brown bear fishing for salmon in the rapids of a coastal river, will be one of your greatest memories of Alaska.

In Alaska, the interior brown bear *(Ursus arctos horribilis)* is commonly known as the grizzly bear and is distinguished by its silver-tipped coat, massive shoulder hump, and dished face. A large adult can stand nine feet tall and weigh 900 pounds and will live 15 to 30 years. The coastal brown bear (*Ursus arctos middendorfi*) is an even larger bear than the grizzly, because of both genetics and the rich diet of sea-run salmon, coastal berries, and succulent vegetation.

A grizzly or brown bear in any given range visually recognizes every other adult grizzly or brown bear in the area, and instantly knows its place in the respective social hierarchy. Social position determines order of access to prime feeding sites such as berry patches, salmon streams, or wolf kills. Fights in the wild are rare—most often bears communicate through body posturing and vocalization so as to avoid conflict. In June, during the breeding season, aggressive interactions increase between males. Body language is very important, as are facial expressions.

Most often you will see bears at a great distance. Look for a somewhat circular form that moves ponderously and low to the ground over the landscape—not at all

Kodiak brown bears looking for lunch in the island's wildlife refuge.

A coastal brown bear cub grazes on spring succulents.

in the long-legged manner of animals such as moose and caribou. Bear sign includes digging sites (where the bears have torn up the tundra to get at plant roots), day beds (excavated sleeping pits in the tundra or forest floor), trails (look for snagged hair on tree branches), kill sites (always avoid these), and winter dens (very hard to find in the subarctic and arctic). Often you will see sows and cubs—avoid them! Bears can easily outrun humans, and are strong swimmers as adults, although cubs can drown while following their mothers in swift glacial streams and rivers (especially in their first spring, when they are so tiny.) Generally, grizzlies and brown bears are visible in Alaska from May through September, after which they retire to winter dens.

Authorities estimate there are about 30,000 brown bears and grizzlies in Alaska. On Kodiak Island, southwest of Anchorage, there are several thousand brown bears, and in years past, the bears outnumbered the people. In other parts of Alaska the bears have low-density populations; in the Arctic a grizzly may have a home range of 1,800 square miles.

Brooks Falls, Katmai National Park and Preserve *map site: 13*
Brown bears catch and feed on salmon in the Brooks River and at Brooks Falls. Commercial jets fly into King Salmon; from there you'll need to take a floatplane. Reservations are required and must be made months in advance. Contact Katmai National Park and Preserve, P.O. Box 7, #1 King Salmon Mall, King Salmon, AK 99613; 907-246-3305. Visitors who cannot get into Brooks Camp (the official and only overnight lodging for the Brooks River and Falls) can contact commercial air charters in Anchorage, Soldotna, and Homer. These outfits fly to lesser-known regions of Katmai National Park and to private bear-viewing lodges like Hallo Bay and Katmai Wilderness Lodge. *See the "Southwest" chapter.*

Dalton Highway *map site: 24*
Grizzly bears often are seen in the vicinity of the Chandalar Shelf and Atigun Pass. In early summer they hunt Dall sheep lambs on Atigun Pass. Later in the season they move about in the greenery eating shrubs. In the autumn, look for reddish-colored blueberry patches. Grizzlies can often be seen gorging themselves on the abundant berries in these distinctive areas. *About 300 miles north of Fairbanks. See the "Arctic" chapter.*

Denali National Park and Preserve *map site: 21*
Best viewing begins just past Mile 32 on the national park road, in what is known as Igloo Canyon. Sable Pass, at the head of the canyon, is another good place to find bears, as is all of the country from the Toklat River to the Eielson Visitor Center at about Mile 66. *Park entrance is 237 miles north of Anchorage on the George Parks Highway. See the "Interior" chapter.*

Kodiak Island *map site: 14*
The sprawling Kodiak National Wildlife Refuge is a top brown-bear viewing destination. Access is via the town of Kodiak, by floatplane to either the Fraser or O'Malley River viewing areas. Brown bears gather at both locations during salmon runs from early July through early August. Registration is required. *Contact Kodiak National Wildlife Refuge headquarters just south of the town of Kodiak for information. 907-487-2600. See the "Southwest" chapter.*

McNeil River State Game Sanctuary *map site: 12*
The falls on the McNeil River State Game Sanctuary are known for their concentrations of brown bears; up to 50 bears can be seen at one time as they feed on the salmon. There is tent camping only, with no public facilities beyond an outhouse. Viewers are escorted at all times by highly trained and helpful Fish and Game personnel. *Alaska Peninsula southwest of Anchorage, with access primarily by floatplane. Entrance to the Sanctuary is limited to the months of June, July, and August and is determined by a lottery. Application deadline is April 1. Contact the State of Alaska Department of Fish & Game for applications and additional information (907-267-2244; www.wildlife.alaska.gov/mcneil). See the"Southwest" chapter.*

Stan Price State Wildlife Sanctuary, Admiralty Island *map site: 3*
Bears feed here on salmon from mid-July through mid-August. The sanctuary is located at Pack Creek on Admiralty Island. Access from Juneau via floatplane or

boat. *Registration is recommended and information can be obtained from the State of Alaska Department of Fish & Game in Anchorage or the Admiralty Island National Monument in Juneau, 907-586-8790. See the "Southeast" chapter.*

■ CARIBOU

The sudden, unexpected migrations and equally sudden disappearances of caribou baffle wildlife biologists. Alaska has a number of large "herds" (more accurately, regional populations), including the Mulchatna Herd, the Porcupine Herd, and the Central Arctic Herd. Their annual migrations can easily cover over 1,000 miles.

The 800,000 caribou in Alaska prefer wet tundra and mountains during the summer and are sometimes seen near roads. During the winter they descend to valleys where the snow level is lower and forage is easier to reach. Caribou are social animals. Groups may range in size from several to several thousand.

Denali National Park and Preserve *map site: 21*
Caribou can be encountered anywhere in the park. They are often seen along the Park's only access road in the following locations: by Primrose Ridge just above the Savage River turnout at Mile 14; the Toklat River gravel bar; Highway Pass; Thorofare Pass; and in the highlands around Wonder Lake. *Park entrance is 237 miles north of Anchorage on the George Parks Highway. See the "Interior" chapter.*

Dalton Highway *map site: 24*
Look for caribou north of Atigun Pass between late July and early September. As the days shorten, the main herd moves south from its summering area on the coastal plain near the Arctic Ocean. At times you will see caribou in every direction—tens of thousands on the arctic coastal plain. *Dalton Highway runs from Livengood, just north of Fairbanks, to Prudhoe Bay. See the "Arctic" chapter.*

Denali Highway *map site: 20*
Caribou are seen throughout the summer here, especially near Tangle Lakes. Denali Highway runs between Richardson Highway to the east and George Parks Highway on the west. Try pullouts at miles 13, 50, and 117. *See the "Interior" chapter.*

A caribou skull lies on autumn tundra in Kobuk Valley National Park. The Western Arctic caribou herd, 500,000 strong, is Alaska's largest.

■ DALL SHEEP

Dall sheep navigate treacherous sheer rock cliffs and nimbly run, jump, and gallop across rock pinnacles with thousands of feet of vertical relief below. The lambs are especially vulnerable to predation in May, shortly after birth, and are a favored delicacy of the Alaskan wolf. About half of them do not survive their first winter.

Yellowish white in color, the Dall sheep of Alaska appear almost as dots of snow on the tundra and rocks. The areas they inhabit—the rugged mountains of the subarctic and arctic—offer some of the most spectacular scenery on the continent. Despite their preference for the wildest mountains, Dall sheep can be seen at a number of points from gravel or paved roads.

Anchorage Area *map site: 16*
Just southeast of the city on the Seward Highway, Dall sheep step down off the cliffs and graze along the side of the roads. *See the "South-Central" chapter.*

Dalton Highway *map site: 24*
A small herd of Dall sheep grazes on or near the top of Atigun Pass, which is the place where the Dalton Highway crosses the Arctic Divide in the Brooks Range. Sometimes these Dall sheep are literally in the road. *Dalton Highway runs from Livengood, just north of Fairbanks, to Prudhoe Bay. See the "Arctic" chapter.*

Denali National Park and Preserve *map site: 21*
A hike up Primrose Ridge from the Savage River turnout will normally reward you with a sight of the sheep. From the road itself they can be seen in Igloo Canyon, Sable Pass, and Polychrome Pass. The big rams are in the area before Memorial Day and after Labor Day—they spend the summer in the higher mountains to the west. *Park entrance is 237 miles north of Anchorage on the George Parks Highway. See the "Interior" chapter.*

Glenn Highway *map site: 17*
Look for Dall sheep in the Eklutna/Twin Peaks area (access via the Glenn Highway Mile 26.3 exit), and in the Sheep Mountain Closed Area near Mile 106 and Mile 116. *Glenn Highway (Alaska Route 1) runs from Anchorage east to Tok, where it connects to the Alaska Highway. See the "Interior" chapter.*

DALL SHEEP

Always there are many rams in these lofty pastures, many old veterans with long, gracefully curved horns. There is something entrancing about a mountain-sheep horn, something about its sweep that satisfies our sense of smoothness while the ruggedness of its surface gives its character. The horns of these white sheep are especially free in their sweep, are relatively slender, and often have a pleasing amber hue.

–Adolph Murie, *A Naturalist in Alaska*, 1961

Kenai Peninsula *map site: 10*
Dall sheep are seen often from the Sterling Highway at the Cooper Landing Closed Area at Mile 41.1. They are also sometimes spotted along miles 104 through 106 along the Seward Highway. Hiking further increases your chances to see sheep, but be careful, as brown and black bears are numerous here. *Southwest of Anchorage and accessible by highway. See the "South-Central" chapter.*

■ EAGLES

Four eagle species—the bald eagle, the golden eagle, the white-tailed eagle, and the rare Steller's sea eagle—are found in Alaska. Some golden eagles migrate up to several thousand miles each spring from the Lower 48 to their nesting and feeding grounds scattered across the state. Bald eagles generally migrate a shorter distance, and many are year-round residents in coastal areas of Alaska.

Eagles are monogamous, mate for life, and return to the same nest each year, as long as it has not been disturbed by humans. They nest in steep cliff-faces and also in tall trees, including dead trees. Immature bald eagles have a dark head with some white mottling for the first couple of years; they then acquire the distinctive pure white hood of maturity. In Denali and in the interior, eagles subsist primarily on ptarmigan, arctic ground squirrels, and predator- or road-killed animals such as Dall sheep, caribou, and moose. Along the coast, they prey primarily on fish. Visitors will see eagles stationary on tree perches, in flight at both low and high altitudes, and actively killing prey such as salmon, trout, and Dolly Varden. The wingspan of a mature bald eagle can range from six to eight feet, and the birds can fly with a salmon that weighs as much as they do.

SALMON TRAPS EAGLE

The heaviest load a mature eagle can carry is ten pounds. Occasionally, it will mis-judge a salmon's size and hook into a twelve- or fifteen-pounder. While out in the kayak, I once spotted an eagle down on the water, bobbing over low waves. As I drew closer, I saw a flashing metallic shape underneath—a large salmon hooked to talons. The eagle was gasping for breath, wings spread limply over the pierced salmon. I then burst out laughing as the eagle spun around, then was zipped from side to side by the running fish. Putting comedy aside, I reached down and flopped both eagle and big catch into the boat. The spent bird lay over on its side, unable to release the fish because its talons were sunk in up to the hilt. However, it wasn't a good set: the sharp curves, missing the spinal cord, were buried into side meat. When the salmon flopped, the eagle squawked as it was thrown about. I quieted both by clubbing the fish over the head, and then pushed victor and vanquished overboard onto the near-est beach.

–Michael Modzelewski, *Inside Passage,* 1991

Only in recent years has the bald eagle, the national symbol of the United States, finally been removed from the endangered species list in the Lower 48 states; they were never endangered in Alaska, where the current population is esti-mated at 40,000.

Alaska Chilkat Bald Eagle Preserve   *map site: 6*
The largest concentration of bald eagles in the world is found at the Chilkat Preserve. Up to 3,000 eagles flock here every autumn and can be observed into the winter, feeding on salmon and carrion. *North of Haines on the upper arm of the Lynn Canal, 80 air miles from Juneau. See the "Southeast" chapter.*

Inside Passage, aboard ship or ferry   *map site: 1*
Visitors who travel to Alaska via the Inside Passage of Southeast Alaska will see bald eagles on a daily basis in the saltwater bays and channels. *There is no road access to this area but a variety of cruises to choose from. See the "Southeast" chapter.*

Juneau   *map site: 4*
When salmon are spawning in the streams and rivers around Juneau, concentrations of bald eagles can be seen. Good viewing can be found on Douglas Island as well as

on Eagle River north of town in summer and autumn. *Juneau can be reached by marine ferry or by plane, but it cannot be accessed by road. See the "Southeast" chapter.*

Kenai Peninsula *map site: 10*
Bald eagles are quite common along the sea coast and on major streams and rivers, especially on the Kenai River. Park at one of the campgrounds near Cooper Landing and walk down to the river to look for eagles. Another possibility is to drive up to Captain Cook State Recreation Area north of Kenai, where bald eagles often fish in the intertidal areas. *See the "South-Central" chapter.*

Prince William Sound *map site: 8*
Any of the boat charters that leave daily in the summer from Seward should lead you into prime bald eagle habitat. *Reached by boat from Valdez; or drive from Anchorage to Portage (one hour south) and take the Alaska Railroad to Whittier, then board boat or ferry (reservations necessary) for Prince William Sound. See the "South-Central" chapter.*

A bald eagle scouts for prey in Homer, Alaska

■ Moose

The largest members of the deer family, moose stand up to six and a half feet tall at the shoulder and weigh up to 1,800 pounds. Because they feed on submerged aquatic plants, they wade at the edge of streams, rivers, lakes, beaver ponds, and muskeg, dipping their muzzles down into the water, then raising their heads to chew and look around. Though shy and solitary, they assemble in small bands in winter and tramp the snow firm in a small area to form a "moose yard."

Moose are among the most easily seen large animals in Alaska and are found from the coastal regions to the highest mountains, from the forested interior to the Arctic Slope. Even at a distance they are easily recognized, with their stiff-legged, shuffling gait. In the winter they often amble down into cities, sometimes climbing up on rooftops to nibble at tree branches appearing above the snow.

Moose sign to look for in the wild includes the large cloven tracks (especially in soft substrates such as mud, sand, and snow); day beds in swampy areas and out on the wet tundra; winter hair, antler velvet, or antlers that the moose have shed; and old bones and skulls from wolf or grizzly kill sites. Moose calves are especially vulnerable to wolf and grizzly predation in the first week following birth, which normally occurs in May. This is the time of year when you are most likely to see grizzlies and wolves in hot pursuit of a young calf. Cow moose will aggressively attack predators threatening their young, and are a force to be reckoned with. Breeding season occurs in September and October, when the bulls assemble harems and challenge each other—often violently—for the right to breed the cows.

During the fall rut, bull moose can be aggressive, and cow moose accompanied by calves may charge if crowded.

Chena Hot Springs Road *map site: 23*
The 56-mile Chena Hot Springs Road offers some of the best moose viewing possibilities in Alaska. Mornings and evenings are always a good time to look for moose along this road, part of the immense Chena River State Recreation Area. *North of Fairbanks and off the Steese Highway at Milepost 4.9. See the "Interior" chapter.*

Chugach State Park *map site: 16*
Moose are frequently seen throughout Chugach State Park, which is located in the eastern suburbs of Anchorage. Virtually any trail into the park will lead you into

prime Alaskan moose habitat. *From downtown Anchorage follow the Glenn Highway and exit at Eklutna Road (Milepost A 26.3). Continue 10 miles to reach the park's largest lake or exit Glenn Highway at Arctic Valley Road (Milepost A 6.1) and continue 7.5 miles to enter the park. Chugach State Park office: 907-345-5014. See the "South-Central" chapter.*

Dalton Highway   *map site: 24*
Moose are found along the length of the Dalton Highway and are almost always seen in the vicinity of Coldfoot and in the region around the Yukon River. *Dalton Highway runs from Livengood, just north of Fairbanks, to Prudhoe Bay. See the "Arctic" chapter.*

Denali National Park and Preserve   *map site: 21*
Moose are widespread here. Especially good spots include the timberline forest around Riley Creek Park Headquarters, the area around the bridge over the Teklanika River, Sable Pass, and all of the country from the Eielson Visitor Center west to Wonder Lake. The shores of Wonder Lake offer some the finest viewing opportunities, as the moose are seen feeding around a large picturesque lake with Denali in the background. These sites are on the park bus route. *Park entrance is 237 miles north of Anchorage on the George Parks Highway. See the "Interior" chapter.*

Denali State Park   *map site: 19*
Moose can frequently be seen along the George Parks Highway, which passes through Denali State Park. Other good spots in the park accessible by trail include Troublesome Creek and Byers Lake. *Adjacent to the southern border of the national park, Denali State Park may be approached via the George Parks Highway or the Alaska Railroad. For information call Alaska State Parks, 907-745-3975. See the "South-Central" chapter.*

Wrangell–St. Elias National Park and Preserve   *map site: 18*
Moose are visible along the McCarthy Road, which runs east from Chitina at the end of the Edgerton Highway. Be especially alert along Sculpin Lake, Moose Lake, and Long Lake. *Located in Southeast Alaska, the national park is reached via the Richardson Highway, which runs from Valdez to Delta Junction. See the "South-Central" chapter.*

■ Musk Oxen

Musk oxen were eradicated in Alaska early in the 19th century, but they have now been restored in several areas, including the Arctic National Wildlife Refuge in northeastern Alaska, Nunivak Island in the Bering Sea, and other sites in western Alaska. They have flourished in their natural habitat since the Pleistocene era, when they shared the tundra with woolly mammoths and saber-toothed cats. With fur 15 to 20 inches long that is reinforced by a dense undercoat, thick skin, and a layer of insulating fat, the musk ox can live comfortably with a wind chill factor of 80 degrees F below zero or even colder. The animal, with its peculiarly down-sloped horns and long shaggy coat of silken hairs, can weigh between 400 and 850 pounds. Despite its name, the musk ox has no musk, nor is it an ox.

Musk oxen are social animals that live in small herds and form a highly effective protective circle around their young when attacked by arctic wolves.

Gift shops at the University of Alaska, Fairbanks, and elsewhere sell small packets of the unusual soft underhair, called qiviut, which the Eskimos spin into yarn for woven and knitted clothing.

Large Animal Research Station, University of Alaska, Fairbanks *map site: 22*
A small herd of musk oxen is housed here along with caribou and reindeer. *Off Yankovich Road, off Ballaine Lake Road. Contact the Office of University Relations, 907-474-7581. See the "Interior" chapter.*

Musk Ox Farm, Palmer *map site: 16*
The cooperative maintains a small herd and collects the qiviut for village artisans who weave it into garments. Each village has a distinctive decorative pattern. Guided tours are given daily from May 9 through late September (closing date varies); *East of Palmer on the Glenn Highway at Milepost 50.1. Contact the Musk Ox Development Corporation, 907-745-4151. See the "South-Central" chapter.*

■ Polar Bears

Standing up to 10 feet tall and weighing in excess of 1,200 pounds, the polar bear is an awesome predator. Semi-aquatic, it lives on drifting oceanic ice floes, and unlike the brown bear and black bear, it is almost exclusively carnivorous, eating seals, whales, walruses, and other marine mammals. The soles of its feet are hairy, both insulating it from cold and facilitating movement across ice. Like most bears, polar bears tolerate the presence of other bears only near an abundant food source, such as a whale carcass. For most of the year, polar bears actually live on the ice and snow, far from the shore, hunting for marine mammals.

Females give birth to between one and four two-pound cubs in winter in a den of ice or snow, often inland in caves excavated from snow drifts or in soft earthen banks. In the Arctic National Wildlife Refuge, these natal den sites can be located as far as 30 miles from the nearest salt water (and provide one of the reasons for concern about coastal oil drilling). Cubs remain with their mother for several years, but after that polar bears are solitary animals. Under the terms of the Marine Mammal Protection Act, local Eskimos are permitted to hunt this rare animal.

Kaktovik *map site: 25*
Polar bears can be observed on the outskirts of this Eskimo community on the Arctic Ocean in the fall, when whales are killed and butchered. Access is via commercial airline to Kaktovik, and there is lodging available in town. The polar bear viewing season runs from mid-September through mid-October. You can also see them in Barrow along the beach, but be certain to keep your distance—polar bears are, of course, potentially dangerous. *See the "Arctic" chapter.*

■ SEA LIONS

The Steller's sea lion, named for the naturalist who first wrote about it when he explored Alaska with Vitus Bering in 1742, is the largest of the eared seals. On average, it grows to 11 feet and weighs 2,200 pounds; bulls can reach 13 feet and 2,400 pounds. Steller's sea lions inhabit coastal waters from the southern end of the southeast panhandle to the Bering Sea and live in large colonies on rocky points and capes. Like seals, they are protected from indiscriminate hunting and can be hunted only by Native Alaskans. Females can live up to 30 years, and males to 20. Populations in some areas have mysteriously declined in recent years.

Glacier Bay National Park and Preserve *map site: 5*
Sea lions can be seen in the Inland Passage at the foot of glaciers in Glacier Bay. Approximately 100 miles northeast of Juneau by boat or plane. Permits for pleasure boats are required. *Contact park headquarters, 907-697-2230. See the "Southeast" chapter.*

(following pages) Steller's sea lions socializing on the rocky shores of Glacier Island, in Prince William Sound.

Kenai Fjords National Park   *map site: 11*

Charter boats based in Seward will take you into Resurrection Bay, where sea lions are readily seen. Because Seward is a three-hour drive from Anchorage, this is probably the best opportunity for visitors to see the sea lion in Alaska. *A number of charter boats operate out of the Seward Small Boat Harbor. See the "South-Central" chapter.*

Prince William Sound Area   *map site: 8*

If you take a boat charter in the Sound, you will see sea lions along rocky islands and shoreline. *Board boat or ferry at Valdez. See the "South-Central" chapter.*

■ SEA OTTERS

Sea otters' playfulness indicates a highly developed brain, especially in the frontal lobes associated with cognition, or thought. Though hunted to near extinction by the end of the 19th century, sea otters have made a comeback in Southeast Alaska, where they now thrive. They are also returning strongly all along the Pacific coast of Canada and the Lower 48. Currently, there are more than 150,000 sea otters in Alaska. They are most often seen along the shore in giant sea kelp beds, where they hunt for shellfish.

Sea otters are continually grooming themselves, rubbing water-resistant oil from subcutaneous glands onto their fur to make a more effective barrier to water. They are a wonderful animal to watch, as they float in huge groups in kelp beds—nursing pups, occasionally diving for shellfish, or peacefully napping in the rolling swells. Some sea otters employ a rudimentary form of tool technology, using rocks to crack open shellfish, which the otters place on their chests for the opening process.

Inside Passage, aboard ship or ferry   *map site: 1*

Visitors who travel to Alaska via water often see otters in the saltwater bays and channels of Prince William Sound, Glacier Bay, or the outer coast near Sitka. *There are a variety of cruises to choose from, as well as the Alaska state ferries. See the "Southeast" chapter.*

Kenai Fjords National Park   *map site: 11*

From Seward (a three-hour drive from Anchorage) take a charter boat into Resurrection Bay, where both sea lions and sea otters can be seen. *A number of charter boats operate out of the Seward Small Boat Harbor. See the "South-Central" chapter.*

Prince William Sound *map site: 8*

Sea otters can sometimes be seen in the vicinity of the Valdez docks. It was in this area that the *Exxon Valdez* grounded on Bligh Reef in 1989, causing the worst oil-spill disaster in U.S. maritime history. Many sea otters and other wild animals perished as a result. *At northern extent of Gulf of Alaska. Board boat or ferry at Valdez. See the "South-Central" chapter.*

■ WALRUS

Walruses live in groups of up to one hundred and frequent relatively shallow water, beaches, and ice floes. Occasionally, they feed on seals and other marine animals, but their diet consists mainly of clams, which they dig for with their long tusks and shovel into their mouths with stiff whiskers. Their tusks, which both sexes possess, are also used for hauling themselves onto the ice, and rarely for fighting. The male walrus is much larger than the female and can reach a maximum length and weight of about 12 feet and 2,770 pounds.

Walrus Islands State Game Sanctuary *map site: 15*

About 10,000 walruses summer at the Walrus Islands, along with up to 1,000 Steller's sea lions and hundreds of thousands of puffins, auklets, gulls, cormorants, kittiwakes, and murres. There is also a small population of red foxes. *Located on Round Island, a windy, remote island about 70 miles southwest of Dillingham. Reached by charter boat from Dillingham via the Eskimo village of Togiak. See the "Southwest" chapter.*

■ WATERFOWL

The migratory waterfowl and shorebirds of Alaska are a miracle of nature. The **golden plover,** for example, migrates south to Antarctica each year and then returns to Alaska in the summer. Other migrations—ducks, geese, cranes—are no less amazing, and involve the mass movement of large bird populations across thousands of miles of open sea, coastal mountains, and vast interior regions. Alaskans hopefully await the arrival of the first birds every May, and sadly note the departure of the great flocks each August. In many ways, summer can be defined by the presence of the migratory birds. One of my favorites is the **common loon,** which nests on inland lakes and ponds. This loon is strikingly beautiful, and its black-and-white checkered

Harlequin ducks on Kodiak Island.

plumage is best described as surreal. The bird has a haunting, yodeling song that echoes forlornly over the subarctic waters in the twilight hours. Once mated, the male and female loon construct a nest of twigs and feathers in the reeds and share nesting responsibilities—one adult feeding while the other warms the eggs or hatchlings. It's always wonderful to see the parents and young birds paddling around the lake. One of the best places to look for loons is Wonder Lake in Denali National Park and Preserve.

Colorful **tufted puffins** are found in great abundance along the Pacific coast of Alaska. Puffins have thick dark bodies, distinctive white-feathered faces, and bright orange beaks that resemble those of parrots. Puffins are social birds, and their extensive nesting colonies—built into rocky ledges overlooking the sea—are widespread, particularly in Resurrection Bay and the Kenai Fiords area. Puffins feed widely on the food resources of the open sea and coastal bays and estuaries, eating everything from crabs to young salmon. Puffin facsimiles are a favorite at gift shops in places like Homer and Kenai—kids love them.

Copper River Delta *map site: 7*
Each spring millions of migratory birds on their way north stop at this vast, 400-square-mile river delta. Snow geese, sandhill cranes, arctic terns, jaegers, great blue herons, and bald eagles are only a few of the bird species that spend time here. The Copper River Delta hosts an annual shorebird festival in May. *Located west of Cordova. Access by Copper River Highway, boat, or floatplane. Contact the U.S. Forest Service, Cordova Ranger District, 907-424-7661. See the "South-Central" chapter.*

Creamer's Field, Fairbanks *map site: 22*
Creamer's Field Migratory Waterfowl Refuge, a former farm, is one of the best places to observe migratory waterfowl such as ducks, geese, and enormous flocks of sand hill cranes. Each May and September these planted fields are aswarm with tired, hungry birds either just arriving or preparing to leave. *Located on College Road near the offices of the State of Alaska Department of Fish & Game. See the "Interior" chapter.*

Kenai Fjords National Park *map site: 11*
A tour boat from Seward will take you through Resurrection Bay, where tens of thousands of colorful seabirds can be observed. *Seward is a three-hour drive south from Anchorage. Tours depart from the Seward Small Boat Harbor. See the "South-Central" chapter.*

Potter Marsh, Anchorage Area *map site: 16*
Geese, ducks, trumpeter swans, and other waterfowl can sometimes be seen here. The best time of year to visit is between the first week of April and mid-September. Noise from the freeway running along one side of the marsh and gunfire from the rifle range across the road make this place less than tranquil, however. *Located on the Seward Highway just east of town; turnoffs at Mile 117.4 and Mile 116. See the "South-Central" chapter.*

■ WHALES AND ORCAS

Humpback whales winter in the warm waters around Baja, Mexico, and Maui, Hawaii, where visitors sometimes observe them giving birth. As spring advances over the northern hemisphere the whales respond to an ancient migratory urge and swim north. By mid-June they arrive at their rich summer feeding grounds in Alaska. At this time they are often seen by summer visitors traveling at sea. If there are humpback whales in the vicinity of your fishing boat or cruise ship you will know about it.

First, whales sometimes breach—rocketing out of the water and crashing onto their sides with a resonant splash. Additionally, you will see their spray spouts as they come up to breathe. You may also see their flukes just before they slide beneath the surface. There are few experiences in this world as magnificent as seeing a whale at sea.

Humpbacks are not toothed whales, like sperm whales or orcas, but rather have fringed baleen plates set in their jaws. By straining water through these extensive natural filters, the humpbacks are able to feed on swimming crustaceans and small fish. Humpbacks have been observed schooling and moving through water in such a way as to concentrate their food sources; the giant mammals then take turns diving through the concentrated krill. Marine biologists operating in the northern Pacific waters and utilizing hydrophones suspended from research boats have recorded the beautiful songs of humpbacks. These songs have not yet been deciphered, but the fact that many of these long compositions are repeated, virtually note for note, year after year, is intriguing. There are perhaps 2,000 humpback whales in the north Pacific, with several hundred migrating to southeastern Alaska every summer.

Orcas, or killer whales, can grow over 20 feet long. They are easy to identify when they surface because of the prominent dorsal fin, which, on males, may be as high as six feet. Biologists use the distinctive black-and-white marking on the dorsal fin to identify particular orcas in their field study areas. Orcas have large teeth that resemble sharpened ceramic coffee mugs in size and surface appearance.

These large ocean-going predators travel in "pods"—small groups roughly conforming to an extended family—and have a highly evolved social structure. There are two distinct varieties of orca: resident (which eat only fish) and transient (which prey on whales, seals, sea lions, and even birds. The two types never intermingle. The orca is actually, from a taxonomic standpoint, a gigantic dolphin (in much the same way that a wolverine is a giant weasel). It is thought that at least 300 to 400 killer whales live along the Pacific Coast of Alaska, although these numbers fluctuate considerably.

Glacier Bay National Park and Preserve and Juneau Area *map site: 5*
Whales are abundant in Glacier Bay and the areas around the park, including Icy Strait, Chatham Strait, and Lynn Canal, from early July through September. Whale-watching cruises are available in Juneau. One researcher claims to have observed the same whale returning to Glacier Bay for 12 consecutive years. *Southeast Alaska at northern end of Inside Passage. Inquire at park headquarters (907-697-2230) or book a tour out of Juneau. See the "Southeast" chapter.*

Inside Passage *map site: 1*

Whales are seen along the Marine Highway most often in the spring and fall, when they are migrating either north or south. *See the "Southeast" chapter.*

Prince William Sound *map site: 8*

Whales are often observed in the southwestern part of Prince William Sound, near Montague Strait and the Gulf of Alaska. *Reached from Valdez at northern extent of Gulf of Alaska. See the "South-Central" chapter.*

■ WOLVES

Adult Alaskan wolves range in size from 90 to 140 pounds. Signs most often encountered in the wild include their five-toed, dog-like tracks, kill sites (which will not be covered with ground debris, as with a bear kill site), natal den sites (often old fox dens that have been enlarged), summer rendezvous sites (a day-bed area for the pack), and scent-marking sites (which have a pungent smell and are often located near or on prominent rocks or trees). Pups are born in the late spring. For the first few weeks, the mother remains with the cubs, while the rest of the extended family, which may include non-blood-related members, hunts. When the adult wolves return, they regurgitate their food for both the mother and the cubs as the latter are weaned from the mother's milk. Eventually, the mother resumes hunting, and in mid-summer the pack abandons the natal den site for the summer rendezvous sites, from which they hunt.

Dalton Highway *map site: 24*

Wolves are sometimes seen on Atigun Pass, where they hunt Dall sheep, and on the coastal plain, where they hunt barren-ground caribou. Wolves are trapped and hunted in this area, so they are not as easily seen as in the national parks. The caribou migration on the coastal plain begins in early August; at that time the Porcupine Herd of around 120,000 animals moves south toward the foothills of the Brooks Range. Wolves, closely following the herd as it moves south, can be seen along the Dalton Highway in this region at that time. *Dalton Highway runs from Livengood, just north of Fairbanks, to Prudhoe Bay. For a more specific location of the herd, check with the BLM office in Fairbanks or with the State of Alaska Department of Fish & Game in Fairbanks, 907-459-7200. See the "Arctic" chapter.*

WOLVES ARE LISTENING

The wolves must have seen me first. In the slanted sunlight of late evening, they couldn't miss a bright orange tent, a snowmachine, and a man on the valley floor. I looked up, wondering what had spooked the sheep, and saw them: ten wolves, strung out along the ridge, silhouetted against the snow. They worked across the snowfield, down into a draw, and out of sight.

I went back to camp chores, feeling lucky. Even far back in the western Brooks Range, most packs have learned the hard way about men. But these wolves didn't run, though they paused and stared toward me. Maybe there was something about the way I stood or even what I thought that reassured them. If wolves are experts at anything, it's reading intentions.

I cooked dinner and watched the upper Noatak Valley slide into the twilight that, in late April, passes for night. As I sat alone, a chorus of howls rose from the mountain, then faded into the wind.

I awoke the next morning to more howls, much closer now. Stumbling from the tent into the bright blue day, I scanned the ridge behind me. There, a head on the skyline, five hundred yards above me in the rocks. I was being watched, and no doubt discussed. Scanning, I found other wolves as they crested the ridge. They apparently wanted to move downhill, on a course that would take them right through camp.

Slowly, one at a time, in almost imperceptible movements, they made their way down, one here, two there. If I sat and watched, they moved little or not at all, feigning indifference, plopping down and curling up as if for a quick nap. When I ducked into the tent and checked five minutes later, they'd shifted closer.

After a half hour of this, I'll admit I was getting edgy. The wide sweep of the Noatak Valley echoed with silence. I didn't exactly feel threatened, but how many people have sat calmly, alone, as a dozen wolves worked their way into camp?

All the warnings I'd heard from older Eskimos swirled back. Clarence, the master wolf hunter, had admonished me to be careful around large packs. When I replied that I wasn't afraid of wolves, and tried to counter with my white-guy-feel-good-about-wolves-they-are-our-brothers statistics, Clarence grew suddenly irritated. "Quiet! Wolves are listening right now!" His tone of voice was the same as when he'd warned me I'd unknowingly crossed some dangerous ice.

I suppose I should have waited. But what if I just sat here and they passed just on the other side of that knoll? I shouldered my camera tripod and hustled to intercept them.

From the crest I spotted one gray loping off, pausing to look back. The others seemed to have evaporated. This was wolf behavior I understood. I watched and waited, was about to give up, when I spotted another lying in the brush, close enough to make me start. But though I was in plain sight a few dozen yards away, the young male ignored me, gazing off down the slope. When I moved closer, he rose, stretched, and regarded me with casual interest. When I inched closer, he moved off an equal distance. After a few minutes of this inter-species two-step, he trotted off, apparently bored by my company.

Suddenly he stopped, intent on something. He gathered himself, pounced, and came up with an ordinary-looking stick. Shaking his head like an overgrown puppy, he paraded away.

When I looked back up the hill, the rest of the pack was retreating, circling west. One big black and a limping gray seemed especially wary; they stood on the skyline, looking down. Then they were gone.

As I trudged back to camp, I kicked myself for not staying put. Then again, maybe the pack wouldn't have come any closer. I'd never know, but this much was true: we'd each taken steps toward the other, and something like peace had passed between us.

Back in Ambler, old Nelson Greist would shake his head and laugh at my earnest explanation. "Maybe they try to eat you," he said. "You just never know it."

–Nick Jans, *A Place Beyond,* 1996

Denali National Park and Preserve *map site: 21*

A good place to look for wolves is the open country that ranges from Sable Pass on the east to Thorofare Pass on the west. In the past several years, wolves have often been seen in the Teklanika campground area (Mile 29) and along the road nearby. Wolves are most active at night and in the twilight hours. Another prime location from which to watch for them is near the bridge over the East Fork of the Toklat River, as well as near the bridge on the Toklat River. There is an active wolf den about a mile upstream from the East Fork bridge; this entire area is off limits to cross-country hiking, but with good binoculars the wolves can often be seen at dawn or dusk. There is also an active wolf den downstream of the bridge over the Toklat River, also an excellent area for wolf viewing. *See the "Interior" chapter.*

■ SAFETY AND REGULATIONS

Remember that it is illegal to possess migratory bird feathers and to collect antlers and skulls from national parks. The body parts of endangered marine mammals (and most marine mammals are endangered) are also protected by federal law.

Red foxes are among the residents of Denali National Park and Preserve.

A STORY IN THE SNOW

To one who lives in the snow and watches it day by day, it is a book to be read. The pages turn as the wind blows; the characters shift and the images formed by their combinations change in meaning, but the language remains the same. It is a shadow language, spoken by things that have gone by and will come again. The same text has been written there for thousands of years, though I was not here, and will not be here in winters to come, to read it. These seemingly random ways, these paths, these beds, these footprints, these hard, round pellets in the snow: they all have meaning. Dark things may be written there, news of other lives, their sorties and excursions, their terrors and deaths. The tiny feet of a shrew or a vole make a brief, erratic pattern across the snow, and here is a hole down which the animal goes. And now the track of an ermine comes this way, swift and searching, and he too goes down that white shadow of a hole. . . .

–John Haines, *The Stars, The Snow, The Fire,* 1977

These laws are designed to protect wildlife from illegal activities, such as poaching, which are unfortunately a significant problem in Alaska. If you have any questions regarding souvenirs found in the field, feel free to inquire with state or federal agencies or local law enforcement officials. Hikers should also understand that it is a federal crime to be in possession of an eagle feather. Authorities trying to protect wildlife have no way of knowing whether a person in the backcountry found the feather on the ground or killed a bird to get it.

■ WORDS OF CAUTION

Make noise while hiking: sing, carry a whistle, or converse loudly in bear country.

Keep food and garbage properly stored and away from your sleeping area.

If you encounter a bear, don't run. Back away slowly and speak to the bear in a low, firm voice.

If you encounter a moose, don't crowd it. If it advances purposefully toward you, making eye contact and with head lowered, you should run.

HABITAT ZONES

RAIN FOREST OF THE SOUTHEAST

The Panhandle's rain forest of evergreen hemlock and Sitka spruce is the habitat of the forest-dwelling black bear, deer, flying squirrels, owls, woodpeckers, and songbirds. Millions of salmon return from the ocean to spawn in freshwater creeks, and bald eagles wait to snatch them from the water. Along the edge of the rain forest, in the waterways of the Inside Passage, live whales, porpoises, seals, and sea lions.

Sitka spruce forest

White spruce forest

SPRUCE-HARDWOOD FOREST OF THE INTERIOR

Between the coastal rain forest and the treeless tundra of Alaska's north and west is a low forest of birch, white spruce, aspen, fir, pine, and poplar trees. The forested lowlands are home to bears, moose, and wolves. Dall sheep and golden eagles are found in the mountain peaks and treeless tundra of higher elevations.

Wet Tundra of the Arctic

Dwarf shrubs and a variety of grasses and mosses grow on soggy tundra. Legumes are common near streams and lakes. Vast herds of migratory caribou, grizzlies, swans, ducks, geese, loons, jaegers, and snowy owls can be found here. Millions of mosquitoes breed in the swampy muskegs of these areas, providing food for hungry migratory birds that fly thousands of miles to summer here. On the icy sea of the far north, polar bears feed on seals and walrus.

Wet tundra

Dry Tundra

Higher elevations in the Arctic and subarctic regions support dry alpine tundra, which is characterized by barren ground and rock as well as by such vegetation as lichens, grasses, sedges, berries, and some herbs. Willows grow along the streams. Feeding on these shrubs and grass are caribou herds, moose, Dall sheep, grizzlies, ptarmigan, and various songbirds.

Dry tundra

S O U T H E A S T
A N D   T H E   I N S I D E   P A S S A G E

Alaska's long and narrow southeastern panhandle is made up of myriad islands, of quiet deep bays with breaching whales, and of ancient forests thick with moss, where great bears lumber silently. Skies are forever lowering under some new Pacific squall, then rising unexpectedly to reveal great snowcapped mountains. Seal pups are born at the edge of glaciers that themselves "calve" into the sea. Here, too, lies the most beautifully situated state capital in the United States: Juneau, which remains, even at the dawn of the 21st century, unconnected by road to the rest of the continent.

The best way to travel in Southeast Alaska is by ferry or cruise ship up the Inside Passage. Most leave from Bellingham, Washington (one and a half hours north of Seattle, and one hour south of Vancouver B.C.) and travel north to Ketchikan, Petersburg, Juneau, Skagway, and Haines.

■ **THE INSIDE PASSAGE**   *maps pages 84, 85, 118, & 119*

The Alaska Marine Highway System begins in Bellingham, Washington, and runs through the picturesque green islands of Puget Sound and up the incised coast of British Columbia. After you pass the Canadian port of Prince Rupert and re-enter American waters south of Ketchikan, the coast becomes increasingly rugged. For the next couple of days you will travel through a wonderland of islands both large and small, expansive bays and inlets, massive glaciers, towering mountains. Everywhere the northern coastal forests will amaze you—lush and green as a tropical rain forest. Sometimes you will spot wildlife—moose, bears, deer—going about their affairs along the beaches and coves. Out on the water you will often see seals, sea lions, killer and humpback whales, sea gulls, and bald eagles in primordial abundance.

There will be stops, of course, and time to explore the crowded waterfronts that smell of fish, salt air, brewing coffee, diesel engines, and wood-burning cabin stoves. But then you will be back on the water—in a world too vast to be captured in a photograph or scribbled about on a postcard. North of Ketchikan, turning west into Clarence Strait, you will enter one of the last great wilderness areas on

Sea kayakers at Auke Bay, near Juneau.

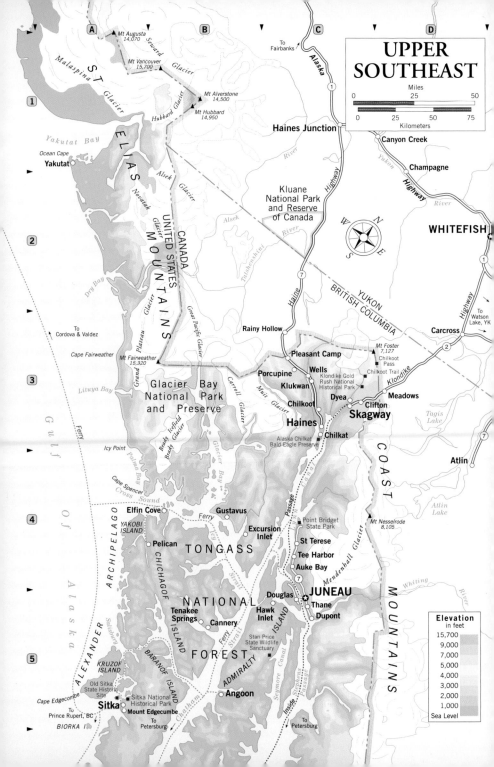

UPPER SOUTHEAST

Miles
0   25   50

Kilometers
0   25   50   75

A   **B**   **C**   **D**

Mt Augusta
14,070

To
Fairbanks

Alaska

Malaspina
Glacier

Seward Glacier

ST

Mt Vancouver
15,700

Hubbard Glacier

Mt Alverstone
14,500

Mt Hubbard
14,950

Haines Junction

Canyon Creek

Champagne

Yukon River

Highway

1

ELIAS

Yakutat Bay

Ocean Cape
Yakutat

Alsek

Glacier

Novatak Glacier

UNITED STATES

CANADA

Kluane
National Park
and Reserve
of Canada

Alsek River

Tatshenshini River

N
W   E
S

WHITEFISH

Highway

To
Watson
Lake, YK

2

To
Cordova & Valdez

Dry Bay

Cape Fairweather

MOUNTAINS

Grand Plateau Glacier

Great Pacific Glacier

Mt Fairweather
15,320

Haines

Rainy Hollow

YUKON

BRITISH COLUMBIA

Carcross

Lituya Bay

Gulf

Carroll Glacier

Brady Icefield

Brady Glacier

Glacier Bay
National Park
and Preserve

Pleasant Camp

Porcupine

Wells

Klukwan

Chilkoot

Mt Foster
7,127

Klondike Gold
Rush National
Historical Park

Chilkoot Trail

Chilkoot
Pass

Klondike

Meadows

Dyea

Clifton

Skagway

Tagis
Lake

3

Cape Fairweather

Icy Point

Ferry

Glacier Bay

Palma Bay

Muir Glacier

Haines

Alaska Chilkat
Bald Eagle Preserve

Chilkat

Skagway

Atlin

7

Cape Spencer

Cross Sound

Ferry

Elfin Cove

YAKOBI
ISLAND

Pelican

Gustavus

Excursion
Inlet

Point Bridget
State Park

St Terese

Tee Harbor

Auke Bay

Mt Nesselrode
8,105

COAST

Atlin
Lake

4

of

ARCHIPELAGO

CHICHAGOF ISLAND

TONGASS

NATIONAL

Tenakee
Springs

Cannery

Lisianski Strait

Ferry

Icy Strait

Chatham Strait

Douglas

Hawk
Inlet

JUNEAU

Thane

Dupont

Mendenhall Glacier

Whiting River

MOUNTAINS

7

Alaska

ALEXANDER

KRUZOF
ISLAND

Old Sitka
State Historic
Site

Cape Edgecumbe

To
Prince Rupert, BC

BIORKA I.

Sitka National
Historical Park

Sitka

Mount Edgecumbe

To
Petersburg

BARANOF ISLAND

FOREST

ADMIRALTY
ISLAND

Stan Price
State Wildlife
Sanctuary

Angoon

Seymour Canal

Inside Passage

Stephens Passage

To
Petersburg

5

Elevation
in feet

15,700
9,000
7,000
5,000
4,000
3,000
2,000
1,000
Sea Level

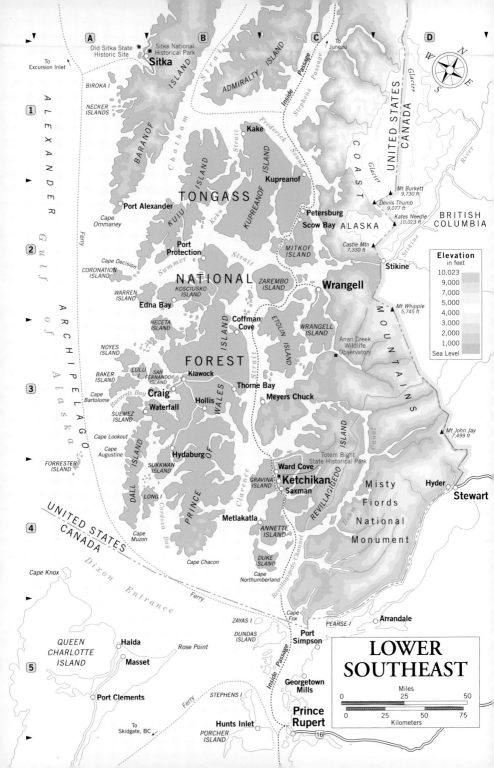

LOWER SOUTHEAST

Miles
0   25   50

0   25   50   75
Kilometers

A   B   C   D

1   2   3   4   5

Elevation
in feet

10,023
9,000
7,000
5,000
4,000
3,000
2,000
1,000
Sea Level

To Excursion Inlet

Old Sitka State Historic Site
Sitka National Historical Park
Sitka
BIROKA I
NECKER ISLANDS

ADMIRALTY ISLAND

Chatham Strait

To Juneau

Inside Passage
Stephens Passage

Kake
Frederick Sound

Kupreanof

Petersburg
Scow Bay
ALASKA

BARANOF ISLAND

KUIU ISLAND
Ketu Strait
KUPREANOF ISLAND

TONGASS

Cape Ommaney

Port Alexander

Cape Decision
CORONATION ISLAND

Port Protection

Summer Strait

NATIONAL

MITKOF ISLAND

ZAREMBO ISLAND

Wrangell

WARREN ISLAND

KOSCIUSKO ISLAND

Edna Bay

HECETA ISLAND

Coffman Cove

WRANGELL ISLAND

Anan Creek Wildlife Observatory

FOREST

NOYES ISLAND

BAKER ISLAND
LULU I
SAN FERNANDO ISLAND

Klawock
Thorne Bay

PRINCE OF WALES ISLAND

Stikine Strait

ETOLIN ISLAND

Meyers Chuck

Cape Bartolome
SUEMEZ ISLAND

Craig
Hollis
Waterfall

Cape Lookout
Cape Augustine

Hydaburg
SUKKWAN ISLAND
LONG I

Clarence Strait

Bucareli Bay

FORRESTER ISLAND

DALL ISLAND

Cordova Bay

Cape Muzon

Totem Bight State Historical Park

Ward Cove
Ketchikan
Saxman
GRAVINA ISLAND

REVILLAGIGEDO ISLAND

Behm Canal

Metlakatla
ANNETTE ISLAND

DUKE ISLAND

Cape Chacon

Cape Northumberland

Revillagigedo Channel

UNITED STATES
CANADA

Dixon Entrance

Ferry

Cape Knox

ZAYAS I
DUNDAS ISLAND

Cape Fox

PEARSE I
Arrandale

Hyder
Stewart

Misty Fiords National Monument

Mt John Jay 7,499 ft

MOUNTAINS

Mt Whipple 5,745 ft

Stikine

Castle Mtn 7,330 ft

Kates Needle 10,023 ft
Devils Thumb 9,077 ft
Mt Burkett 9,730 ft

Stikine River

COAST

Glacier

Glacier River

UNITED STATES
CANADA

BRITISH COLUMBIA

ALEXANDER ARCHIPELAGO

Gulf of Alaska

Ferry

Port Simpson

Inside Passage

Georgetown Mills

QUEEN CHARLOTTE ISLAND

Halda
Masset
Rose Point

Port Clements

To Skidgate, BC

STEPHENS I

Hunts Inlet
PORCHER ISLAND

Prince Rupert

16

YOU CAN'T MAKE HAY WHILE IT RAINS

I never saw a richer bog and meadow growth anywhere. The principal forest-trees are hemlock, spruce and Nootka cypress, with a few pines. . . . I have found southeastern Alaska a good, healthy country to live in. The climate of the islands and shores of the mainland is remarkably temperate and free from extremes of either heat or cold throughout the year. It is rainy, however, —so much so that hay-making will hardly ever be extensively engaged in here. . . . The most remarkable characteristic of this summer weather is the velvet softness of the atmosphere. . . . I never saw summer days so white and so full of subdued lustre.

–John Muir, *Travels in Alaska,* 1879

After Fishing *(ca. 1960), Colcord (Rusty) Heurlin.*

earth. Prince of Wales Island will be to the west—the third-largest island in the United States—and to the east there will be a rich profusion of smaller islands, all part of the immense Tongass National Forest. Farther north you will pass Admiralty Island, where most valleys have more bears than people. Approaching Juneau through spectacular Stephens Passage, on a clear day, you'll spot to the east the forbidding peaks and glaciers of the Tracy Arm–Fords Terror Wilderness.

Much of this area is included in the Tongass National Forest. About one-third of the Tongass has been designated "commercial forest lands," which are slated to be clear-cut sooner or later, but the forest also contains a dozen large wilderness areas, including much of Admiralty Island, small portions of Baranof Island and Prince of Wales Island, and Misty Fiords National Monument.

Among the attractions of the Tongass are the 150 public recreational cabins maintained by the U.S. Forest Service, which are reached only by floatplane or boat.

The towns of Southeast Alaska partake of two worlds—the sea and the land. They are surrounded by glaciers and mountains and forests, and yet they are as much a part of the salt water as the herring gulls and the hermit crabs. The people who live in them work in the forests, on the sea, or in commerce, including tourism. They are isolated from the mainland highways, connected to the rest of the country only by satellite dishes, telephones, and computers. But the towns of the Panhandle differ from other island and coastal towns in the United States. Because these hamlets are on the busy Marine Highway and are also easily accessed from the air, visitors will not find the xenophobia—the distrust of outsiders—that sometimes exists in isolated rural or bush communities. There is a worldliness about these Southeast towns, a tolerance of differences, a warm friendliness, and a natural generosity.

■ KETCHIKAN *map page 85, C-4*

Ketchikan's economy is based on three industries: salmon fishing, logging, and tourism. The town has found itself in the national news frequently in the past decades at the center of an intense debate over clear-cutting so-called high volume old-growth forest—the biggest and oldest and most valuable trees. (Such forest land constitutes only 4 percent of the total Tongass area). In 1990 federal legislation restricted harvests and forced large multinational companies to shut down pulp mills in Ketchikan and Sitka. This was good news for salmon (whose spawning streams were being destroyed because of siltation), but bad news for people working in the timber industry. Since then, pro-timber interests have waged a concerted campaign to roll back protections, and court battles continue.

The population of Ketchikan is 7,922, making it the fifth-largest population center in Alaska. The town rambles along the coast for quite a distance, never more than a dozen blocks wide, and climbs the hills on wooden stairways that offer pretty views over the neighboring islands.

Ketchikan began as a Tlingit salmon fishing camp, called *Kitschk-Hin,* or "The Creek of the Thundering Wings of an Eagle." It subsequently became a center for salmon canneries. Today, you'll find the remnants of wilder days, including a former red-light district that features a bordello turned into a museum, **Dolly's House** (24 Creek Street; 907-225-6329); and a lively local bar, the Sourdough. The **Totem Heritage Center** (601 Deermount Street; 907-225-5900) has 33 totem poles, the largest collection of historic totems in the United States. Two totem parks, one at Saxman and another at Totem Bight State Historical Park (907-247-8574), display tribal houses and poles in scenic, outdoor settings. The city walking-tour map is available at the **Ketchikan Visitors Bureau** (131 Front Street; 907-225-6166 or 800-770-3300), on the cruise ship dock on Front Street. A number of local tour operators offer tours by boat or floatplane to the spectacular **Misty Fiords National Monument,** which is 30 miles east of Ketchikan. As with Petersburg, Sitka, and Juneau, Ketchikan has daily jet service from Seattle and Anchorage via Alaska Airlines.

■ Misty Fiords National Monument
map page 85, C/D-3/4

At the southern end of the Tongass National Forest, directly beside the Canadian border, is a magnificent wilderness of some 2.3 million acres known as Misty Fiords National Monument. The name powerfully evokes the place—perpetually misty and characterized by a multitude of deep fjords. Thundering waterfalls drop thousands of feet from sheer rock cliffs. Mountains rise vertically from the cold salt water to the snowfields. Everywhere the northern rain forest vegetation is lush and green.

Reached from Ketchikan, this area is a favorite for boating and for fishing. Camping can be tough because the tides range upward of 20 feet, and it can be a challenge to find dry flat areas. One of the most popular ways of visiting Misty Fiords is on a larger-sized boat, where passengers can sleep comfortably on board. Wildlife includes black and brown bears, Sitka deer, and mountain goats, with the waters offering the normal Pacific complement of whales, seals, and sea lions. The area is also known for its bald eagle population.

Picturesque Creek Street, in Ketchikan, was the town's red-light district in the early 1900s. Now many of its small houses, built on stilts over the water, have been turned into shops, cafés, and bed-and-breakfasts.

■ PRINCE OF WALES ISLAND   *map page 85, B-2 to 4*

At 2,231 square miles, Prince of Wales Island is easily the largest island in Southeast Alaska. In fact, it is the third-largest island in the United States—behind the big island of Hawai'i and Kodiak Island. Because of the wet maritime climate, much of Prince of Wales Island is heavily forested. In recent decades up to a dozen active logging camps operated on the island. More recently, though, timber harvesting has declined for several reasons: available allotments have been clear-cut, public sentiment has turned against harvesting wood at a loss for export to Japan, and Congress in response has begun to rein in the industry. As a result of the logging industry, there is a gravel road system that connects the three primary towns—Craig, Klawock, and Thorne Bay—as well as other areas where both logging and mining have taken place. Alaska state ferries serve the town of Hollis, on the east side of the island. Although the timber and mining industries historically go from boom to bust and back again, the salmon industry has provided a renewable natural resource that faithfully supports many of the permanent residents on Prince of Wales Island. The island is a favorite with sport fisherman, big-game hunters, and sea kayakers.

Craig is located on the west side of Prince of Wales Island about 60 miles west of Ketchikan. Like many of the smaller villages in the region, Craig began its life as a Tlingit fishing camp in the years before the Russian empire arrived. Today, Craig is an important regional center for the logging and fishing industries. Visitors use the town as a base of operation for fishing and hunting expeditions into the backcountry. There is a lodge in Craig (see page 123), as well as restaurants and a store.

■ WRANGELL   *map page 85, C-2*

A good-sized town of about 2,300 inhabitants, Wrangell is located in close proximity to the Stikine River, which drains from British Columbia to the sea. The Stikine is one of the most scenic rivers in the Pacific Northwest. Like many of the towns in the region, Wrangell owes its existence to the expansive Russian fur empire of the 18th and 19th centuries. Upon arriving on the ferry, you'll find the **Wrangell Visitor Center** in the new James and Elsie Nolan Center (244 Front Street; 907-874-3901). Farther along, on Front Street, is the **Kiksetti Totem Park,** which pays homage to the rich Indian cultures of the region. More totems are on **Chief Shakes Island,** at the end of Shakes Street, including some

The lush forests of Prince of Wales, Admiralty, and Chichagof islands receive more than 150 inches of rain a year in some locations.

house posts in the Chief Shakes Tribal House, a 1939 replica of a traditional tribal house. **Petroglyph Beach State Historic Park,** with ancient, cryptic designs carved into its boulders, is worth a short guided tour, and the Anan Creek Wildlife Observatory is accessible by a short floatplane trip or by jet boat. There are three hotels, several bed-and-breakfasts, and a number of gift shops in Wrangell. As with other southeastern towns on the state ferry system, Wrangell can be used as a jumping-off point for a number of outdoor activities, including sport fishing, sea kayaking, camping, hiking, and wildlife photography. There are about a dozen Forest Service cabins available for renting in the Wrangell area (see page 140).

Famous **Anan Creek Wildlife Observatory** (800-367-9745) is only 28 miles by plane or hired boat from Wrangell. During the summer salmon runs, you can observe black bears and often brown bears. (For more information, see page 56.)

■ PETERSBURG   *map page 85, C-2*

Picturesque little Petersburg, on Mitkof Island south of Juneau, is often referred to by Alaskans as "Little Norway" for its beautiful fjord-like setting and neat, white, Scandinavian-style homes and storefronts. Magnificent views open to the eye in every direction: to the east across Frederick Sound to Horn Mountain and the Horn Cliffs on the mainland; to the north and west, mountainous Kupreanof Island. In the six-block downtown area, you'll find a **Tongass National Forest office** (907-772-3841), the **Sons of Norway Hall, Clausen Memorial Museum** (corner of Second Street and Fram Street), and the **Harbor Bar** (at the corner of Dolphin Street and Nordic Drive). The main attraction is the **Frederick Point Boardwalk,** which leads from the Sandy Beach Recreation Area through classic southeastern hemlock forest and moose muskeg to a salmon stream, where you can watch the fish spawn, in season. Visitors can use Petersburg as a base of operations for sport fishing, camping, sea kayaking (Le Conte Glacier is a popular destination), photography, or hunting trips.

■ SITKA   *map page 85, A/B-1*

Sitka (pop. 8,835), on Baranof Island, has a mild, damp climate moderated by the sea. Even in the short dark days of January, the average daily temperate in Sitka is a balmy (by Alaskan standards) 33 degrees Fahrenheit. This contrasts markedly with Fairbanks, where the average daily temperature in January is between 2 and 18

Petroglyphs on the beach at Wrangell.

SITKA JACK'S HOUSE

We visited "Sitka Jack," an arrant old scoundrel, but one of the wealthiest men of the Sitka tribe. Of course his house stood among the largest, at the fashionable end of the town. These houses were built of planks, three or four inches thick, each one having been hewed from a log, with an adze formed by lashing a metal blade to the short prong of a forked stick. In constructing the native cabin, the planks are set on edge and so nicely fitted that they need no chinking. The shape of the house is square; a bark roof is laid on, with a central aperture for chimney. The door is a circular opening about two feet in diameter. It is closed with a sheet of bark or a bear-skin or seal-skin. On arriving at Sitka Jack's hut we crawled through the door, and found ourselves in the presence of Jack's wives, children, and slaves, who were lounging on robes and blankets laid on a board flooring which extended along each side of the room. A dirt floor about seven feet square was left in the center, and on this the fire burned and the pot of halibut boiled merrily. Our arrival was hailed with stolid indifference. The family circle reclined and squatted as usual, and went on with the apparently enjoyable occupation of scooping up handfuls of raw herring-roe, which they munched with great gusto.

—[Author unknown], "Among the Thlinkits in Alaska,"
The Century Magazine, July 1882

The interior of a Tlingit house in 1787 as depicted by John Webber, Captain Cook's shipboard artist.

degrees below zero. Like other Southeast towns, Sitka is often drenched in rain, receiving more than 100 inches a year. This site historically was used by Tlingit Indians, and in 1799 Russian fur baron Alexandr Baranov (for whom the island is named) built a fort here to anchor his trade in sea otter pelts.

Today, a large part of the attraction of Sitka is its Russian and Tlingit past. The city has a number of historic sites and museums and is of special interest to history buffs. Visitors can see a replica of the old **Russian Blockhouse**, which the Russians used as a protective stronghold against Indian attacks, and an original log cache built in 1835. **St. Michael's Cathedral** (907-747-8120), at the center of Lincoln Street downtown, is an exact replica of the original built in the 1840's by Bishop Innocent Veniaminov of the Russian Orthodox Church; the cathedral's displays include a collection of church treasures and art. The **Russian Bishop's House** (907-747-6281), built in 1842 as a residence for the Russian Orthodox bishop—Bishop Veniaminov was its first occupant—is also on Lincoln Street, although it is technically a part of the **Sitka National Historical Park** (106 Metlakatla Street; 907-747-6281), at the end of Lincoln Street within easy walking distance of the downtown area. The historical park, with a visitors center and a small museum, preserves both Sitka's Tlingit and Russian past on its acreage, and contains a totem pole assemblage as well.

Also, in the downtown area (downtown here denoting an area a few hundred yards long and about the same wide) you will find a **Tongass National Forest office** (204 Siganaka Way; 907-747-6671), which offers brochures and information regarding hiking and outdoor attractions; the well-known **Pioneer Bar** on the waterfront (on Katlian Street); the **Sheldon Jackson Museum** (907-747-8981), with its world-class collection of artifacts and old totems; and the **Isabel Miller Museum** (907-747-6455), focusing on the history of Sitka and its people. Another popular attraction is the **Alaska Raptor Center** (1000 Raptor Way; 907-747-8662), where injured eagles and other birds are cared for and exhibited.

Sitka's two harbors are filled with brightly painted fishing boats and face numerous pine-covered islands. Above them to the west rises Mount Edgecumbe, an extinct volcano with a pyramid shape. To the east are rugged snowcapped peaks, often shrouded in clouds.

The area is famous for ocean sport-fishing. King and coho (silver) salmon and monster halibut are the main attractions. Expertly captained charter boats are available; brochures can be picked up at the Tongass National Forest office.

(following pages) Crescent Harbor in Sitka, with Mount Verstovia in the background.

■ JUNEAU AND VICINITY *maps page 84, C-5, and page 99*

> The calm bay was full of the fantastic, beautiful harlequin ducks,
> geese were returning from their feeding-grounds near the shore, and
> on the land itself, varied thrushes and sparrows were singing in the
> trees. We dodged among the reefs, slipped through great quantities
> of sea-weed, everywhere abundant. . . . It had cleared and the day
> was beautiful and sunny.
>
> –Charles Sheldon, *Wilderness of the North Pacific,* 1909

A city of 30,711 people (a state capital smaller than 17th-century Boston), Juneau is a cosmopolitan community, with high-rise buildings, cultural facilities, legislative assembly chambers, and shopping malls. Yet Mother Nature is everywhere—in a sprawling glacier, the cold northern sea, mysterious dark spruce and hemlock forests, soaring snowcapped peaks, and abundant wildlife. Part of the reason Juneau remains beautiful is the seamless way wild nature and human culture blend into an integrated whole in which neither is diminished.

All of this is particularly remarkable when you consider that Juneau, like so many other Alaskan towns from Fairbanks to Nome, began as a disorganized mining camp. The historians tell us that in 1880 a couple of misfit miners named Dick Harris and Joe Juneau discovered gold in the stream that now runs through the center of town, rushing past Tenth Street and Ninth Street on its way to the Gastineau Channel. They were directed to the area by none other than John Muir, who noticed the local rocks' similarity to those in California's gold-bearing areas.

For a time the state capital was located in Sitka, but in 1906 common sense dictated the capital be moved to Juneau, where all the action was. Nearly $100 million worth of gold was extracted from Juneau before the mines closed in 1944.

Juneau is a compact, friendly town to walk around in. It is also the only state capital in the country where the governor's mansion is only nine blocks from prime bear habitat. The downtown streets are laid out in a grid, surrounding a creek that annually hosts spawning salmon. In the residential areas on the slopes above, the streets bend with the steep contours, conforming to the vagaries and vicissitudes of the rather jumbled landscape. The local air is heavy and moist, and it smells of seashore and spruce forest. In summer, the flower gardens are spectacular, and the scent of blossoms tinges the air.

■ DOWNTOWN JUNEAU WALKING TOUR

Visitor Information   *map this page, C-2*

If you arrive by cruise ship, you'll dock by Marine Park. Here at the visitors kiosk you can pick up a map illustrating a downtown walking tour. Maps, brochures, and information are also available at the **Juneau Visitors Center** (101 Egan Drive, inside the Centennial Hall Convention Center; 907-586-2201 or 888-581-2201). Before you set out on your tour, be certain you have your umbrella or a raincoat—rain is a fact of life in this temperate, maritime

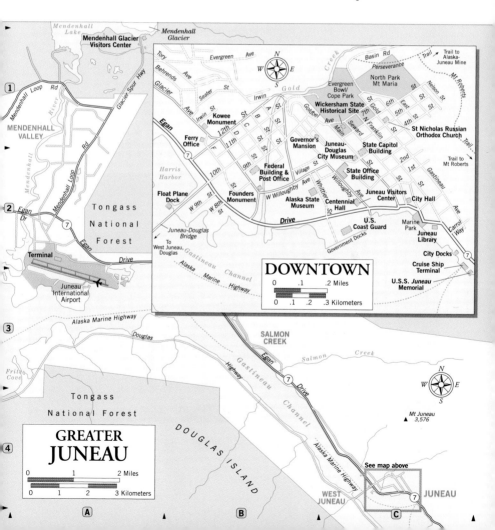

rain forest. Note that the state ferry terminal is 13 miles north of downtown, a long ride by taxi or bus.

Red Dog Saloon
You might want to start your tour at the popular **Red Dog Saloon,** just across the street from Marine Park. Overflowing with stuffed animal heads, furs, and memorabilia, with a sawdust-covered floor, it was built decades ago as a tourist attraction—and is. (Food and service are generally good, by the way). *278 South Franklin Street; 907-463-3658.*

State Capitol Building   *map page 99, C-2*
The home of the Alaska Legislature was built in the 1930s and has been recently renovated. Tours are available. Behind it stands one of Juneau's finest totem poles, the "five-story totem"—named for its unusual height. *Fourth Street between Seward and Main streets; 907-465-2479.*

Governor's Mansion   *map page 99, B/C-1/2*
The mansion, at the corner of West Seventh Street and Calhoun Avenue, is open to the public only for one day each year, in December, when its famous Christmas

During the summer months, downtown Juneau is enlivened by visitors, many of whom end up retiring to the Red Dog Saloon.

decorations and lights make it a popular stop even for locals. An impressive, white colonnaded structure built in 1912, it's worth a walk past. *716 Calhoun Avenue.*

St. Nicholas Russian Orthodox Church *map page 99, C-1*
Built in 1894, the small, onion-domed church is the oldest original Russian Orthodox church in Southeast Alaska. It's open daily for summer tours, and visitors are welcome to attend Sunday services. *326 Fifth Street; 907-586-1023.*

Wickersham State Historical Site *map page 99, C-1*
At the top of the hill behind the capitol is the one-time home of pioneer judge James Wickersham, who between 1909 and 1933 spent seven terms as Alaska's non-voting delegate to Congress. The main floors of the house, a large Victorian built in 1898, are open to the public. *213 Seventh Street; 907-586-9001.*

Alaska State Museum *map page 99, B/C-2*
One of the state's most impressive museums. Here, along with the natural history exhibits and scale models of historic ships, you can see a 40-foot walrus-hide umiak, or skin boat, used by Eskimos to hunt whales, a recreated Tlingit tribal house, and other Native artifacts. *395 Whittier Street; 907-465-2901.*

Gold Mining
The **Juneau–Douglas City Museum** (155 South Seward Street; 907-586-3572), across from the capitol, features gold mining history and a hands-on museum that's especially interesting for kids. If you become fascinated with the city's gold-mining past, walk up to see the ruins of the old **Alaska-Juneau Mine** at the end of Basin Road (the north end of Cope Park), or to the nearby **Glory Hole** accessed by the Perseverance Trail (see page 102). Another possibility, across the Gastineau Channel is the **Treadwell Mine** on Douglas Island. You can reach the island by taxi or city bus if you don't have a rental car. Other people try their hand at gold-panning in one of the public creeks (the Forest Service office will provide directions and guidance or you can arrange to take one of the commercial tours. (For more details, see pages 128 and 129.)

■ FISHING INDUSTRY

Macaulay Salmon Hatchery
Known to locals as the DIPAC hatchery (for Douglas Island Pink and Chum, Inc.), this privately run, modern facility has a glass-sided fish ladder, saltwater aquariums,

and informational displays. It's a very popular place to visit, and highly recommended. About three miles north of town via Egan Drive. *2697 Channel Drive; 907-463-4810.*

■ HIKING AROUND JUNEAU *map page 99, C-2*

Bears
The city of Juneau overlaps prime black bear habitat, and bear sightings are frequent. Don't crowd bears, and use common sense if you encounter one. No one in Juneau has ever been seriously injured by a black bear; you don't want to be the first. Most bears will retreat, but consider all bears, even those that seem passive, to be dangerous.

Perseverance Trail *map page 99, C-1*
Reached by walking up Basin Road from the center of town, this trail leads you into typical coastal rain forest habitat. Towering spruce and hemlock trees overhung with moss rise from a lush understory—a thick carpet of wild blueberries, devil's club (a native shrub with painfully sharp thorns), and innumerable wildflowers. Those with enough hiking experience and physical fortitude can continue up the Perseverance Trail to 3,576-foot **Mount Juneau.**

Douglas Island
Douglas Island, across Gastineau Channel, has developed hiking and cross-country skiing trails. The more remote trails require overnight trips into the wilderness; they can be accessed by sea kayak, chartered boat, or air charter.

Farther Afield
You can go by boat or plane to Glacier Bay National Park and Preserve, landing in the rustic community of Gustavus. Other options include Admiralty Island National Monument, any of a variety of remote sport fishing camps, or a wilderness cabin in Tongass National Forest. Numerous charter boat companies can take you fishing, whale watching, or sightseeing.

A trolley tour is one way to see downtown Juneau. Here, on South Franklin Street, are some of the oldest buildings in the city, including the 1913 Alaskan Hotel.

■ **MENDENHALL VALLEY**   *map page 99, A-1/2*

About 10 miles west of town on Egan Drive lies the lovely Mendenhall Valley. The valley is dominated by the Mendenhall Glacier, which drains south from the interior peaks of the Coastal Mountains. Not only is this an area of geological importance, it is also an important wildlife habitat; spawning salmon, black bear, beaver, and mountain goats are commonly seen (the latter at a distance). A beautiful visitors center is maintained near the base of the glacier, and there is a top-notch Forest Service campground on the west shore of the lake. The nearby 3,789-acre Mendenhall Wetlands State Game Refuge protects one of the few large salt marshes between the Fraser River in British Columbia and the Gulf of Alaska. It is an important resting area for migratory waterfowl and also provides habitat for bald eagles, herons, and a variety of smaller birds. Guided raft or kayak trips down the river afford fine views of the glacier and brief stretches of whitewater.

■ **ADMIRALTY ISLAND**   *maps pages 84 & 85*

Mention Admiralty Island to anyone in Alaska and the first association that comes to mind is the great coastal brown bear, *ursus arctos middendorfi,* an animal that grows to mind-boggling proportions on the extravagant diet of sea-run salmon, berries, vegetation, and scavenged marine mammal carcasses. Ninety percent of Admiralty Island is managed as the Admiralty Island National Monument and is home to hundreds of brown bears, making it one of the famous spots in Alaska for those interested in observing wildlife.

■ **STAN PRICE STATE WILDLIFE SANCTUARY**   *map page 84, C-5*

Most visitors to Juneau interested in seeing the big bears head for the **Stan Price State Wildlife Sanctuary** at Pack Creek, on 100-mile long Admiralty Island. This sanctuary is located about 28 miles south of Juneau, making for a short air flight. Like much of the Alexander Archipelago of the Alaska Panhandle, the Pack Creek area is a dense, jungle-like forest of spruce and hemlock with clear-running streams that support annual runs of pink and chum salmon. The estuary and tidal flats are also good places to look for bears out in the open. Primitive camping is permitted in the sanctuary in various designated areas. Most visitors choose to make day visits from Juneau.

■ ANGOON   *map page 84, B-5*

Set on a peninsula on the west side of Admiralty Island, about midway between Juneau and Sitka, is the village of Angoon. It is one of the major Tlingit Indian communities in the Southeast (with 572 inhabitants), and the only permanent community on the island, and yet it is a very small village, with only three miles of roadway. Informal dress and manners prevail among the local residents, who pursue a modern, yet traditional, lifestyle that utilizes such resources as salmon, shellfish, deer, bear, and berries. There are also two lodges, a couple of stores, and a bed-and-breakfast in Angoon.

In this 1900's image, a Tlingit artist in Angoon paints a totem pole carved in a killer whale design.

■ CHICHAGOF ISLAND *map page 84, B-4/5*

■ TENAKEE SPRINGS *map page 84, B-5*

Located on the east side of Chichagof Island, **Tenakee Springs** is best known for its natural hot springs. Accommodations are available at the Tenakee Inn. Camping is possible in the adjoining Tongass National Forest. The area is popular with sport fishermen, big-game hunters, and sea kayakers. With only around 100 residents, Tenakee Springs is representative of the truly small villages in southeastern Alaska.

■ HOONAH *map page 84, B-4*

Across Icy Strait from Glacier Bay National Park and Preserve, and on the northern shore of Chichagof Island, you will find the predominantly Tlingit village of Hoonah, population 860, which features an airstrip, several lodging options, a restaurant or two, and well-stocked stores. Hoonah is often used as a jumping-off point for big-game hunters and sport fishermen. A small seining and trolling fleet is based in Hoonah, plying the coastal waters for salmon and halibut. Sportfishing and sightseeing charter boats are locally available. A brand-new cruise ship destination and visitors complex has been built at nearby Point Sophia, complete with stores, tours of the historic cannery from which the complex was built, and entertainment by local Tlingit dancers.

■ GUSTAVUS *map page 84, B-4*

The community of Gustavus serves as the gateway to Glacier Bay National Park, and is connected by air and by regular marine taxi runs from Juneau. For decades the residents resisted incorporation into a formal township, but, due to a steadily growing population (nearly doubled in 25 years to its current 429), have since given in. Folks here are known for their independence, friendliness, and a laid-back attitude. There are several good lodges and bed-and-breakfasts in the area, plus a small grocery store; public campgrounds are at nearby Bartlett Cove. Everything from sea kayaks to bicycles, boats to airplanes can be chartered or rented from local businesses, and a number of tour operators conduct visitors into the nearby park. There is even a rustic golf course (rubber boots recommended in the rainy season).

■ GLACIER BAY NATIONAL PARK AND PRESERVE

maps page 84, A/B-3, and page 108

Surrounded by towering mountains (including 15,320-foot Mount Fairweather), Glacier Bay is a magnificent spectacle. Although the park is about the same size as Yellowstone National Park—3.3 million acres—it differs from its southern cousin in that Glacier Bay cannot be reached by road. Visitors travel the 50 miles west of Juneau either by airplane or by boat. By far the most popular way to visit is by cruise ship or by smaller day-tour craft. Drop-off and pick-up services are available in Gustavus for kayakers, hikers, and campers.

> When the sunshine is shifting through the midst of the multitude of the icebergs that fill the fiord and through the jets of radiant spray ever rising from the tremendous dashing and splashing of the falling and upspringing bergs, the effect is indescribably glorious. Glorious, too, are the shows they make in the night when the moon and stars are shining. The berg-thunder seems far louder than by day. . . . But it is in the darkest nights when storms are blowing and the waves are phosphorescent that the most impressive displays are made.
>
> –John Muir, *The Trip of 1880*

As John Muir's journal indicates, the chief attraction of this national park is the magnificent bay surrounded by active glaciers. In fact, Muir, who made a number of trips to the area beginning in 1879, was the first scientist to seriously study the glaciers. Muir had first studied glaciers in the Sierra Nevadas, particularly in what has become Yosemite National Park, and was astounded by the beauty and diversity of the glaciers in this particular bay. The glaciers have retreated far up the bay since Muir's time, the most rapid glacial retreat ever documented.

As impressive as the geology of Glacier Bay is the wildlife, which ranges from northern Pacific marine mammals—orcas, humpback whales, sea otters, seals, and minke whales—to the host of subarctic terrestrial mammals, including moose, wolves, grizzly and black bears, coastal blacktail deer, lynx, mink, and beaver. More than 200 bird species are found in the bay, and fishing (halibut, Dolly Varden, salmon) can be excellent. And just as interesting as the wildlife is the plant life.

GLACIER BAY
NATIONAL PARK
AND PRESERVE

0   5   10 Miles
0   5   10   15 Kilometers

1794 Historical extent of glaciation

CANADA
UNITED STATES

Muir Glacier

Riggs Glacier

Carroll Glacier

Rendu Glacier

Casement Glacier

Muir Inlet

Adams Inlet

Tarr Inlet

Rendu Inlet

Queen Inlet

Wachusett

RUSSELL
ISLAND

Lamplugh Glacier

Reid Glacier

Glacier

Bay

Tidal
Inlet

Brady Icefield

Brady Glacier

Wood
Lake

Abyss
Lake

DRAKE
ISLAND

WILLOUGHBY
ISLAND

Beartrack Cove

BEARDSLEE ISLANDS

Visitor Center
Glacier Bay Lodge

Park
Headquarters

Airport

Gustavus

Dundas
River

Berg
Bay

Dundas
Bay

North Passage

Dixon Bay

Graves Bay

Taylor Bay

INIAN
ISLANDS

South Passage

LEMESURIER
ISLAND

Icy   Strait

PLEASANT
ISLAND

Cape Spencer

1976
1972
1960
1948

1929

1929

1907

1949

1907

1907

1892

1860

1860

1857

1845

1966

1892

1966

1966

1892

1892
1880

1892

1907

1892
1879
1907
1892
1907
1919

1860

1966

1892

1794

1794

1961

1750-80

N
W   E
S

Sweet Air of the Glacier

There is no air so indescribably, thrillingly sweet as the air of a glacier on a fair day. It seems to palpitate with a fragrance that ravishes the senses. I saw a great, recently captured bear, chained on the hurricane deck of a steamer, stand with his nose stretched out toward the glacier, his nostrils quivering and a look of almost human longing and rebellion in his small eyes. The feeling of pain and pity with which a humane person always beholds a chained wild animal is accented in these wide and noble spaces swimming from snow mountain to snow mountain, where the very watchword of the silence seems to be "Freedom." The chained bear recognized the scent of the glacier and remembered that he had once been free.

In front of the glacier stretched miles of sapphire, sun-lit sea, set with sparkling, opaline-tinted icebergs. Now and then one broke and fell apart before our eyes, sending up a funnel-shaped spray of color—rose, pale green, or azure.

At every blast of the steamer's whistle great masses of ice came thundering headlong into the sea—to emerge presently, icebergs. Canoeists approach glaciers closely at their peril, never knowing when an iceberg may shoot to the surface and wreck their boat. Even larger craft are by no means safe, and tourists desiring a close approach should voyage with intrepid captains who sail safely through everything.

–Ella Higginson, *Alaska, the Great Country,* 1908

Because of the rapid glacial retreat, it is possible to observe the dynamics of plant succession firsthand and up close, as lichens, moss, and grasses work to create soils suitable for primitive grasses and eventually more complicated vascular plants such as fireweed, alder, and wild blueberries.

The largest sea wave ever to hit shore occurred in Glacier Bay National Park, which is located over the tectonically active point where the Pacific and North American plates converge and create enormous friction. In 1958, a landslide set off a colossal sea wave in Lituya Bay, which is on the other side of the Brady Icefield from Glacier Bay, sloshing 1,740 feet (the height of a 140-story building) over Cenotaph Island and up over the north side of the bay. The killer wave literally took everything back into the sea as it retreated—trees, plants, animals, and soil. Only the sheer, slick bedrock on the mountainside remained—a truly awesome example of the power of nature.

There are many activities that can be pursued in Glacier Bay National Park and Preserve, including sea kayaking, boat or aerial touring, sport fishing, hiking, camping, and landscape or wildlife photography. Visitor numbers to most park areas are regulated by permit, so inquire ahead.

■ HAINES   *map page 84, C-3*

Many—perhaps most—who take the ferry from Bellingham, Washington, eventually ride it all the way to Haines, which sits at the head of Lynn Canal about 70 miles north of Juneau.

Haines entered modern history in World War II, when engineers built the Haines Highway from the sleepy little port north to the Canadian Yukon to join the Alaska Highway, then known as the Alcan. In Haines you will find the **Haines Convention and Visitors Bureau** (122 Second Avenue South; 800-458-3579) on Second Avenue near Willard Street, as well as the usual assemblage of hotels, restaurants, and stores nearby. Fishermen will find abundant opportunities to pursue their sport around Haines (information available at the visitors bureau). Although there is much to see in the way of culture—the **Sheldon Museum and Cultural Center** (Corner of Front and Main streets; 907-766-2366), the art galleries near the visitors bureau—the star attraction of Haines is the **Alaska Chilkat Bald Eagle Preserve**, one of five state parks in the area (for information, contact the Haines Ranger Station; 907-766-2292). Each winter thousands of bald eagles flock to this area in order to feed on salmon in the Chilkat River. Some of the best views are around Mile 20 on the Haines Highway. The season peaks from October through January.

About 120 miles north of Haines is **Kluane National Park**—the Denali of the Canadian subarctic. Dall sheep, moose, and grizzlies are observed here regularly.

■ SKAGWAY   *map page 84, C-3*

Skagway is to the east of Haines at the head of Lynn Canal, about 90 miles north of Juneau. If you take a cruise ship to Alaska, you will most likely stop in Skagway, one of the most popular and interesting ports. Like many towns in Alaska, Skagway owes

Steve Hites runs history-focused sightseeing tours in Skagway; here he poses in front of the town's Arctic Brotherhood Hall.

Skagway prospers as the summer of 1898 approaches and the Klondike gold rush begins to peak.

its existence to the gold rush days. It was here that Jack London began his famous trek into the Yukon gold mines, an adventure that resulted in his world-famous works, *The Call of the Wild* and "To Build a Fire." Begin your tour at the **Skagway Convention and Visitors Bureau,** in **Arctic Brotherhood Hall** (Broadway, between Second and Third avenues; 907-983-2854). The former lodge building dates from 1899 and is hard to miss with the thousands of pieces of driftwood on its facade. Follow through with a walking tour of the downtown streets, where numerous restored turn-of-the-century buildings make up a portion of the **Klondike Gold Rush National Historical Park.** You can join one of the National Park Service ranger-led tours by stopping in at the **Visitor Center** (Broadway and Second Avenue; 907-983-2921), housed in the old White Pass and Yukon Railroad Depot. Also in the historic district is the **City of Skagway Museum** (700 Spring Street; 907-983-2420), where mining artifacts, exhibits, and videos tell the history of Skagway. The National Historical Park also includes the nearby gold rush town site of Dyea and the first section of the infamous Chilkoot Trail, where hopeful (and often hapless) would-be miners, laden with supplies, trudged up a steep mountain pass toward imagined riches.

SLIPPERY SOAPY SMITH

Alaska's most notorious outlaw, and "America's last frontier badman of legend" according to chronicler William Bronson, was a confidence man by the name of Jefferson Randolph Smith, popularly known as "Soapy" Smith. He got his name as a result of a trick he used in Colorado mining towns where he sold bars of soap by convincing dupes that $20 bills were concealed in the wrappers.

The facts surrounding his sojourn in Alaska appear to be as slippery as the man himself. According to pioneer Judge James Wickersham, Soapy settled in the Skagway and Dyea region in 1897. He quickly assembled a confederacy of crooks, strong-arm men, and tricksters, and began robbing the miners flooding the region on their way to the Klondike gold rush. Soapy and his men virtually took over Skagway and were on "friendly" terms with the town's only lawman, a U.S. marshal. Soapy's henchmen began systematically bilking money from the transient population through scams, fraud, highway robbery, and murder.

Paradoxically, Soapy gave away as much money as he made and was considered a philanthropist by some residents (he was careful not to rob the locals). But when Klondikers returning from the mines began avoiding Skagway because of its reputation, local business owners decided Soapy was more of a liability than an asset. In July of 1898, a vigilante group had a showdown with Soapy and his men. Most were rounded up and booted out of town (including the crooked marshal). Three ringleaders were tried and sentenced to many years in the Washington State Penitentiary and Soapy was shot to death on Skagway Pier by citizen/vigilante Frank Reid. Reid also died in the shootout and remains the town's greatest hero—his gravestone reads, "He gave his life for the honor of Skagway."

The Soapy Smith gang of Skagway.

During the evening, the liveliest show in town is **"The Days of '98,"** performed in Eagles Hall (Sixth Avenue and Broadway; 907-983-2545), which for more than 70 years has been dramatizing the life and death of Soapy Smith, the scoundrel boss of early Skagway. Before leaving town, you can visit the cemetery where Soapy is buried. (Note that Frank Reid, the vigilante who was killed while dispatching him, rates by far the handsomer monument.) Some of the locals enjoy impersonating historical figures, so don't be surprised if you run into Soapy above ground, too. You might even meet "Robert Service"—actually, an actor playing the part of the famous gold rush poet, who will be happy to oblige you with a recitation.

In curious contrast to its wild and woolly past, the town is rather neatly laid out in orderly blocks, with wide streets that are largely empty—empty, that is, until a cruise ship or busload of tourists arrive, instantly filling the curio shops and small art galleries. Yukon moose wander into town from time to time from the surrounding mountains.

In the 1890s humanity streamed into this town en route to the gold fields of the Yukon. Most came aboard steamers from Seattle, disembarked along the Alaska coast, and followed trails inland over the coast range.

Downtown Skagway at night.

GAZING FROM THE DECK

No other excursion that I know of may be made into any other American wilderness where so marvelous an abundance of noble, newborn scenery is so charmingly brought to view as on the trip through the Alexander Archipelago to Fort Wrangell and Sitka. Gazing from the deck of the steamer, one is borne smoothly over calm blue waters, through the midst of countless forest-clad islands. . . . We seemed to float in true fairyland, each succeeding view seeming more and more beautiful. . . . Never before this had I been embosomed in scenery so hopelessly beyond description.

–John Muir, *The Alexander Archipelago*, 1880

Nine miles north of Skagway, along an old Indian route, runs one of the most famous and historic trails in Alaska, the **Chilkoot Trail.** Originating near the water's edge at what is now Dyea and climbing over the 3,246-foot Chilkoot Pass at the U.S.–Canadian border before it drops down to the Yukon River, it is an arduous 32-mile trek that takes three days to complete. Despite the difficulties of this hike, thousands of miners and entrepreneurs made the trip, hoping to reach the gold fields of the Yukon. It's an exposed route, which should be regarded with caution, but it's followed by thousands of hikers every summer.

From Skagway itself runs an old trail over White Pass. The suffering endured by hopeful prospectors and their 3,000-odd horses and dogs (many of whom died) on the trail was horrendous: the trail was renamed **Dead Horse Trail** in 1897.

Unlike all other towns of the Southeast except Haines, Skagway is connected to the mainland by a road, the Klondike Highway. This spectacular route closely follows the old Dead Horse Trail to the picturesque gold rush town of Carcross (98 miles), Canada, and to Whitehorse (183 miles).

The easiest way to catch a glimpse of the old Dead Horse Trail without having to break a sweat (or a leg) or to crane your neck from a car, is to take a ride on the old **White Pass and Yukon Route Railroad.** Completed in 1900, the spectacular narrow-gauge railway almost single-handedly kept Skagway from turning into a ghost town after the Klondike gold rush ended. For more than eight decades, it transported goods and travelers from Skagway's port up the Skagway River Gorge, with a lunch stop (often including moose steaks) midway. Although the completion of the Alaska Highway temporarily halted its run, the train now makes daily tourist excursions up the pass, and even to Whitehorse. (See page 136.)

Gold-seekers, in endless procession, making the arduous climb over Chilkoot Pass to reach the gold fields of the interior during the gold rush of 1898. The White Pass and Yukon Route Railroad was constructed in 1900 to render such a climb unnecessary.

■ YAKUTAT   *map page 84, A-1*

Yakutat is far up the Gulf of Alaska along the wave-swept outer coast of the upper-most part of the Panhandle, where rugged peaks rise from sea level and there are few sheltering bays. Most people see the region from the airplane as the pilot wings westward from Juneau toward Anchorage and points to the Malaspina glacier around Mount St. Elias, informing you that the glacier is larger than the state of Rhode Island. In Yakutat you will find a few lodges, cafés, bars, and stores. The area is well known for its big-game hunting and for its sport fishing, especially for steelhead and salmon. The Yakutat Forelands area is ranked as one of the finest bird-watching areas (cranes, geese, ducks, trumpeter swans) on the whole coast, especially during peak migration times in the spring and fall. Later salmon runs attract bald eagles and brown bears. (Best visited by plane; see pages 120 and 137.)

■ TRAVEL INFORMATION

■ GETTING THERE AND GETTING AROUND

Much of Southeast Alaska consists of islands and inlets that are accessible only by water or air. The Southeast's major city (and the state's capital), Juneau, is served by only one major carrier, Alaska Airlines. The area is also served by the Alaska state ferry system, cruise ships, and tour boats originating in Bellingham, Washington, and Prince Rupert, Canada. The total length of the Canadian–U.S. Inside Passage is more than 1,000 miles; the Alaskan part is 550 miles. By car, the Panhandle's northernmost towns of Haines and Skagway can be reached by driving north from the U.S. border on the eastern side of the coastal mountain range through British Columbia and part of the Yukon via the Alaska Highway.

By Ferry

Alaska has an excellent public-ferry system akin to a marine bus service. The ferries connect Bellingham, Washington, and Prince Rupert, British Columbia, with

A cruise ship meets the White Pass and Yukon Route Railroad at Skagway.

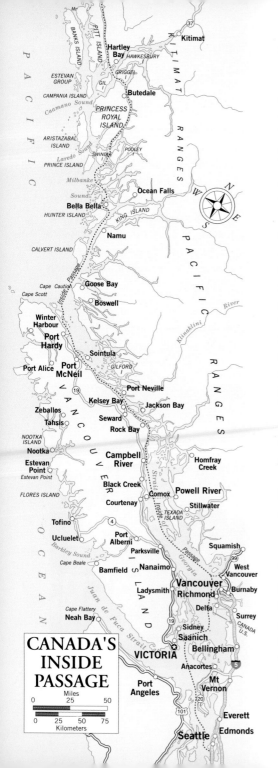

CANADA'S
INSIDE
PASSAGE

Miles
0   25   50

0   25 50 75
Kilometers

many of the major towns along Alaska's Inside Passage. A one-way trip in peak season (May through September) from Bellingham, Washington, to Skagway, the Southeast's northernmost town, takes three days.

In summer the cabins and car decks are usually full, so make your reservations at least six months in advance—or allow for plenty of flexibility in your schedule. Generally, stops in ports do not allow enough time for shore excursions, so you may want to customize your trip by adding stop-overs (a port-to-port rate may increase your fare, but it may be worth the extra expense). The Alaska ferry terminals will provide a computer printout describing the sights and accommodations of all the towns en route.

Alaska Marine Highway System. *Juneau: 907-465-3941 or 800-642-0066; www.akmhs.com.*

B.C. Ferries. *Victoria, British Columbia: 250-386-3431; www. bcferries.bc.ca.*

Cruise Ships and Ocean Liners

Cruises provide spacious, often luxurious accommodations on their tours of the Inside Passage. Fares vary according to style and taste, starting around several hundred dollars per person per day, usually all inclusive. "Shoulder season" travel—that is, near the beginning and the end of peak season, typically before Memorial Day and after Labor Day—can result in considerable savings, sometimes as much as 50 percent. So can bookings made months ahead of time. Ocean liners and cruise ships provide entertainment, activities, and formal and informal dining. Smaller cruise ships and specialty vessels are able to traverse the shallow coves and narrow waters where the big ships can't go. Many of these have a staff of naturalists onboard to give informal lectures on natural history along the way. Because of the great variety in cruise options, you may need to work with a travel agent or contact individual companies for details of itineraries, tours, and add-ons.

By Charter Boat

Tour boat companies connect passengers with the Southeast's smaller towns and remote villages. Arrangements often may be made upon arrival in these towns. To plan in advance, contact local visitors bureaus for information; these are listed by town under "Food, Lodging, & Tours" beginning on page 122. *In Juneau call 907-586-2201; www.juneaualaska.com.*

Floatplanes on the Taku River at Taku Glacier Lodge.

By Plane

From Juneau it is possible to travel to Haines, Skagway, Glacier Bay National Park and Preserve, Angoon, Hoonah, and other points on Southeast islands by commuter carriers offering intrastate scheduled air service. The airlines sometimes offer packages in conjunction with the ferry service, allowing travelers to fly in and ferry back. Inquire at **Alaska Airlines** (800-426-0333; www.alaskaair.com) for chartered flights from Juneau or at the **Federal Aviation Administration** (907-271-2000) in Anchorage for a list of certified air taxi operations throughout Alaska, including the following: **L.A.B. Flying Service** (907-766-2222; http://labflying.com/); **Air Excursions** (907-789-5591); and **Wings of Alaska** (907-789-0790; www.wingsofalaska.com).

By Car

Few southeast communities are accessible by road. If you're planning to visit the region en route to Anchorage or Fairbanks via the Alaska Highway, consider transporting your car via ferry from Seattle or Bellingham to Skagway, at the end of the Panhandle. From there it is a day's drive to Fairbanks, where you can turn north to the Arctic or south toward Anchorage.

Charges for cars brought aboard the ferry are based on the number of passengers and the size of the vehicle. Although it may cost as much as $600 to take a car the 1,000 miles of the Inside Passage, travelers must also calculate how long, as an alternative, it would take to drive the Alaska Highway, as well as the cost and wear and tear on the vehicle. Many travelers determine that, despite the high cost, it is actually more economical—in terms of time and traveling costs—to take the ferry. Make reservations for the busy summer travel season as far in advance as possible; six months is recommended.

■ CLIMATE

The defining characteristic of Alaska's Panhandle is rain, which falls year round. Near the coast, especially along the southernmost islands, annual rainfall can exceed 15 feet, with the bulk of it falling in the fall and winter months. Temperatures are cool in the summer, and chilly but seldom frigid in the winter. The three stations below are all at sea level and represent the southern end of the Panhandle (Ketchikan), the central portion (Juneau), and the northern end (Glacier Bay National Park and Preserve).

SUNLIGHT

SUMMER MAXIMUM	SUNRISE	SUNSET	# OF HOURS
Juneau	3:51 AM	10:09 PM	18:18
Ketchikan	4:04 AM	9:32 PM	17:28

WINTER MINIMUM	SUNRISE	SUNSET	# OF HOURS
Juneau	8:46 AM	3:07 PM	6:21
Ketchikan	8:12 AM	3:18 PM	7:05

TEMPS (F°)	AVG. JAN. HIGH	LOW	AVG. APRIL HIGH	LOW	AVG. JULY HIGH	LOW	AVG. OCT. HIGH	LOW	RECORD HIGH	RECORD LOW
Glacier Bay	26	16	45	33	62	48	46	37	76	-4
Juneau	28	16	48	30	65	48	48	36	90	-22
Ketchikan	40	30	51	36	65	51	53	42	95	-8

PRECIPITATION (INCHES)	AVG. JAN.	AVG. APRIL	AVG. JULY	AVG. OCT.	ANNUAL RAIN	ANNUAL SNOW
Juncau	3.7	2.9	4.1	7.7	53	99
Ketchikan	13.9	12.1	8.1	22.3	154	20
Glacier Bay	3.9	3.5	5.5	8.9	71	145

■ FOOD, LODGING, & TOURS

RESTAURANT PRICES

Per person, without drinks, tax, or tip

$ = under $15   **$$** = $15–$25   **$$$** = over $25

ROOM RATES

Per room, per night, double occupancy

$ = under $70   **$$** = $70–$100   **$$$** = over $100

ANGOON *map page 84, B-5*

Population: 572
Visitors information: 907-788-3653 (City Office)

◆ LODGING

Favorite Bay Inn Bed & Breakfast. Comfortable, family-style B&B, associated with Whaler's Cove Lodge. Canoe and kayak rentals. Fishing trips arranged. *Next to the sea plane float in the harbor; 907-788-3123 or 800-423-3123; www. favoritebayinn.com.* **$$**

Kootznahoo Inlet Lodge. Basic motel with housekeeping units overlooking Kootznahoo Inlet and a restaurant. *911 Kilisnoo Road; 907-788-3501.* **$$**

◆ WILDERNESS LODGES

Admiralty Island Cabins. There are 14 public-use cabins in Admiralty Island National Monument available on a first-come, first-served basis for $25–$45 per night, permit required. Apply up to 180 days in advance; no bedding, wood, or cookware supplied. It's strongly recommended that you reserve as early as possible for best possible choices. *Contact Juneau Ranger District, 907-586-8800 for specific cabin information and help in choosing. Reserve through 877-444-5777 or www. reserveusa.com (go directly to the "Browse Using Maps" function to figure out where cabins and campgrounds are located).*

Thayer Lake Wilderness Lodge. Remote lodge on the shores of a freshwater lake in Admiralty Island National Monument; accessible only by plane. Main lodge and two independent lakefront cabins. *Reservations: P.O. Box 8897, Ketchikan, AK 99901; 907-247-8897.* $$$

CRAIG   *map page 85, B-3*

Population: 1,397
Visitors information: 907-755-2626; www.princeofwalescoc.org

◆ LODGING

Oceanview Bed & Breakfast. Comfortable, spacious rooms with a beautiful view and convenient location. *601 Oceanview; 907-401-0113; www.oceanviewbnb.com.* $$-$$$

Haida Way Lodge. A rustic lodge with 25 rooms located in downtown Craig. *501 Front Street; 907-826-3268; www.sea-biz.com/haidawaylodge.* $$

GUSTAVUS   *map page 84, B-4*

Population: 429
Visitors information: (currently no phone listing); www.gustavus.com

◆ LODGING

Aimee's Guest House. Centrally located, on the river. Two apartments. Attached to co-op gallery that features local artists. *907-697-2306; www.islandnet.com/aimee.* $-$$

Blue Heron Bed and Breakfast. Beautiful setting. Deluxe (upstairs) rooms with views of meadows and mountains, and also two cottages. *907-697-2293; www.blueheronbnb.net.* $$$

Glacier Bay Country Inn. Built from hand-logged timber, this lodge has a modern mountain ambience and a gourmet restaurant that culls from its own kitchen garden. The lodge also can arrange flightseeing tours and charter-boat service into Glacier Bay. *Between the airport and Bartlett Cove; 907-697-2288 (summer) or 800-628-0912; www.glacierbayalaska.com.* $$$

Glacier Bay Lodge. In Glacier Bay National Park, close to the boat dock and beach; beautiful rain forest views. Offers packaged adventure tours. Highly rated, and advance reservations are a must. Restaurant. *At Bartlett Cove; 907-697-2225.* $$$

Gustavus Inn. In town, this romantic old inn has a picturesque garden and an excellent restaurant. *On the main road; 907-697-2254 or 800-649-5220; www.gustavusinn.com.* $$$

◆ Tours

Spirit Walker Expeditions. Day and overnight kayak trips, including whale watching in kayaks. *907-697-2266 or 800-529-2537; www.seakayakalaska.com.*

Cross Sound Express. Twice-daily whale watching and wildlife cruises. Operates May–September, reservations required. *907-766-3000 or 888-698-2726.*

Glacier Bay Cruises. One-day tours of Glacier Bay on modern, comfortable boat. Very popular, including with area locals. *907-697-4000 or 888-BAYTOUR.*

HAINES *map page 84, C-3*

Population: 1,811
Visitors information: 907-766-2234 or 800-458-3579; www.haines.ak.us

◆ Restaurants

Bamboo Room. Coffee shop serving breakfast, burgers, sandwiches, and seafood. *Second Avenue, near Main Street; 907-766-2800.* $

Fireweed Restaurant. Organic world cuisine, specializing in Italian food. *37 Blacksmith Road; 907-766-3838.* $$

Lighthouse Restaurant. Restaurant with a view of Lynn Canal and a colorful bar where the local commercial fishermen gather. *Front Street on the harbor; 907-766-2442.* $$

◆ Lodging

Captain's Choice Motel. In town, overlooking Portage Cove. *Second and Dalton streets; 907-766-3111 or 800-478-2345; www.capchoice.com.* $$

Hotel Hälsingland. This hotel, popular with European tourists, occupies a Victorian-style building that was once the officers quarters of old Fort Seward (a decommissioned U.S. Army post). *On the parade grounds, Fort Seward; 907-766-2000 or 800-542-6363; www.hotelhalsingland.com.* $–$$

◆ Tours

Chilkat Guides. Knowledgeable guides host a four-hour float trip through the Chilkat Bald Eagle Preserve indicating wildlife and landscape features; picnic lunch included. *Beach Road at Portage Street; 907-766-2491; www.raftalaska.com.*

Sockeye Cycle. Bike rentals and three-hour mountain-bike tours through scenic (and hilly) Haines. *24 Portage Street; 907-766-2869; www.cyclealaska.com.*

JUNEAU *map page 84, C-4/5*

Population: 30,711
Visitors information: 907-586-2201 or 888-581-2201; www.traveljuneau.com

◆ RESTAURANTS

Breakwater Inn. Prime rib and Alaskan seafood, overlooking Aurora Boat Harbor. *1711 Glacier Avenue; 907-586-6303 or 800-544-2250; www.breakwaterinn.com.* $$–$$$

Douglas Cafe. Casual dining in a relaxed, friendly atmosphere. Voted best burger in town by Juneau 2007 restaurant poll. *Across the bridge from Juneau in Douglas, 916 3rd Street; 907-364-3307.* $$

El Sombrero. Mexican food in large portions, friendly ambience. A local favorite. *157 South Franklin Street; 907-586-6770.* $–$$

The Hangar on the Wharf. Waterfront restaurant and bar popular among residents. Great views, solid service and food. *Merchants Wharf; 907-586-5018.* $$

Silverbow Inn Bakery and Backroom Restaurant. Locally favored coffee and breakfast spot with excellent fresh breads in the bakery; restaurant features local seafood. Also a comfortable bed-and-breakfast. *120 Second Street; 907-586-4146 or 800-586-4146; www.silverbow.com.* $$–$$$

Tokyo. A very popular Japanese-American restaurant featuring sushi, steaks, and tepanyaki grill. *In Mendenhall valley area, 9116 Mendenhall Road; 907-463-3119.* $$–$$$

Thane Ore House Salmon Bake. An all-you-can-eat salmon bake and the "Gold Nugget Review" musical comedy. Closed October through April. *Four miles south of town, 4400 Thane Road; 907-586-3442.* $$

Wild Spice. Eclectic, international "adventure cuisine" featuring such dishes as Balinese squid and Kenyan saffron pork. Also steaks, Alaska seafood, and creative desserts. *140 Seward Street; 907-523-0344.* $$–$$$

◆ LODGING

Alaska Wolf House. Beautiful cedar home on hillside overlooking Gastineau Channel. Sumptuous breakfasts, gracious hosts. *1900 Wickersham Avenue; 907-586-2422; www.alaskawolfhouse.com.* $$–$$$

Best Western Country Lane Inn. Just a few blocks from the airport, with easy access to town; complimentary continental breakfasts. *9300 Glacier Highway; 907-789-5005 or 888-781-5005; www.countrylaneinn.com.* $$$

Best Western Grandma's Feather Bed. A country-themed inn with a restaurant on premises that serves breakfast and dinner. *2358 Mendenhall Loop Road; 907-789-5566 or 888-781-5005; www.grandmasfeatherbed.com.* $$$

Glacier Trail Bed and Breakfast. Lovely home situated only 100 feet from Mendenhall Lake and with spectacular views of Mendenhall Glacier. Three guest rooms, including one apartment suitable for a family. The innkeepers are quite knowledgeable about natural history and wilderness excursions. *1081 Arctic Circle Drive; 907-789-5646; www.juneaulodging.com.* $$

Goldbelt Hotel. Modern hotel with deluxe rooms; distinguished by its carved wooden murals. 106 rooms, dining room, lounge. *51 West Egan Drive; 907-586-6900 or 800-478-6909; www.goldbelttours.com.* $$$

Juneau International Hostel. One of the finest youth hostels in Alaska, offering dorm space for 48 people, a comfortable community room, kitchen and laundry facilities. Open year-round, with maximum stay of three nights. *For reservations mail request plus $10 per-person deposit to: 614 Harris Street, Juneau, AK 99801; 907-586-9559; www.juneauhostel.org.* $

Pearson's Pond Luxury Inn. Upscale, award-winning B&B, beautiful setting and many amenities. In Mendenhall Valley. Smoke free. *4541 Sawa Circle; 907-789-3772 or 888-658-6328; www.pearsonspond.com.* $$–$$$

Prospector Hotel. Modern hotel near museum with large rooms, great views, and popular bar and restaurant. *375 Whittier Street; 907-586-3737 or 800-331-2711; www.prospectorhotel.com.* $$–$$$

Westmark Baranof Hotel. The hotel's lobby is known for its art deco style and original artwork by Sydney Lawrence and other Alaskan artists. Unique décor on each floor; 194 rooms; fine restaurant. *127 North Franklin Street; 907-586-2660 or 800-544-0970; www.westmarkhotels.com.* $$$

◆ WILDERNESS LODGES

The Cove Lodge. Remote lodge catering to fishermen, but also offering scuba, kayaking, and photography adventures. *Reservations address: 91 West Nebraska Avenue, St. Paul, MN 55117 (winter) or P.O. Box 17, Elfin Cove, AK 99825 (summer); 800-382-3847; www.covelodge.com.* $$$

Johns Hopkins Glacier empties into Glacier Bay under a towering mountain spire some 8,000 feet above.

Elfin Cove Lodge. Remote lodge on Chichagof Island accessible from Juneau by plane or private boat. Offers full fishing packages. *Reservations address: 42476 Salmon Creek Road, Baker City, OR 97814 (winter) or P.O. Box 44, Elfin Cove, AK 99825 (summer); 800-422-2824; www.elfincove.com.* $$$

Pybus Point Lodge. On the southeast tip of Admiralty Island, this family-oriented lodge offers guided fishing expeditions. Accessible by plane or private boat. *Reservations address: Box 33497, Juneau, AK 99803; 907-790-4866 or 800-947-9287; www.pybus.com.* $$$

♦ **TOURS**

Adventure Bound Alaska. Daily cruises to Tracy Arm, arguably the most dramatic fjord and glacier destination in Southeast Alaska. Excellent value combining wildlife, scenery, and expert piloting and narrative by Captain Steve Weber. Mid-May through mid-September. *215 Ferry Way, Juneau, AK 99801; 907-463-2509.*

Alaska Discovery Wilderness Adventures. One of Alaska's oldest and most respected wilderness-expedition companies. Provides kayaking, rafting, camping, and bear-watching tours locally and statewide. Reservations recommended. *5310 Glacier Highway; 907-780-6226 or 800-586-1911; www.akdiscovery.com.*

Alaska Travel Adventures. Scenic rafting on the Mendenhall River; gold panning, sea kayak tours, sportfishing, and all-you-can-eat salmon bake. *9085 Glacier Highway; 907-789-0052 in Alaska or 800-323-5757 outside Alaska; www. alaskaadventures.com.*

Coastal Helicopters. Available for charter, glacier viewing, heli-fishing, heli-skiing, and photography tours. *8995 Yandukin Drive; 907-789-5600 or 800-789-5610; www.coastalhelicopters.com.*

CruiseWest. Nine-day "Wilderness Waterways" cruise starts and ends in Juneau, and includes a one-day tour of Glacier Bay and a stop in Sitka. Stops in places not visited by larger cruise ships, such as the Indian village of Kake and remote bays where guests can make excursions in inflatable skiffs. Caters to luxury-inclined "adventure travelers." May through September. *907-586-6300; www. cruisewest.com.*

Orca Enterprises. Specializes in whale-watching and marine life tours. Modern, fast jet boats of modest size get you close to the action. Well organized and professional. *489 Franklin Street; 907-789-6801 or 888-733-6722; www. alaskawhalewatching.com.*

Wings of Alaska. Year-round scheduled or charter airline servicing Southeast, wheels and floats. *8421 Livingston Way, Juneau; 907-789-0790; www. wingsofalaska.com.*

KETCHIKAN *map page 85, C-4*

Population: 7,922
Visitors information: 907-225-6166 or 800-770-3300; www.visit-ketchikan.com

◆ RESTAURANTS

Annabelle's Famous Keg & Chowder House. Local seafood in the historic Gilmore Hotel; features Alaskan seafood and homemade cannery bread, plus a collection of 1920s memorabilia from Ketchikan's onetime red-light district. *326 Front Street; 907-225-6009.* $$-$$$

Diaz Café. Informal, eclectic, friendly. Local hangout. *335 Stedman Street; 907-225-2257.*

Salmon Falls Resort. Serving fresh seafood caught in local waters; octagonal dining room supported by a piece of pipe originally intended for the Alaska pipeline. Open from May through mid-September. *Mile 17, North Tongass Highway; 800-247-9059; www.salmonfallsresort.com.* $$$

◆ LODGING

American Youth Hostel. Summer only (June through August); bring your sleeping bag. Showers and kitchen facilities; reservations recommended. *First Methodist Church at Grant and Main streets; 907-225-3319.* $

Best Western Landing. Right in the heart of town, across from the Marine Ferry Terminal, with a restaurant in the building. *3434 Tongass Avenue; 907-225-5166 or 800-428-8304; www.landinghotel.com.* $$–$$$

Gilmore Hotel. Built in 1927 and now on the National Historic Register; 38 rooms; city-center waterfront views. *326 Front Street; 907-225-9423 or 800-275-9423; www.gilmorehotel.com.* $$$

New York Hotel. Historic inn with beautiful rooms and convenient downtown location. *207 Stedman Street; 907-225-0246; 866-225-0246; thenewyorkhotel.com.* $$$

◆ WILDERNESS LODGES

Waterfall Resort. Coastal fishing resort with luxurious accommodations 62 miles west of Ketchikan. Full bath, wet bar, refrigerator, television, and billiards.

Accessible by plane or private boat. *Prince of Wales Island. Reservations address: P.O. Box 6440, Ketchikan, AK 99901; 907-225-9461 or 800-544-5125; www. waterfallresort.com.* **$$$**

WestCoast Cape Fox Lodge. Above Ketchikan and Tongass Narrows; 72 spacious rooms with views and the Heen Kahidi Dining Room with floor-to-ceiling windows overlooking Ketchikan. *800 Venetia Way; 907-225-8001 or 866-225-8001.* **$$$**

Yes Bay Lodge. Offers saltwater and freshwater fishing, family-style meals. Accessible by plane or private boat. 50 miles northwest of Ketchikan. *Reservations address: P.O. Box 8660, Ketchikan, AK 99901; 907-225-7906 or 800-999-0784; www.yesbay.com.* **$$$**

◆ CAMPGROUNDS

Six U.S. Forest Service campgrounds are to be found north of town on North Tongass Highway and Ward Lake Road; remote cabins (accessible by plane or boat) are also available. *For information, call the Ketchikan Ranger District, 907-225-2148; for reservations, 877-444-6777 or www.reserveusa.com (go directly to the*

John Neary harvests bears' bread, a wild fungus, from the forest near Stink Creek.

"Browse Using Maps" function to figure out where cabins and campgrounds are located).

◆ Tours

Alaska Seaplane Tours. Air-taxi service providing tours into Misty Fiords, kayak drop-offs, and more. *866-858-2327; www.alaskaseaplanetours.com.*

Classic Alaska Charters. Charter a 40-foot yacht for guided tours and fishing adventures. *907-225-0608; www.classicalaskacharters.com.*

Southeast Exposure. Provides four- to eight-day kayaking trips into the Misty Fiords, from April through mid-October. *37 Potter Road; 907-225-8829; www. southeastexposure.com.*

PETERSBURG *map page 85, C-2*

Population: 3,224
Visitors information: 907-772-4636 or 866-484-4700; www.petersburg.org

◆ Restaurants

Helse. Open from 8:30 A.M. to 4:30 P.M. only, serving simple fare such as sandwiches, milk shakes, ice cream, and coffee. *Sing Lee Alley and Harbor Way; 907-772-3444.* $

Pellerito's Pizzeria. The pizzas here are made from scratch; there's also a good selection of microbrewery beers. *1105 South Nordic Drive, across from the ferry terminal; 907-772-3727.* $$

Rooney's Northern Lights. Serving breakfast, lunch, and dinner; on the waterfront. Standard fare, family atmosphere. *203 Sing Lee Alley, across from Sons of Norway Hall; 907-772-2900.* $$

Studebaker's Pizza. Good take-out pizza, free delivery. *1258 Howkan Street; 907-772-5000.* $$

◆ Lodging

Broom Hus. A B&B occupying a small Scandinavian-style house built in the 1920s. Open from February through mid-September; it offers a homemade continental breakfast and beautiful views. *411 South Nordic Drive; 907-772-3459; www.broomhus.com.* $$

Scandia House. Petersburg's Norwegian influences are evident in this early 20th-century hotel, rebuilt after a fire in 1995. There are 33 rooms, some with kitchenettes. One block from boat harbor. Car and boat rentals. *110 Nordic Drive; 907-772-4281 or 800-722-5006; www.scandiahousehotel.com.* $$–$$$

Tides Inn. Largest hotel in town; modern rooms; complimentary breakfast. *First and Dolphin streets; 907-772-4288 or 800-665-8433; www.tidesinnalaska.com.* $$

◆ CAMPGROUNDS

The U.S. Forest Service's **Ohmer Creek Campground,** on the Mitkof Highway 22 miles south of town, has 10 sites for tents or trailers. In addition, there are some 20 remote public-use cabins around the Petersburg area, from $25-45 a night. Make reservations up to 180 days in advance. *For information on specific cabins or sites or help in choosing, call the Petersburg Ranger District, 907-772-3871; for reservations, 877-444-6777 or www.reserveusa.com (on the Web site, use the "Browse Using Maps" function to help you zoom in on an area).*

◆ TOURS

Alaska Passages Adventure Cruises. Custom cruises on a classic 65-foot motor yacht, five nights and up. Activities include whale watching, glacier viewing, kayaking, sport fishing, and hiking. Highly recommended. *P.O. Box 213, Petersburg, AK 99833; 907-772-3967 or 888-434-3766; www.alaskapassages.com.*
Tongass Kayak Adventures. No-experience-needed paddle trips around the harbor, plus extended trips. *907-772-4600; www.tongasskayak.com.*

SITKA   *map page 84, A-5*

Population: 8,835
Visitors information: 907-747-5940; www.sitka.org

◆ RESTAURANTS
Backdoor Café. A small espresso shop behind Old Harbor Books that also serves homemade baked goods. Local hangout. *104 Barracks Street; 907-747-8856.* $
Bayview Restaurant. Specializing in pasta, steaks, deli sandwiches, hamburgers, and fresh seafood. Outdoor deck overlooks the harbor. Also open for breakfast. *407 Lincoln Street; 907-747-5440.* $
Channel Club. The steaks here are legendary, but if you don't have an appetite for red meat you'll be delighted by the large salad bar. *Mile 3.5, 2906 Halibut Point Road; 907-747-9916.* $$–$$$

Totem poles near Kasaan, Prince of Wales Island.

Highliner Coffee. Cybercafé with historical nautical décor roasts own beans on premises and serves baked goods. *Seward Square Mall, No. 5; 907-747-4924; www. highlinercoffee.com.* $–$$

Ludvig's Bistro. Mediterranean dishes and Alaska seafood. A local favorite. *256 Katlian Street; 907-966-3663.* $$–$$$

◆ Lodging

Alaska Ocean View Bed and Breakfast. Ocean view, delicious breakfasts, and smoke-free rooms. *1101 Edgecumbe Drive; 907-747-8310 or 888-811-6870.* $$–$$$

Cascade Inn. About 2.5 miles from the center of town, on the waterfront. Rooms have individual balconies and beautiful views of Mount Edgecumbe. *2035 Halibut Point Road; 907-747-6804 or 800-532-0908; www.cascadeinnsitka.com.* $$

Sitka Youth Hostel. Twenty beds. Open June–August only. *Reservations by phone or by writing: P.O. Box 2645, Sitka, AK 99835; 303 Kimsham Street; 907-747-8661.* $

Westmark Shee Atika. The artwork displayed throughout the hotel is a tribute to the history, legends, and talent of the Tlingit people. Many of the rooms overlook Crescent Harbor; the restaurant looks out over the Sitka Sound and the local fishing fleets. *330 Seward Street; 907-747-6241 or 800-544-0970; www.westmarkhotels. com.* $$$

◆ Wilderness Lodges

Rainforest Retreat. Modern cabins situated in a remote stand of old-growth forest 40 miles south of Sitka; guests can relax, hike, and enjoy health-consciously pre-pared meals featuring vegetarian specialties—or, for half price off the normal rate, they can cook for themselves in the shared kitchen. Accessible by plane or private boat. *Reservations: P.O. Box 8005, Port Alexander, AK 99836; 907-568-2229.* $$$

◆ Campgrounds

Sealing Cove RV Park, run by the city of Sitka, has space for 26 RVs and is open from May through September. *Adjacent to Sealing Cove Boat Harbor on Japonski Island, 7 miles south of ferry terminal, short distance from downtown Sitka; 907-747-3439.*

Sitka Sportsman's Association RV Park, has space for 16 RVs, and is open year round. *One block south of ferry terminal on Halibut Point Road, 7 miles north of town; 907-747-6033.*

Starrigavan Campground at Milepost 7.8 on Halibut Point Road (.75 mile from ferry terminal) and **Sawmill Creek Campground** at Milepost 5.4 on Sawmill Creek Road (14 miles southeast of ferry terminal) are U.S. Forest Service campgrounds. *For information, call 907-747-4216, for reservations, 877-444-6777 or www.reserveusa.com.*

◆ TOURS

Boat Company. Custom, all-inclusive "soft" adventures by charter boat. *360-697-4242; www.theboatcompany.com.*

Sitka Wildlife Quest. A half-day wildlife cruise, on which travelers can view sea otters, whales, bears, and sea birds. Other cruise packages are also available. Open May to early September. *907-747-8100 or 888-747-8101; www.allenmarinetours.com.*

SKAGWAY   *map page 84, C-3*

Population: 862
Visitors information: 907-983-2854; www.skagway.org

◆ RESTAURANTS

Red Onion Saloon. Pizza, beer, and live rock music in what was once a bordello. Closes in winter. *Second Avenue at Broadway; 907-983-2222.* $

Stowaway Café. Fine dining, featuring local fish served Alaskan and Cajun style. Closed from October through April. *Congress Way, a 10-minute walk south of town center; 907-983-3463.* $$$

Sweet Tooth Café. This tiny café/saloon is a Skagway favorite, providing pastries and eggs from as early as 6 A.M. Don't miss the cinnamon rolls. *Broadway at Third Avenue; 907-983-2405.* $

◆ LODGING

Chilkoot Trail Outpost. Well-appointed log cabins located out of town in the Dyea valley. Gracious hosts; complimentary breakfast; serene setting removed from Skagway's bustle. *907-983-3799; www.chilkoottrailoutpost.com.* $$$

Historic Skagway Inn. This Victorian inn, in the Klondike Gold Rush National Historical Park, was originally established as a brothel in 1897; rooms are named after notable women from the gold rush era. *Broadway and Seventh Street; 907-983-2289 or 888-752-4929; www.skagwayinn.com.* $$

Westmark Inn. Features period furniture, brass trim, and historical photos. The hotel restaurant has an extensive wine list and diverse menu. Closed from October through April. *Third and Spring streets; 907-983-2291 or 800-544-0970; www. westmarkhotels.com.* $$–$$$

The White House. Historic inn dating from 1902. Private baths and rooms decorated with antiques and handcrafted quilts. Two blocks from downtown. *475 Eighth Avenue; 907-983-9000; www.atthewhitehouse.com.* $$$

◆ TOURS

Packer Expeditions. Guided hiking trips long and short, using helicopter and train for bush country access. Locally owned and operated. *907-983-2544; www. packerexpeditions.com.*

TEMSCO Helicopters. Helicopter flightseeing tours of nearby sights; includes a landing on a glacier and a guided tour on the "river of ice," where a guide will walk you through the interesting features of the glacial terrain. Dogsled rides. *907-983-2900; www.temscoair.com.*

White Pass and Yukon Route Railroad. Narrow-gauge railroad established during the gold rush era takes passengers on a three-hour round-trip excursion (from May through September) to 2,865-foot White Pass summit. For the best view, sit on the left when leaving Skagway. There's also an eight-hour excursion to Lake Bennett, in British Columbia. *800-343-7373; www.whitepassrailroad.com.*

WRANGELL   *map page 85, C-2*

Population: 2,308
Visitors information: 907-874-2381, 907-874-3901, or 800-367-9745; www.wrangell.com

◆ RESTAURANTS

Diamond C Café. Inexpensive food in a diner atmosphere. *223 Front Street; 907-874-3677.* $

◆ LODGING

Bruce Harding's Old Sourdough Lodge. Situated on the docks and family-run, with homey rustic rooms, and open living room/dining room. *1104 Peninsula Street; 907-874-3613 or 800-874-3613; www.akgetaway.com.* $$

Stikine Inn. Standard rooms but convenient location and great harbor views. Coffee shop, restaurant, and gift shop. *One block from ferry terminal, Stikine Avenue; 907-874-3388 or 888-874-3388; www.stikine.com.* $$

Tongass National Forest Cabins. A dozen cabins in the Wrangell area, more than 150 in all of Tongass National Forest. Rustic but comfortable, renting from $25-45 per night. Reserve up to 180 days in advance. Accessible by boat, floatplane, helicopter, or hiking trail. *For information, contact the Wrangell Ranger District, 907-874-2323; for reservations, 877-444-6777 or www.reserveusa.com (on the Web site, use the "Browse Using Maps" option to help you locate where you'd like to go).*

◆ LODGING

Alaska Isle B&B. Convenient location; standard amenities; choice of one- or two-bedroom suite. *325 Church Street; 907-874-2002.* $$

◆ TOURS

Stikeen Wilderness Adventures. Guided jet boat tours and transport to Anan Creek Bear Observatory. Local expert guides. Highly recommended. *107 Front Street; 907-874-2085 or 800 874-2085; www.akgetaway.com.*

YAKUTAT *map page 84, A-1*

Population: 680
Visitors information: 907-784-3323 (City Hall)

◆ RESTAURANTS

Glacier Bear Lodge. A lounge and restaurant with rooms in a forest setting. Two miles from airport; 907-784-3202 or 866-425-6343; *www.glacierbearlodge.com.* $$

Yakutat Lodge. Lodge and restaurant. Guided fishing and hunting trips. *By airport; 907-784-3232 or 800-925-8828; www.yakutatlodge.com.* $$

◆ LODGING

Blue Heron Inn. Stay with a local sport fishing guide and his family. Guiding service and vacation rentals. *On Yakutat Bay in town; 907-784-3287; www.johnlatham. com.* $$

Leonard's Landing Lodge. Cabins and restaurant on water by the boat harbor. *Five miles from the airport; 907-784-3245; www.leonardslanding.com.* $$

■ FESTIVALS AND EVENTS

■ FEBRUARY
Tent City Winter Festival, Wrangell. Held on the first weekend in February to celebrate the role Wrangell played in the gold rush; food, crafts, and beard-growing and tall-tales contests. *907-874-3901.*

■ APRIL
Alaska Folk Festival, Juneau. A mix of music, food, and handmade crafts. *907-463-3316; www.alaskafolkfestival.org.*

■ MAY
Jazz and Classics Festival, Juneau. Performances by nationally known musicians. *907-463-3378; www.jazzandclassics.org.*
Little Norway Festival, Petersburg. In celebration of Petersburg's Norwegian heritage; features folk dancing, folk food, costumes, halibut-filleting contests, and Viking raids. *907-772-4636.*

The Tlingit tribal meeting house in Saxman.

■ **JUNE**

Gold Rush Days, Juneau. A two-day celebration including logging competitions between miners and loggers, a children's carnival, food booths, and a closing night dance. *907-586-2201.*

Sitka Summer Music Festival. A three-week event, with chamber-music artists from all over the world performing to standing-room-only crowds. Brown-bag and "coffee" concerts accompany the main evening concerts. *907-747-6774 (June only) or 907-277-4852; www.sitkamusicfestival.org.*

■ **AUGUST**

Blueberry Arts Festival, Ketchikan. Arts and crafts, blueberry pies, blueberry crêpes, blueberry cheesecakes. Slug race, pie-eating contest, and spelling bee. *907-225-2211.*

Southeast Alaska State Fair, Haines. Popular regional event featuring crafts, home-made foods, a horse show, and a parade. *907-766-2234 or 800-458-3579; www. seakfair.org.*

■ **OCTOBER**

Alaska Day Festival, Sitka. A three- to five-day festival celebrating the 1867 purchase of Alaska from the Russians. Festival highlights include a costume ball, Russian dancing, parade, and ceremonial reenactment of the purchase. *907-747-5940.*

■ **NOVEMBER**

Sitka Whalefest. A weekend of whale-watching tours, seminars by eminent visiting biologists and researchers, marine art shows, and other doings. *907-747-7964; www.sitkawhalefest.org.*

SOUTH-CENTRAL

South-Central Alaska encompasses two worlds—the crenellated coastline of the northern Pacific and the complicated mountain country south of the Alaska Range. Here is everything from seaweed-covered beaches to permanently frozen glacial ice fields. In this region you will find some of the tallest peaks in North America, and by my count about one hundred of the most beautiful valleys. Some of the fjords on the Kenai Peninsula look like pictures from Norway. Nearby old-growth rain forests appear to have been transplanted from the Amazon. There are soaring trees in those coastal forests with enough wood in one tree to build a good-sized country church, and there are ancient wind-flagged krummholz (stunted) trees at timberline that could fit in your hat. Retiring moose call this place home, as do wolves and grizzlies. In the rivers you will find the biggest salmon in the world.

The core city of **Anchorage** offers the amenities of a sizable metropolis, and highways lead to the **Kenai Peninsula,** which juts out south of Anchorage between Cook Inlet and Prince William Sound. Many people consider this the most beautiful area in Alaska, and it has several delightful towns, in particular Homer and Seward. A tour boat or fishing charter will take you out to explore the coastline of **Prince William Sound** and to see its glaciers, fjords, and wildlife. To reach this area drive south to Portage and from there drive or take the train to Whittier. Or travel north, then east of Anchorage via the Glenn Highway. At Glennallen the road meets the Richardson Highway which turns south to Valdez.

Many visitors instead drive or take the train north from Anchorage to **Denali National Park and Preserve** (described on page 211 in the following chapter).

■ ANCHORAGE AND VICINITY

■ HISTORY

Anchor-age: the name says it. Anchorage was in the beginning a convenient place for ships to rest awhile from the stormy north Pacific, a protected stretch of salt water at the head of a long inlet, surrounded by forest and meadow. A place to throw out the heavy rusted anchor, lower the wooden longboats, and venture forth in search of fresh water, fresh meat, fresh berries—anything so long as it did not taste of sea. The Russians visited, and the British, and later the Americans.

Seldovia, a small village on the Kenai Peninsula across Kachemak Bay from Homer, must be reached by air or sea. Thus isolated, it retains the charm of an earlier Alaska.

Everyone seemed to like it, but not even aboriginal Alaskans built a permanent settlement. Then in 1914, the future arrived in the form of a pioneering federal railroad north into the gold-and-silver mining country around Fairbanks. Anchorage was the logistical center between Fairbanks and the railroad's southern terminus at Seward, and the rest, as they say, is history.

In the 1930s, concerted efforts were made to turn the Matanuska Valley north of Anchorage into an agricultural paradise—cattle, barley, potatoes. Most of these well-intentioned attempts did not meet with success, but the various government-sponsored experiments at least drew hordes of hardy homesteaders into the area. Other events—especially support activities surrounding the Aleutian battles of World War II and the growing popularity of Mount McKinley National Park, now Denali National Park and Preserve—conspired to bring Anchorage more and more toward center stage in Alaska.

(following pages) Facing the Columbia Glacier across Prince William Sound.

Downtown Anchorage in 1915.

By the 1970s, Anchorage had become an important international air crossroads, the state's financial and commercial center, and the corporate headquarters for the oil pipeline running from Prudhoe Bay south to Valdez. Revenues from the pipeline brought an enormous amount of money into the state, and especially into Anchorage. Increasingly, Juneau—the state capital—began to fade behind the rising star of its big sister to the north. In 1974, state residents voted to move the capital to Willow, a small town north of Anchorage; but then, in the often contradictory spirit of democracy, they refused to fund the project. As a result, Juneau remains the ever-remote seat of government.

■ ANCHORAGE TODAY

Downtown Anchorage has a haphazard, frontier feel to it. Stern hotels overlook parking lots and empty lots; a few oil company office buildings and a federal building rise above disheveled cottages and new apartment buildings. The excellent art and history museum (more attractive inside than outside) and an architecturally interesting performing arts facility exude a public spirit also evident in parks ablaze

ART AND CULTURE IN ANCHORAGE

In Anchorage, cultural juxtapositions abound. Inupiat teenage girls adopt gangsta styles fresh out of South Central L.A. Samoan, African-American, and Korean churches spring up in unlikely buildings in less likely mini-malls. Horse-drawn carriages vie with Segway scooters for local tours. A bank that once gave away a .44 Magnum with every $10,000 certificate of deposit is now a donut shop. Seedy neighborhoods once lined with massage parlors are becoming trendier by the minute as real estate values rise. Lacking major historical sites to visit, tour-bus drivers take passengers through suburban neighborhoods, pointing out trophy homes and gardens of local executives.

"Fine art" muddles through somehow, although a flood of "moose and mountains" imagery tends to dominate the market. Books seriously examining the recent massive transformation of Alaska exist but require a little seeking out.

In Anchorage, artists nonchalantly cross disciplines and genres. A friend who was the concertmaster for the Anchorage Opera also played fiddle with a rock band called Sportin' Woodies. Another friend writes travel books and news articles, puts out a political magazine called *POL*, and sits on the Anchorage Municipal Assembly. A young poet and Denali train waitress is an accomplished jazz dancer. In one week I judged a high school poetry contest, opened my painting studio as part of a city-wide tour, and played an Earth Day festival as a rhythm guitarist in a band named after a trailer court.

There is a unique vibrancy and piquancy to the arts here. You only have to look as far as Tom Bodette of NPR fame and John Adams, Alaska's notable musical composer, and on to celebrated author John Haines. Many lesser-known but talented artists, writers, performers, and artisans are part of the mix, some locally well known, others laboring in relative obscurity.

Anchorage symphony, opera, and concert associations present increasingly vigorous programs, featuring both surprisingly high-quality local talent and international touring productions. Small theaters, including the venerable **Cyrano's** crank out regular productions, fed in part by a nationally respected University of Alaska (Anchorage) theater program. Private galleries like the **Decker-Morris** and the **International Gallery for Contemporary Art** push to expand visual horizons. Cafés like **Kaladi Bros., Side Street, Q [Qupqugiaq] Cafe,** and **The Firehouse** provide occasional forums for poetry slams and live readings. More mainstream bookstores like **Cook Inlet Books, Borders Books, Title Wave Books,** and **Barnes**

and Noble frequently host signings and readings by both Alaskan and "outside" authors.

Anchorage offers an eclectic variety of live music, featuring everything from standard bar bands to summer bluegrass festivals to mainstream jazz. High-energy local groups like the Photon Band inspire cult-like followings, and the quality of musicianship and original songwriting is often surprising. National mega-pop star Jewel (more popular outside the state than in it) is an Alaska product who once played local clubs. Venues range from intimate clubs to the larger **Moose's Tooth Restaurant** auditorium, which seats several hundred. And every so often, a headline national act rolls into town, filling the **George M. Sullivan Sports Arena** (the largest local hall) with frenzied fans. A semi-underground scene of alternative dance clubs and all-night raves contrasts with mainstream country-and-western clubs like **The Pines.** From practically zero 30 years ago, the music scene in Anchorage continues to thrive and expand. The *Anchorage Daily News* "8" section and the *Anchorage Press* give extensive listings of just about every little event in town.

–Jamie Bollenbach (updated by the editors, 2007)

with flowers in the summer. Good restaurants and hip bars are lively in the evening. Nearby are both upscale and dingy arts and crafts shops, fur outlets, pawn shops, a memorial to homicide victims, and dive bars (outside of which drunks reel around and curse each other). On a gray summer Saturday, downtown can appear damp and half-empty, except at the Saturday Market in the parking lot by the Hilton. But if the clouds part and the setting reveals itself, the effect is exhilarating. To the west lie the gray waters of Cook Inlet, rimmed with sand and clay cliffs topped by birch and spruce. In every other direction rise the jagged, snowcapped Chugach Mountains.

As with so many other cities, the local commercial life of Anchorage has been sucked into the neighborhoods where most people live, and like their counterparts in the Lower 48, shoppers head to nearby malls rather than drive into the old downtown. This residential part of Anchorage can be difficult for the visitor to penetrate, and there isn't much incentive to do so, as artery boulevards are lined with the same chain food outlets, blank-walled discount stores, and landscaping-free malls that pockmark the rest of the United States. Yet if you know someone to help you negotiate the terrain, they'll point out with great enthusiasm such places as the New Sagaya City Market, a specialty food store and café where you can sit outside and mingle with the hip crowd; the solarium of Bell's Nursery café; and a great Thai restaurant in a remodeled Dairy Queen.

More than half of Alaska's residents live in Anchorage and its surrounding suburbs. The majority of the city's approximately 260,000 inhabitants trace their ancestry to Europe, yet there is a large population of Native Alaskans here—Eskimo, Athabaskan, Aleut, and Tlingit, as well as African-Americans, Russians, Hispanics, and folks from the Pacific Rim countries (Korea, Japan, Taiwan). The result of this mixture is a cosmopolitan, multicultural community in a city that retains the sort of informality associated with the frontier.

■ EXPLORING ANCHORAGE *map page 149*

Log Cabin and Downtown Visitor Information Center *map site: 1*
The Anchorage Convention and Visitors Bureau runs this visitors center, which is open daily during the summer tourist season. The place explodes with pamphlets, brochures, maps, and coupons. *Fourth Avenue and F Street; 907-274-3531 or 800-478-1255.*

Next door, at the 1936–vintage **Old City Hall,** there are signs telling you where to meet for the **Historic Downtown Walking Tour.** This tour of historic Anchorage is offered by Anchorage Historic Properties (907-274-3600), a non-profit historic preservation organization, Mondays through Fridays at 1 P.M. in June, July, and August. No reservation is needed; just meet at the Old City Hall at 524 West Fourth Avenue.

Alaska Public Lands Information Center *map site: 2*
In the Old Federal Building, also at Fourth Avenue and F Street, the center features informational videos, wildlife exhibits, and historical displays, and also includes a good selection of books, maps, posters, and videotapes for sale. The highly trained desk staff can provide free and detailed information on public lands across the state. *605 West Fourth Avenue; 907-271-2737.*

These two visitors centers are at the center of downtown's shop and restaurant district. Flowerpots overflowing with beautiful bright flowers hang from the surrounding Fourth Avenue lampposts in summer.

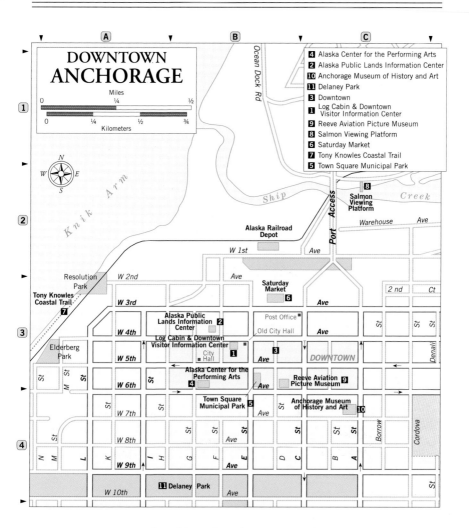

DOWNTOWN ANCHORAGE

Miles
0   ¼   ½

0   ¼   ½   ¾
Kilometers

4 Alaska Center for the Performing Arts
2 Alaska Public Lands Information Center
10 Anchorage Museum of History and Art
11 Delaney Park
3 Downtown
1 Log Cabin & Downtown Visitor Information Center
9 Reeve Aviation Picture Museum
8 Salmon Viewing Platform
6 Saturday Market
7 Tony Knowles Coastal Trail
5 Town Square Municipal Park

Downtown Area: Fourth, Fifth, and Sixth avenues, A to H streets. *map site: 3*
The downtown Anchorage area is an eclectic mix of hotels, public buildings,
tourist-oriented galleries and gift shops, local watering holes, and eateries to suit
every taste and wallet. Want a carved chunk of fossil mammoth ivory? A garish
wolf-fur hat, complete with glass eyes and tail? An Asian-made Eskimo doll or plush
toy for the grandkids? A multi-thousand-dollar bronze of a diving whale or above-
the-couch-sized framed photograph of a grizzly? Hot dogs from a street vendor,

haute cuisine, local draft ale and a good sandwich—you'll find it all downtown. As far as tourist shopping and galleries go, this is certainly the area. There's also a locally owned bookstore, Cook Inlet Books, which has a fine collection of Alaskana, and a modest-sized but worthwhile mall. The farther you wander down Fourth Avenue, the rougher-looking the neighborhood; street crime is rare, however. The scattered bars and street folks are part of the local ambience.

Alaska Center for the Performing Arts   *map site: 4*
The center was built in the mid-1980s and furnished by Alaskan craftsmen. The largest of its three theaters, the Evangeline Atwood Concert Hall, seats more than 2,000 and has a dramatic starburst-patterned ceiling that radiates from the stage like the aurora borealis. Check the schedule to see what new plays, musicals, dances, or symphonic performances are currently being featured. *621 West Sixth Avenue, at G Street; 907-263-2900 or 800-478-7328.*

A typical summer day at the visitors center in downtown Anchorage.

Town Square Municipal Park *map site: 5*
In the summertime this park, just east of the performing arts center, is abloom with flowers so improbably colored, you'd swear they'd been dipped in paint. Rather, this color is testimony to the effect of 20 hours of daylight and plenty of rain.

Saturday Market *map site: 6*
Held on summer Saturdays in the parking lot across from the Hilton. Nearly 300 vendors set up their blue-and-white tents, and sell a wide variety of foods and crafts, both Alaskan and imported—including 3-foot carved bears, Philly cheese steaks, Russian piroshki, barbecued oysters, popcorn, wolf-fur boots, knives, and implements made from antlers, to hats and scarves made from qiviut (underfur of the musk ox). *E Street at the corner of Third.*

Tony Knowles Coastal Trail *map site: 7*
This lovely paved trail is reached by walking west down Third Avenue to the southern end of Resolution Park, where the trail begins. Named in honor of former Anchorage mayor and two-term governor Tony Knowles, it's a fine example of the many parks within the city limits that offer a taste of wilderness. Following it, you'll see lovely residential neighborhoods, views across Cook Inlet, wildflowers, trees, and, honking in the tidal flats, dozens of Canada geese. In winter and early spring, you also stand an excellent chance of seeing a moose. Some Anchorage lodgings provide their guests with bicycles; if yours does, take advantage of the offer and bike the trail, which extends south for 11 miles along the western shores of the inlet, connecting to the myriad trails of sprawling, 1,500-acre Kincaid Park. On the way, you'll pass through Earthquake Park, so named when the 1964 earthquake caused a massive downward slump. The signs of the quake are becoming less visible with time, but interpretive signs and the impressive view make it a worthwhile and popular stop. If your hotel fails to provide you with wheels, you can remedy the problem with a visit to Downtown Bicycle Rental (333 West Fourth Avenue; 907-279-5293).

Salmon Viewing Platform *map site: 8*
During the summer months, salmon migrate up Ship Creek, and they can be observed easily from this platform, reached by continuing north on C Street across the railroad tracks to the bridge over Ship Creek. The banks are often crowded with fishermen, shoulder to shoulder as they fish for big king salmon—quite a sight to behold in the midst of a major American city. Salmon in the 50-pound class have been caught here.

Reeve Aviation Picture Museum *map site: 9*
This photo archive has more than a thousand photos of Alaska's most famous bush pilots. *343 West Sixth Avenue between D and C streets.* (Also well worth a visit for aviation buffs is the **Alaska Aviation Heritage Museum**, housing a collection of classic aircraft, near the airport at 4721 Aircraft Drive; 907-248-5325.)

Anchorage Museum of History and Art *map site: 10*
This major facility offers an outstanding collection of historic and contemporary Alaskan art, and a special section for children. The wide interior atrium is a truly inviting space, airy and light. Alaskan artisans display and sell their wares here, and the ambience is such that it's easy and pleasant to stand about and talk to them about their work. A café serves informal food at tables around a fountain (which is supposed to look like it's built of ice, but looks more like glass bathroom tiles).

Among the many treasures in the collection of the Anchorage Museum of History and Art are this Haida argillite box made by John Cross, circa 1900, and the seal-oil lamp (right), roughly 1,000 years old, found on the Kenai Peninsula.

Downstairs galleries exhibit the works of Sydney Laurence, Thomas Hill, and Fred Machetanz, well-known Alaskan painters whose romantic and realistic visions of an earlier era convey a sense of the mythic and spiritual effect the Alaskan landscape can have on those who live here. Upstairs, the crafts of Native Alaskan and early Russian communities are artfully displayed in domestic settings that give these tiny artifacts life and meaning. Especially beautiful are a narrow nude female figure caved in walrus ivory that served as a needle case and an ancient stone bowl that served as a seal-oil lamp. *West Seventh Avenue and A Street; 907-343-4326 or 907-343-6173 (for recorded information).*

Delaney Park *map site: 11*
South of the art museum in a long narrow greenbelt from A to P streets between Ninth and 10th avenues—the Park Strip—lie lovely bicycle and walking trails that wind through woods and meadows and eventually meet up with the Tony Knowles Coastal Trail.

Alaska Native Heritage Center *map page 144, A/B-3*
In a beautifully landscaped, 26-acre park in northeast Anchorage, this impressive site offers a taste of Alaska Native culture and history to visitors not traveling to the remote bush. Guests can tour five historically re-created village sites, which provide a glimpse into a lifestyle now largely lost to the modern world. The center features contemporary Native dancing, game and craft demonstrations, and storytelling, along with a variety of exhibits and a nicely done short film on Native culture. Guides and staff are friendly and informative, and the gift store carries a line of Native crafts from across the state. In summer there's a complimentary shuttle from the Log Cabin and Downtown Visitor Information Center, from the Anchorage Museum of History and Art, and several other locations. *8800 Heritage Center Drive; 907-330-8000 or 800-315-6608.*

ALASKA POLITICS

Nothing fits neatly in Alaska politics. Idealistic, reactionary, frontier-practical, isolated, and often apathetic or actively paranoid, Alaskans insist on their own interpretation of everything. The people sort of lead, candidates sort of follow, and parties limp behind. Without a major sports team, politics has to suffice for entertainment. Most voters are Independents, and cross-party coalitions frequently determine the leadership of the state legislature.

Alaskans have voted for every Republican presidential candidate since 1968; still, three of the last six governors were moderate Democrats. The current governor, Republican Sarah Palin, is the state's first woman to hold that office. Perhaps the most popular of all modern Alaska governors was a light-hearted moderate Republican named Jay Hammond, who was narrowly elected in 1978. With a bush pilot past, a white beard, and a penchant for wearing flannel shirts and jeans to official events, Hammond was an endearing character and a genuine populist. His legacy includes helping to establish the state's famous Alaska Permanent Fund, now a $40 billion reserve of public money from oil revenues from which every Alaskan receives an annual dividend check.

As a territory in the 1950s, Alaska was left-leaning enough that a New York congressman claimed the future state's two senators and one representative would be "selected by communist agents." Alaska's current representative in Washington, Don Young (R), who originally lost an election in 1972 to Rep. Nick Begich (who was deceased at the time), is famous for impersonating rabbits dying in leg traps, speaking obscenities in front of school children, and declaring happily that perseverance will beat out intelligence in the end.

Third parties such as Libertarians, Greens, or even Bull-Moose Republicans often bubble up. The "Alaska Independence Party" actually elected former Nixon Secretary of the Interior Walter Hickel as governor in 1990, but his adopted party's platform of "Alaska sovereignty" never resulted in substantive policy. Moderate Democrat Tony Knowles had a two-term run (1994–2002) during which Alaska grew steadily but changed little. Governor Murkowski then waged a no-holds-barred autocratic agenda that alienated Alaskans. Palin, as charismatic as Murkowski was unpopular, seems a moderating influence.

The 1971 **Alaska Native Claims Settlement Act** (ANCSA) set up 13 public corporations whose stockholders consist of the 80,000 Alaskans of at least one-quarter Native heritage. These corporations provide their stockholders with stock dividends, jobs, resources, health care, and other quasi-governmental services, and are major players in Alaska politics. The act, which gave control of 44 million acres of Alaska land to Natives, fostered major divisions within these highly diverse ethnic groups. Many Native corporation shareholders, residents of remote bush villages, still live a subsistence-oriented, hunter-gatherer lifestyle; they feel that the so-called "Brooks Brothers Natives"—suit-wearing, white-talking executives who head their corporations—have lost track of their roots in their pursuit of the bottom line. However, because a majority of the Native corporations raise revenue by developing the resources of their lands, thereby providing dividends and jobs to shareholders, many Alaskan aboriginal peoples find themselves on both sides of such issues as clear-cutting trees for export or oil development in the Arctic National Wildlife Refuge.

Another effect of ANCSA has been the revitalization of Native Alaskan culture. Corporations have made it more possible for Native people to remain economically viable in their villages, and as a result, there has been a modest but pronounced renaissance of Native language, arts, and culture.

Oil development transformed Alaska politics forever. The trans-Alaska pipeline—a massive, 1,000-mile project that connected the world-class oil fields near Prudhoe Bay to the ice-free port of Valdez and generated a boom that lasted from the early 1970s through the 1980s—literally flooded the state treasury. It also brought a huge influx of oil-industry workers, many of whom transplanted their unique southwestern sensibilities, giving rise to the once-popular bumper sticker, "Happiness is a Texan leaving with an Okie under each arm." But the corporate structure of big oil was here to stay. Even with the gradual decline of the massive Prudhoe Bay area oil fields over the past two decades, the stakes are still in the billions of dollars, and lobbyists and organized interests are a dominant force in Alaska politics. New fields are being developed, and technologies have improved for recovering available oil. The current struggle between environmentalists, Native groups, and the oil companies to develop oil fields in ANWR (the Arctic National Wildlife Refuge) and the lesser-known, but far more vast NPRA (National Petroleum Reserve–Alaska) is ongoing.

Oil interests, social conservatives, and development groups, such as the mining or lumber industries, have had a common interest in defeating more socially liberal and environmentally protective legislators. The resulting coalition has made the Alaska Legislature increasingly conservative. The pro-development/social conservative alliance continues its efforts to develop environmentally sensitive areas, but the live-and-let-live traditions of a frontier culture remain as a force to be reckoned with.

–Jamie Bollenbach

■ NEARBY HIKING TRAILS

There is great mountain hiking right in Anchorage. The Chugach Mountains rise dramatically from the eastern suburbs, only a few miles from the core area of the city. If you drive east on O'Malley, Huffman, or DeArmoun roads—or virtually any other major road—you will reach trailheads. Once up these trails, you might catch a glimpse of Dall sheep, grizzly bears, black bears, moose, coyotes, wolves, foxes, eagles, hawks, ravens, and ptarmigan, to name just a few. (To avoid surprising large animals and putting them on the defensive, make noise as you walk, talking loudly, whistling, singing, or otherwise making your presence known.) The **Flattop Mountain Trail,** at the end of Huffman Road, is one of the best: a four-mile round trip with a good view from the top. Another fantastic hike is the trail up **Rendezvous Peak,** offering even better panoramic views than Flattop Mountain. The trailhead is at the end of the Arctic Valley Road.

Given all the trails that lead directly into Anchorage, it's not surprising that wildlife lives on the city's fringes and often wanders through suburban neighborhoods. Three hundred moose are thought to live in the Anchorage area year-round, and another 700 come into the city when the snow gets deep. In the winter of 1994, with snow banks reaching to the rooftops, some moose clambered up on top of houses in order to nibble at the lower branches of trees. And Alaska Fish & Game Department biologists confirm at least one pack of wolves living within the city limits of Anchorage.

■ NEARBY SITES OF INTEREST: NORTH

Eagle River Nature Center *map page 144, A/B-3*

The drive here from Anchorage is along a spruce- and cottonwood-lined road that curves below spectacular mountains. The Eagle River Nature Center, a log cabin at the end of the suburban town of Eagle River, has displays about the area's natural history and in the summer offers guided nature walks, including hikes into Chugach State Park along the historic Old Iditarod–Crow Pass Trail. Nearby are views of spectacular mountain scenery and the hanging glacier on Polar Bear Peak. Eagles, bears, and moose all live in the vicinity. *From Anchorage take the Glenn Highway northbound to the Eagle River Loop/Highland Road exit; continue and turn right onto Eagle River Road and drive 10 miles to the center. 32750 Eagle River Road; 907-694-2108.*

Near Anchorage, ice climbing above Turnagain Arm.

Abandoned buildings at Independence Mine State Historical Park, at Hatcher Pass.

Palmer and the Matanuska Valley *map page 144, B-3*

Matanuska Valley (also referred to as Mat-Su Valley) is Alaska's primary farming region, known for the mammoth vegetables that grow here during the summer months, when photosynthesis is a 24-hour event. The valley was homesteaded in the Depression by struggling farm families relocated here by the U.S. government. Palmer, the valley's main town, is noted for its historical buildings. The **Palmer Visitors Center** (723 South Valley Way; 907-745-2880), located in a log cabin and run by the Greater Palmer Chamber of Commerce, provides extensive information on local hiking, boating, rafting, camping, and fishing.

Musk Ox Farm

Just east of Palmer is the **Musk Ox Farm**, where the musk ox is raised domestically. In Alaska, musk oxen were hunted to extinction in 1865 but were successfully reintroduced to several locations across the state 70 years later. Their underfur, qiviut, is hand knit by Native Alaskans to make warm garments. The farm is open to visitors from mid-May through late September (winters by appointment), and there is a gift shop on the premises. *On the Glenn Highway at Milepost 50.1; 907-745-4151.*

Eklutna Historical Park

The line of sofas overlooking the Glenn Highway at Mile 26.3 tells you you're passing Eklutna, population 46 and counting. If it is a sunny day, residents of this Athabaskan Indian village often sit back and watch the four lanes of traffic speed past on their way to or from "Los Anchorage." The town is unique in that it hosts its own historical park, featuring guided tours of a small museum and Russian Orthodox Church, and provides an interesting, unvarnished view of local Native culture and history. The cemetery, where colorful "spirit houses" (the local equivalent of headstones) combine elements of indigenous and Russian Orthodox tradition, is unique, and the mountain-rimmed setting is beautiful. *On the Glenn Highway at Milepost 26.3; 907-688-6026.*

Hatcher Pass

North of Anchorage the road to Hatcher Pass leads 22 miles into the high mountains, through a historic gold mining area, and up to beautiful Summit Lake. This area is popular with the local population for hiking, wildlife observation, and, in winter, skiing and other winter sports. *North of Palmer on the Glenn Highway.*

■ SEWARD HIGHWAY: SOUTHEAST

Driving from Anchorage toward the Kenai Peninsula you drive on one of the most spectacular roads in the country—the **Seward Highway.** Along the way you are treated to views out of a picture book—towering snow-covered peaks rising from cold sea waters where pods of black-and-white orcas can sometimes be spotted hunting for salmon. Beluga whales ride the famous bore tides—high, rapid waves associated with incoming tides that are amazing to watch. Dall sheep are often visible along the highway, and throughout the summer, waterfalls and cataracts plunge from the mountain heights to the thick green valley forests. But drive carefully and keep your eyes on the road—this highway is known for its high accident rate, due mostly to excessive speed and driver inattention. As with many Alaska highways, mileposts provide a reference for travelers. Traveling from Anchorage toward Seward, the miles count down from 127. Going the opposite direction, the countdown is reversed (the mileposts start at one; Anchorage is 127).

The Kenai National Wildlife Refuge is the home of moose, Dall sheep, black bears, bald eagles, and other species. Skilak Lake and the Kenai Mountains are in the distance.

Potter Point State Game Refuge (Potter Marsh)   *map page 144, B-3*
From the wooden boardwalk that winds through a wide green marsh along the
edge of the Seward Highway, strollers occasionally see Canada geese (who nest here
in the summer), trumpeter swans, arctic terns (who fly to Antarctica and back each
year, 10,000 miles each way), ducks, and seabirds. Early spring and summer
evenings are best at this wildlife viewing area, part of the Anchorage Coastal
Wildlife Refuge. Bring your binoculars and bird book. Sometimes park rangers set
up telescopes focused on eagles or hawks—whose eagle-eyes are probably focused
back upon the viewers. The constant sound of gunfire from a nearby rifle range
and the roar of nearby freeway traffic add a vaguely unsettling note to this bucolic
scene. *About 10 miles south of downtown Anchorage on the Seward Highway, at
Milepost 117.*

Chugach State Park   *map page 144, B-3*

Beginning at Mile 115, and for the next 24 miles, you drive through the 495,000-
acre Chugach State Park between the mountains and Turnagain Arm on the Cook
Inlet. (Supposedly Captain Cook came in here, but turned around when he saw
that the inlet didn't connect to William Sound.) There are numerous hiking trails
that lead from the highway up into the park, offering varied terrain and breathtaking views. On the water side of the highway you'll see a pullout at Beluga Point,
popular with windsurfers. Occasionally, the white whales for which the point is
named can be seen, as well as orcas (killer whales). Vast tidal flats here and farther
up Turnagain are potentially dangerous, since the tide moves fast and the mud is
thick. *907-345-5014.*

Alyeska Resort   *map page 144, B-3*

At Mile 90 on the Seward Highway, the spur road to Alyeska Resort leads into a
scenic valley where you can get out and stretch your legs or take some photographs
of the wildflowers or mountains. The Alyeska Prince Hotel has exceptionally beautiful public rooms and lovely terraces leading out to views of the mountains. A
tram ride will take you up to the Seven Glaciers restaurant perched on the mountainside. During the winter Alyeska Resort offers the finest downhill skiing in the
state, in an alpine setting that features long runs, big drops, and plenty of challenges. *907-754-1111 or 800-880-3880.*

Portage Glacier *map page 144, B-3*

Along the Seward Highway, at the far end of Turnagain Arm, you'll meet the turnoff to Portage Glacier. Once the most visited glacier in the state, it has retreated and shrunk so rapidly that it is no longer visible from the visitors center. The **Begich-Boggs Visitor Center** (907-283-2326), manned by Chugach National Forest Service rangers, provides information about the natural wonders in the vicinity. It's still worth the stop and extremely scenic, with good camping, hiking, and picnic possibilities. Portage Valley also has several observation decks where you can see red and dog salmon during their spawning season—the best place is just past the bridge at Mile 4.1, on the turnoff to the campground.

■ KENAI PENINSULA *map page 144, A/B-3/4*

The Kenai Peninsula is a microcosm of Alaska. In it you will find representative samples of nearly every biogeographic province of the state—from permanent glaciers (Harding Ice Field) to crab-filled tide pools (Homer); from high mountain tundra where herds of caribou run (Russian River headwaters) to thick rain forest haunted by brown bears (Kachemak Bay State Wilderness Park); from salmon-filled coastal streams (the Kenai River drainage boasts the largest king salmon in the state, plus blue-ribbon fishing for other species) to mountain lakes supporting prodigious lake trout (Kenai Lake). In short, it's an outdoorsman's paradise.

From mid-June through mid-August the Kenai Peninsula becomes crowded, especially along the salmon streams, where RVs line the margins of the road and fishermen stand shoulder to shoulder in the water. Because the area is only a three- or four-hour drive from Anchorage, the roads, towns, and campgrounds fill up. If possible make reservations in advance. If you're making plans day by day, go anyway: you'll probably find accommodations in one of the many private campgrounds or B&Bs.

The small, coastal community of **Whittier** (see page 173), on Prince William Sound, once only accessible overland by rail, can now be reached by an 11-mile road from Portage, completed in 2000, that features a one-lane tunnel that alternately allows passage by trains, cars traveling to Whittier, and cars returning. A toll is charged, and waits of up to 30 minutes are common. Tunnel information is available at 877-611-2586 and on local radio (AM 530 in Whittier or AM 1610 in Portage).

■ From Portage to Seward

From Portage the Seward Highway turns west and then south onto the Kenai Peninsula. There are numerous turnoffs and side roads and public campgrounds where you can leave the busy road and enjoy the sights.

Hope *map page 144, B-3*

At Mile 56.7 there is a turnoff to the old mining village of **Hope** (another 18 miles distant), and there are several good public campgrounds down this road.

Upper and Lower Summit Lakes

Ten miles farther on you'll drive past Summit Lakes, a good spot for Dolly Varden fishing. This is also a nice place for a restorative picnic if the road is particularly busy.

Kenai Mountains

Ten miles past the lakes you'll find yourself deep in the Kenai Mountains and approaching the turnoff to the Sterling Highway, which leads west to Cooper Landing, Soldotna, Kenai, and Homer.

Moose Pass *map page 144, B-4*

If you continue straight, you'll be on your way to Seward, which is the gateway to Kenai Fjords National Park. The road reaches **Moose Pass** (motel, store, restaurant) at about Mile 29.

Kenai Lake

Five miles farther south you'll see the glacially fed, bright green-blue **Kenai Lake** off to the west—good lake trout fishing here. The rest of the drive consists of a steady descent through a heavily forested valley to the busy fishing town of Seward, at the head of Resurrection Bay.

Exit Glacier

Four miles before you arrive in Seward you'll reach the turnoff to Exit Glacier on the west side of the Seward Highway. This is the easiest and safest glacier to touch in all Alaska, and well worth the trip. Experienced ice climbers can use the glacier for access to or exit from the vast Harding Ice Field (hence the glacier's name, given by an early explorer).

Fall colors along Engineer Lake in the Kenai National Wildlife Refuge, near Cooper Landing.

■ SEWARD   *map page 144, B-4*

Once known primarily as the southern terminus of the Alaska railroad and as the departure point for thousands of prospectors and miners, Seward (pop. 2,830) is today associated with the commercial fishing industry and the tourist business attached to Kenai Fjords National Park (formed in 1980). Seward was severely damaged in 1964 during the Good Friday earthquake, after which a tidal wave more than 100 feet tall thundered in from the sea and pretty well leveled the seafront. Since then, Seward has been rebuilt and is now a charming town of wood-frame houses and fine summer gardens. Facing a deep blue bay and surrounded by snow-capped peaks, with impassable cliffs and ridges that soar up from the back of town, Seward is famous for unstable weather, in both summer and winter.

You'll find the **Kenai Fjords National Park Visitor Center** (907-224-2125, or 907-224-2132 for recorded information) along the boardwalk in the small boat harbor. The Chugach National Forest Service office (907-224-3374) is located at the corner of Jefferson Street and Fourth Avenue. Numerous private charters operating out of Seward can take you on ocean-going tours of the park, or on fishing

Playing with Steller's sea lions at the Alaska SeaLife Center in Seward.

trips, or both. Anything that gets you out on the water and into this fantastic park is highly recommended. Also, sea kayaks can be rented in Seward and transported to remote areas of the park for secluded wilderness adventures. Information on all of this can be obtained at the visitors center.

Also on the waterfront is the **Alaska SeaLife Center,** an educational and research institution with an impressive aquarium that focuses on the marine life of south-central Alaska. *301 Railway Avenue; 907-224-6300 or 800-224-2525.*

■ **KENAI FJORDS NATIONAL PARK** *map page 144, A/B-4*
Stretching more than 100 miles southwest from Seward very nearly to Port Graham, this park is distinguished by its many rocky narrow inlets, or fjords. In these deep cold fjords live sea otters, sea lions, harbor seals, Dall's porpoise, harbor porpoises, sea lions, orcas (killer whales), and gray, humpback, and minke whales. Worldwide, the Steller's sea lion population has declined 75 percent in the last two decades, and the majority of those remaining live off the coast of Alaska. Once while I was sea kayaking in Resurrection Bay a huge bull sea lion surfaced near my kayak and almost swamped the craft. He was much larger than the kayak, and rangers later told me that mature sea lions can exceed 13 feet in length and weigh in the neighborhood of 2,400 pounds.

The horned and tufted puffin colonies are also a sight to behold as the gaudily colored birds fly in and out of their rocky cliffside nests.

■ **WESTERN KENAI PENINSULA**

The Sterling Highway begins at Mile 37 of the Seward Highway and leads west into the Kenai Peninsula. (Note that the first milepost on the Sterling will therefore be 38, and the last will be 179.5, at the tip of the Homer Spit.) The scenic 143-mile-long road provides access to the Kenai River and various coastal communities and sites, including Captain Cook State Recreation Area, Cooper Landing, Soldotna and Kenai, Clam Gulch, Ninilchik, and Kachemak Bay.

The road is two to four lanes and early on traverses lush green valleys ablaze with purple fireweed, hills on either side forested with conifers, rising to green scrub, then brown rock rims. Along the edge of the road are white- or gray-barked alders and aspen. Road signs read GIVE MOOSE A CHANCE, followed by the year's tally of road kill (which often exceeds 300 per year). Although cars and moose are a danger to each other, chances are you'll drive along the highway and see no wildlife at all; keep a sharp eye out nevertheless, both for safety and enjoyment. Due to their penchant for feeding on roadside vegetation, moose frequently seem to appear out of nowhere—sometimes smack in the middle of your lane. Rubbernecking tourists and impatient local drivers make these bottlenecks dangerous. The Sterling Highway continues on through spindly dwarfed forest before turning south along Cook Inlet. It ends at the end of the Homer spit. At certain times of the year—from Memorial Day to Labor Day, essentially—the road carries far more traffic than it was designed for years ago, so always drive cautiously. Huge expanses of dead spruce trees, killed by a cyclic infestation of beetles, are sporadically visible all the way to Homer.

■ STERLING HIGHWAY TO SOLDOTNA *map page 144, A-3*

Kenai Lake *map page 144, A/B-3/4*
West of the Tern Lake Junction you will soon meet up with Quartz Creek and the lovely shore of Kenai Lake, a high glacial lake that is the source of the Kenai River. The glacial till, or ground-up rock, from the glaciers causes the lake to have a distinct blue-green color—the same is true of the river. At Mile 45 you'll pass the Bean Creek Road, which provides access to the Kenai Princess Wilderness Lodge and the Kenai Princess RV Park (907-595-1425 or 800-426-0500 for reservations).

Cooper Landing *map page 144, A/B-3/4*
About one mile farther is the sleepy little community of **Cooper Landing,** which also serves as an important headquarters for several major fishing outfitters and guides serving the Kenai River. There are restaurants and a store here, as well as private and public campgrounds, an RV park, and other visitor services. It is a very friendly place—one of my "homes away from home" in Alaska. The public campgrounds in this area—in fact on the whole peninsula—are very well designed, with many excellent sites available.

Five miles farther down the road is the Russian River Campground, which is very crowded in the summer during the fishing season (by contrast, in May and September the place is virtually empty).

Resurrection Pass Trail
At Mile 53.2 from Anchorage you will find the trailhead for the Resurrection Pass Trail—this is one of Alaska's finest road-accessible wilderness trails, but is infested

with mosquitoes in the summer (the country is also thick with black and grizzly bears). I recommend venturing up this trail (and all others on the Kenai Peninsula) with a topographic map, a compass, bug juice, perhaps a can of bear spray, and a briefing from the forest rangers.

Skilak and Swan Lakes

At Mile 58 there is a side-road south to Skilak Lake, a popular fishing area. Four good campgrounds are found along this 15-mile-long side road, which can offer a pleasant respite from the highway on a particularly busy day. Another side road at Mile 83.4 leads north to the Swanson River and Swan Lake area, a popular canoeing, fishing, and big-game hunting area on the north end of the Kenai Peninsula.

Soldotna *map page 144, A-3*

You'll reach the good-sized town of Soldotna at Mile 95.2, and there you'll find the road lined on either side with parking lots, cinderblock discount outlets, and chain restaurants, all unrelieved by landscaping. Friendly folks and the convenient location mitigate the sometimes bleak, mall-sprawl ambience.

A fresh catch of halibut is weighed in at the dock in Seldovia.

At this point you have a choice—head north in the direction of Kenai and Captain Cook State Recreation Area (excellent beach camping area, but often full), or head south toward Homer. Most choose the latter, and head over the Kenai River bridge toward Kasilof and points south. Along the way, if the sky is clear, you'll see magnificent snow-draped volcanoes that rise above Cook Inlet on the Alaska Peninsula: Mount Redoubt (10,197 feet) and Mount Iliamna (10,016 feet).

■ STERLING HIGHWAY TO HOMER *map page 144, A-3/4*

Tustumena Lake *map page 144, A-3*
South of the little village of Kasilof (another great fishing town on a lovely salmon and steelhead river), there is a turnoff to Tustumena Lake that is worth taking (east side of the road; Mile 111). Tustumena is an ideal place for camping, fishing, and canoeing. A person with a good boat can penetrate nearly 40 miles into the wilderness just by following the lake shoreline—and get lots of opportunities here for observing moose, bears, and bald eagles.

Clam Gulch *map page 144, A-3*
Clam Gulch, at Mile 117.4, is another favorite place in May with the saltwater fisherman—the king salmon pass by here on their way north to the Kasilof and Kenai rivers, and you'll see the ocean dotted with skiffs as freezing-cold fishermen stubbornly troll for them.

Ninilchik and Anchor Point *map page 144, A-4*
Ninilchik, at Mile 135.6, is one of the coast's major ports for fishing outfitters—if you're interested in halibut or salmon fishing at sea, stop here or at Anchor Point, 25 miles farther on.

If you'd like to drop by an old-time roadside bar try the one at the Happy Valley turnoff. Built of stones and cut logs, it's close and dark inside, as if hunkered down against the elements. In the entryway, locals have posted signs describing what they'd like to sell or acquire, such as: "LOOKING FOR WOMAN WHO LIKES TO FISH, CAN CLEAN FISH AND SEW, WHO OWNS A FISHING BOAT." The bar and its eight barstools run the length of the room; the jukebox features the Beatles, Hank Williams, and Buddy Holly. The wall above the two small tables is hung with a wolf skin and there's a snow crab under glass behind the bar.

Ninilchik Russian Orthodox Church, just north of Homer, reflects the Kenai Peninsula's Russian heritage.

■ HOMER   *map page 144, A-4*

At about Mile 167 you will have your first view of one of the prettiest little towns in North America: Homer. First you'll catch glimpses through spruce trees of the deep, cold, blue waters of Kachemak Bay. Then as you crest the hill and head down, you'll see a green swath of land before the bay, a small town, and Homer Spit gracefully curving away from it. Across the bay huge peaks soar from sea level into high steep permanent snowfields, and a light blue river of ice, Grewingk Glacier, flows around a conical mountain. Ships of every size and description are busily going this way and that, wild dark forests lie everywhere, and there are lovely homes, a clean waterfront, and the genuine feel of an artistic community.

In recent years Homer ("Halibut Fishing Capital of the World") has grown beyond all predictions. Once you've spent five minutes in Homer, you'll understand its allure. The inspiration of nature's beauty is everywhere. Painters, sculptors, poets, songwriters, dancers, novelists, playwrights—you will find them here in greater concentration than anywhere else in Alaska. Their presence makes for a nice ambience, a mixture of vitality and creative spirit. The spirit of *nouveau* cooking has also arrived in Homer, and travelers who've been dining for weeks on steak and potatoes, halibut and potatoes, and salmon and potatoes, along with iceberg lettuce salads, will feel they've arrived in a safe harbor. Good restaurants thrive here, as do pretty B&Bs and hillside inns.

As you approach Homer on the Sterling Highway, you will come to a sign pointing downtown at Pioneer Avenue. Continue, and you will see, on the right, the **Homer Chamber of Commerce Visitor Information Center** (201 Sterling Highway; 907-235-7740), which provides maps of Homer and information on hikes, charters, accommodations, and tours. Also on the right, past Main Street, is the new **Alaska Islands and Ocean Visitor Center** (95 Sterling Highway; 907-235-6961), headquarters of the Alaska Maritime National Wildlife Refuge, which encompasses more than 47,300 miles of Alaska coastline and 2,500 islands. Rangers here provide valuable information, including maps of tidal pool areas, brochures on marine life, and specific suggestions for wilderness hikes, sea kayak rentals, halibut or salmon charters, aerial glacier tours. They also have a listing of B&Bs. In the summer there are naturalist-led bird hikes, estuary hikes, and beach walks.

Main Street leads down toward **Bishop's Beach,** a beautiful, wild strand facing Cook Inlet and the volcanoes on the Alaska Peninsula to the west. Following Main Street in the other direction, the road forks, with the left fork (Pioneer Avenue) heading up into the busy municipal center. Excellent art galleries can be found here as well as the **Pratt Museum** (907-235-8635), a fine natural history museum, at one end of Bartlett Street.

Homer Spit

Homer Spit Road aims straight down the center of a narrow, four-mile-long, windy, treeless, gravel spit that is humming with activity. On the west side is its greatest asset (except for the view): a large boat harbor where fishing, commercial, and pleasure boats moor. Also on the spit are logs piled up for shipment to Asia, a chip mill, and huge barges. Warehouses, the offices of private fishing charters and tour boats, and seafood restaurants compete for space with shops selling tourist gimmicks, ice cream stores, public fishing areas, restaurants, and campgrounds (the windiest campgrounds on earth). Lining both sides of the road are parked RVs and cars. At the end of the Homer Spit you can park by Land's End Resort, walk along the stony beach, and gaze over at the wilderness on the other side of Kachemak Bay. Daily ferries cross the bay to the villages of Seldovia or Halibut Cove.

■ PRINCE WILLIAM SOUND   *map page 144, B/C-3/4*

Beautiful Prince William Sound washes the eastern flank of the Kenai Peninsula. Valdez lies at its northern end, the towns of Whittier and Seward to its west and southwest. It is protected from the roiling waters of the Gulf of Alaska by Montague and Hinchinbrook islands.

In Prince William Sound, you can see the magnificent Columbia Glacier, as well as a wide array of marine and terrestrial wildlife, including orcas, harbor seals, humpback whales, and sea otters. Salmon and halibut fishing can be very good in parts of the Sound.

■ WHITTIER   *map page 144, B-3*

On the Kenai Peninsula 17 miles east of Portage, Whittier (pop. 182) provides recreational access to a remote area of Prince William Sound. A recently completed (2000) road link using the existing train route through the 13,000-foot Anton

(following pages) Homer, at the base of Homer Spit, has a scenic setting against the Kenai Mountains.

Prince William Sound

Just as we entered the famous Prince William Sound, that I had so long hoped to see, the sky cleared, disclosing to the westward one of the richest, most glorious mountains I ever beheld—peak over peak, a thousand of them, icy and shining, rising higher, beyond and yet beyond one another, burning bright in the afternoon light, with great breadths of sun-spangled, ice-dotted waters in front. Grandeur and beauty in a thousand forms awaited us at every turn in this bright and spacious wonderland.

–John Muir, *The Harriman Expedition,* 1899

Anderson Memorial Tunnel connects Portage to Whittier, but many travelers still take the train rather than drive between the two towns. Both options are popular; it's a matter of taste and personal logistics. The tunnel, engineered during World War II, was necessitated by the area's extremely steep, mountainous terrain. Trains and cars both depart from the Bear Valley staging area, 6.7 miles from the Seward Highway junction; traffic alternates directions approximately every 30 minutes, often necessitating a wait. The system is computer-controlled, and the safety record is exemplary. There are tolls booths at Bear Valley, as well as a small railway station, an eight-lane staging area, and a large parking lot where you can leave your vehicle if boarding the train. Automobiles can also be put on the train and transported to ferries in Whittier that depart for Valdez, located about a hundred miles to the north and east on the other side of Prince William Sound—a transport option that saves a far longer drive.

The rail line between Portage and Whittier was hurriedly built in 1942-43 to facilitate the movement of troops, fuel, and supplies to the interior of the state in the event of a Japanese invasion. Whittier offered a port that was ice-free during the winter months, remote and difficult to attack from air or sea, and also accessible—once the Anton Anderson and other tunnels were bored through the Kenai Mountains—to the Seward-Fairbanks rail line.

The neatly planned streets of Whittier still retain some of the ordered ambience of a military outpost. Practically every resident lives in a single, multistory concrete building. The town was essentially abandoned by the military in the 1960s, especially after the 1964 Good Friday earthquake and tidal wave destroyed the harbor and many of the buildings. Today in Whittier you will find a hotel, a couple of bed-and-breakfasts, a campground, a few cafés, and some stores. You can rent sea kayaks to explore the local waters, or charter boats for wilderness kayaking, fishing, hiking, or camping expeditions.

One bit of advice when planning a trip to Whittier—pack all the rain gear you own. It's on the wrong side of a rain shadow.

■ VALDEZ   *map page 144, C-3*

Most people reach Valdez via the Richardson Highway—which, on its final approach from Glennallen through the rugged Chugach Mountains and Lowe River Valley, is one of the more beautiful drives in the state. Valdez is set at the base of dramatic, soaring snow-covered peaks. It receives an enormous amount of snow each winter, yet its waters remain ice-free, making it an important port. It's also the southern terminus of the 800-mile-long Alaska Pipeline, from which crude oil is then transported south.

Valdez is the snowiest town in Alaska. Annual accumulations of 30 feet are not uncommon.

The 1964 Good Friday earthquake and subsequent tidal wave wrought enough destruction on Valdez (pronounced val DEEZ) and its environs to require relocating the town site. But it was on a cold overcast day in March 1989—when the oil supertanker *Exxon Valdez* grounded on Bligh Reef, releasing 11 million gallons of North Slope crude oil into Prince William Sound— that the town forever lost its obscurity. If you visit Valdez today you will see little direct evidence of the spill, although most species are fewer in number than in 1989. The good news is that 400,000 acres of habitat will be protected with settlement money from Exxon— if the ongoing court battle over the exact amount of damages, still raging, ever ends.

Valdez is a fairly large town for Alaska (population 4,036). With beautiful neighborhoods nestled in a mountain-rimmed setting, it exudes an air of prosperity. There is an extensive dock area here, as well as pipeline support facilities, governmental offices, and even a community college. As you drive into town, the Richardson Highway becomes Egan Drive; turn right onto Chenega Street and go down a block to the Valdez Convention and Visitors Bureau's **Visitor Information Center** (907-835-4636), at the corner of and Fairbanks Street. Inside you will find lots of good advice about the many things to do during your stay, including boat tours to one of the three local state marine parks, rafting down the Lowe River, hiking around the Valdez Glacier, and fishing for halibut and salmon (summer months offer some of the best fishing on the coast). In winter, Valdez hosts a growing legion of extreme snowboarders and skiers who heli-ski the array of world-class mountains that rise almost straight from the sea. Due to prevailing winds off the ocean, snow is often measured in dozens of feet.

The **Valdez Museum** (217 Egan Drive; 907-835-2764) offers a number of historic and interpretive exhibits; the topics covered include the gold rush of 1898, the oil pipeline construction, and the disastrous *Exxon Valdez* oil spill and its cleanup. There are also a number of artifacts and nicely done scale models, as well as interactive exhibits you can touch (Columbia Glacier ice and a sea otter pelt, for example). The **Museum Annex Warehouse** (436 South Hazelet Street) features an impressive 1:20 scale model of Valdez as it was in 1963, prior to the earthquake that destroyed the town. There is also an interactive earthquake exhibit, as well as photos and displays from that time. The Valdez boat harbor is also a popular and attractive stop, with picnic tables, a promenade, and public restrooms. The coming and going of commercial fishing boats and pleasure craft make for a pleasant backdrop on a nice summer day. **Dock Point Park,** at the east end of the boat harbor, has a beautiful 1-mile walking trail with a scenic overlook.

A trip to the famous **Columbia Glacier**, whose sheer ice face rises 300 feet from the water 25 miles to the west of town, is a popular tour boat destination. At times the flow of ice is so dense that approaching the glacier closer than a mile is difficult. There are also a number of smaller, but equally impressive tidewater glaciers in the area, including Shoup Glacier, just a short skiff ride from town (small boat rentals are available). Marine life—including sea otters, seals, sea lions, and a variety of nesting sea birds—is abundant, though not at pre-oil spill levels. The Valdez area is popular with salmon fishermen during the silver salmon run in July and is also busy during the fall hunting season, as the surrounding Chugach National Forest offers outstanding deer, moose, and bear hunting. You will find all amenities in Valdez, from public campgrounds to well-appointed hotels, fast-food outlets to nice seafood restaurants.

■ CORDOVA AND VICINITY   *map page 144, C/D-4*
Cordova, a town of 2,454 that's six hours by ferry from Valdez, occupies a strategic location for nature lovers. Just east of town is the famous **Copper River Delta State Critical Habitat Area.** To the west is spectacular Prince William Sound, and to the north are the wild Chugach Mountains. More than 20 million migrating shorebirds and waterfowl visit the Copper River's broad delta each spring and fall. The surrounding tidal marshes and wetlands comprise one of the most important migratory bird resting areas in the Western Hemisphere. Other animals that can be seen in the delta, which is reached by the Copper River Highway east of Cordova, include moose, black and brown bears, sea otters, sea lions, harbor seals, and bald eagles. From spring to fall, the waters are filled with runs of red, silver, and king salmon.

From Cordova you can explore west into Prince William Sound. There are endless possibilities for sea kayaking, sport fishing, camping, hiking, and big-game hunting forays. The same is true of the backcountry in the Chugach Mountains, which can be reached by aircraft charter from Cordova.

The town was originally built as the port for the massive and now defunct Kennecott copper mines 196 miles to the north, in what is now Wrangell–St. Elias National Park (see page 182). In the mines' heyday (1922–38), ore was freighted by rail to the ice-free port of Cordova, where it was then shipped south for processing. When the mines closed down, the town of Cordova survived; today, it's an

important fishing and cannery center—the population explodes every summer when cannery workers, many of whom are college students, arrive. (Work in Alaska's canneries is often dangerous, tedious, and underpaid, as U.S. Sen. Hillary Rodham Clinton discovered when she came to work in a cannery during college.) Fresh Copper River red (sockeye) and king salmon caught here are shipped fresh around the world, and are famous for their high quality.

Cordova shares the sort of gorgeous setting common to virtually every Prince William Sound community. On one side is the ocean, with wide tidal flats and a myriad of marine life; on the other three, the spectacular Chugach mountains. Y-shaped Eyak Lake, popular both with salmon and recreational users, is immediately behind town. In July, you can drive along any of several small creeks near town and watch the age-old dance of bright red spawning salmon. A number of nearby hiking trails, including Henley Ridge, the Eyak River Trail, and Sheridan Mountain Trail, all maintained by the U.S. Forest Service, offer recreational opportunities. A word of caution: due to the number of salmon spawning areas, bears are common.

In town you will find a **Chugach National Forest Service** office (612 Second Street; 907-424-7661), a campground, hotels, motels, bed-and-breakfasts, restaurants, a handful of bars, and the customary array of stores. The folks at the forest service office can tell you about recreational cabin rentals, floatplane tours, fishing charters, hunting trips, good berry-picking areas, hiking trails, and, in the unlikely event that you arrive in January, the Mount Eyak Ski Area, which offers a modest but nice one-chairlift run. In the Cordova area, lake, salt water, and stream fishing are accessible without boats, and are often excellent. Species caught include king, silver, and red salmon, cutthroat trout, and Dolly Varden char.

East of town, the famous **Copper River Highway** leads 50 miles across the waterfowl-rich Copper River delta. Since Cordova isn't connected to the highway system, many people don't bring vehicles, but car rentals are available locally, and highly recommended. The road crosses a number of salmon streams and wetlands, and offers opportunities for wildlife viewing, including beavers, moose, bears, and nesting trumpeter swans. For likely areas, inquire at the Forest Service office (above). At Mile 48, there is marked access to the **Childs Glacier Recreation Area,**

Hikers gaze into a pool on Root Glacier in Wrangell–St. Elias National Park.

where it's possible to watch the glacier, constantly undercut by the restless Copper River, calve in spectacular fashion. Caution here: in 1993 a gigantic wave washed through the viewing area. Today, warning signs and placards stress the ongoing danger. Just a tenth of a mile farther up the road is the partial ruin of the **Million Dollar Bridge.** A vital link in the rail line between the Kennecott mines and Cordova, and an engineering marvel in itself (due to the incredible force of the river and calving icebergs from upstream glaciers), the 1,500-foot steel truss structure was completed in 1910, for the then-exorbitant price of $1.4 million. During the 1964 earthquake, the north span of the bridge collapsed. Though temporary repairs have allowed passenger vehicles to drive across, the road goes only another 10 miles, and is poorly maintained. Most people only venture partway across on foot to take in the spectacle of the roiling, turbid river framed by the Childs Glacier, just downstream, and the Miles Glacier above.

■ WRANGELL–ST. ELIAS NATIONAL PARK
AND PRESERVE *map page 144, D/E-3/4*

Wrangell–St. Elias National Park, conjoined with the adjacent Kluane National Park in Canada, forms the largest parkland on the planet. What was long the exclusive domain of prospectors, hard-rock miners, trappers, and big-game hunters was formally designated a World Heritage Site in 1979. Together these two sprawling parks protect more than 19 million acres—an area about four times the size of the state of New Jersey. In Wrangell–St. Elias National Park three great mountain ranges converge—Wrangell, St. Elias, and Chugach. One glacier in Wrangell–St. Elias National Park—the Malaspina—is larger than the state of Rhode Island, and the country around it resembles the frozen cordilleras of the Himalayas. Nearby Mount St. Elias, at 18,008 feet, is the fourth-highest peak north of the Andes. It towers over surrounding mountains—nine of which are among the 16 highest peaks in the United States.

Although much of the Wrangell Mountains owe their origin to volcanism, only Mount Wrangell itself remains active, with distinct vents of steam curling from the menacing summit. The last eruption was recorded in 1930. Associated with this volcanism are layers of valuable minerals, including copper, gold, and silver. In the early part of the century the Kennecott Copper Corporation capitalized on a massive claim, developing the huge **Kennecott copper mill** and **mine complex** near present-day McCarthy. (By the way, an early misspelling on official documents

The abandoned Kennecott copper mine sits on the edge of the massive Kennicott Glacier field, visible in the background covered in rubble.

resulted in the mining company being called "Kennecott" while the nearby glacier and river are spelled "Kennicott.") Still considered the richest copper deposit ever discovered, with more than 70 miles of underground tunnels, the site is now a National Historic Landmark preserved by the National Park Service. The cavernous, weathered mill buildings, built on a steep mountain slope, are dwarfed by surrounding peaks and ridge lines of naked gray rock. Tours are available locally, and the National Park Service offers interpretive tours and slide shows daily in the summer at the Jurick Building in the tiny town of Kennicott (it and **McCarthy,** five miles away, collectively boast a population of 37). This mine area is one of the chief attractions of Wrangell–St. Elias, highly photogenic and unique, well worth the journey in itself. McCarthy, long a ghost town, was resettled in the early 1970s by a number of rugged individualists, and now offers limited facilities for visitors, including a lodge, a guiding business, and an air service.

The park is reached from Anchorage on the Glenn Highway. After passing Glennallen at Mile 189 (from Anchorage), the Glenn Highway shortly comes to an end at the Richardson Highway (which runs north to Delta Junction and south to Valdez). Turn south here; the Park Headquarters is a short drive down the road just north of the tiny town of Copper Center. Continue south another 35 miles down the paved and scenic Edgerton Highway (known locally as the Edgerton Cutoff) to Chitina, where the McCarthy Road begins with a bridge over the Copper River. Chitina also has a Forest Service district ranger station where information is available, and a store that is your last chance to gas up before the 60-mile gravel road to McCarthy. The McCarthy Road parallels the turbid Chitina River. Take your time; the road, narrow in places but well engineered, isn't built for highway speeds. The road stops just short of McCarthy, ending in a gravel parking lot. A foot bridge leads across the river, and there is a shuttle service to carry visitors the five miles to the Kennecott mill and mine complex ruins. The heavily wooded valley is wild and scenic, set between the rugged Chugach Mountains on the south and the soaring Wrangells to the north. Flightseeing tours are very popular, and opportunities for hiking, camping, and photography abound.

The end-of-the-road town of McCarthy, in Wrangell–St. Elias National Park and Preserve, came into being when copper was discovered nearby.

■ NORTH OF ANCHORAGE

■ TALKEETNA *map page 144, B-2*

Talkeetna is a small town located at the end of a road that branches off from the George Parks Highway 99 miles north of Anchorage. At the junction, there's the excellent **Talkeetna/Denali Visitors Center** (800-660-2688) with a helpful staff aid to recommend tours and places to stay.

Talkeetna serves the vast region south of the Alaska Range in a number of ways. Every spring, during the busy mountaineering season, it is the headquarters for those climbing Denali (Mount McKinley), the highest peak in North America. Here the courageous (or insane) climbers arrive with their supplies and board small fixed-wing aircraft for the ride up to the Great Gorge, where they establish their base camps prior to the long and dangerous ascent (for more on climbing Denali, see page 252).

The National Park Service maintains a ranger station at Talkeetna from April through September, and off and on during the winter months.

Talkeetna has a good airport, with a 4,000-foot paved runway, and you can fly here directly from Anchorage on a charter, then board a local flightseeing or air-taxi plane and fly out to land on a glacier or see the great mountain. The airport becomes particularly busy during the big-game hunting season, which in most years runs from late August (Dall sheep) through early October (grizzly, caribou, moose). The Talkeetna Mountains are some of the most famous mountains in the world for big-game hunting—many record-class trophies have been taken from this area, in which the wildlife is carefully managed as a renewable resource.

During the summer fishing season, there is excellent salmon fishing on nearby Montana Creek, on the Susitna River, and upstream on the Talkeetna River. Many fishermen prefer to be transported by floatplane or by boat to more remote wilderness fishing sites, far from the crowds near the road.

You'll find everything you need in Talkeetna—motels, B&Bs, restaurants, stores, and friendly people. It is a small, hard-working community where people tend to have the old values. Two of Talkeetna's most well-known citizens were Don Sheldon and Ray Genet: the first, one of Alaska's great bush pilots, the second, an inveterate mountaineer, who at one time held the record for the most climbs on Mount McKinley and who died at 27,000 feet on Mount Everest. To learn more about Sheldon, Genet, and about the history of the area, visit the **Talkeetna**

Historical Society Museum (907-733-2487) housed in an old red schoolhouse one block off Main Street and opposite the Fairview Inn. Talkeetna also hosts the annual Moose Dropping Festival in July and an annual bluegrass festival in August (see page 207).

■ **DENALI STATE PARK** *map page 144, B-1/2*
Of the nearly 100 state parks scattered across Alaska, Denali State Park (not to be confused with Denali National Park and Preserve) is one of the most accessible and popular. Located on either side of the George Parks Highway about 130 miles north of Anchorage, this 325,240-acre reserve offers visitors a viable alternative to the often packed national park up the road. Visitors at Denali State Park can see wildlife identical to that present in that more famous destination: Dall sheep, moose, caribou, grizzly bear, black bear, fox, lynx, river otter, wolf, eagle, ptarmigan, and raven. But unlike in the national park, where buses often take you right past caribou and bears, seeing more than a moose or two in Denali State Park generally involves getting off the main road and doing some serious hiking, much of it uphill. Bring a good pair of binoculars, good boots, a well-stocked backpack including first aid gear, extra food, bug dope, and a healthy dose of common sense. The good news is: you often have the wilderness to yourself. The bad news: in event of trouble, you're generally on your own. There is a well-maintained campground at Mile 147 near Byers Lake. Trails lead from that campground east to Kesugi Ridge and Curry Ridge, both excellent areas for wildlife observation.

Before leaving Anchorage (or Fairbanks) you should purchase topographic maps if you intend to hike in the backcountry of the park. Denali State Park is a big place—about half the size of Rhode Island—and it is easy to get lost in unfamiliar country. You should also familiarize yourself with proper precautions in bear country, as there will not be as many rangers around to provide instructions as in the national park. The best thing about Denali State Park is that you have some unusual and spectacular views of Denali (Mount McKinley), including Ruth Glacier and the Great Gorge. The view from Curry Ridge is particularly breathtaking. It was from this area that famed Alaskan artist Sydney Laurence painted some of his memorable oil paintings of Denali earlier in the century.

Denali National Park and Preserve, where Mount McKinley is located, is described in the following chapter, beginning on page 211.

■ TRAVEL INFORMATION

■ GETTING THERE

South-Central Alaska is easily accessible by water, land, and air. Anchorage, the state's largest city, is served by several major national and some international airlines, including Alaska Airlines, Delta, and United (see page 351 for the airlines' toll-free numbers).

Driving distance by car from Seattle to Anchorage via the Alaska Highway is 2,435 miles, and quite an adventurous journey. Take a reliable car and be prepared for emergencies. A good guide to this highway route is *The Milepost,* a mile-by-mile guide to sights and services along this and other Alaskan roads, published yearly.

Alaska state ferries originating in Bellingham, Washington, will take you and your car as far as Haines, from which it is a 775-mile drive to Anchorage. Container ships travel from the Lower 48 to Anchorage, but most cruise ships do not. The Alaska Marine Highway System ferries serving the Inside Passage of the Southeast do not connect to the ferries serving Prince William Sound and South-Central Alaska.

■ GETTING AROUND

By Plane

From Anchorage it is possible to travel to rural towns and scenic areas by commuter carriers offering intrastate scheduled air service, or by chartered air service provided by local pilots. Inquire at Alaska Airlines for connectors from Anchorage, or check with your travel agent. Scheduled air-taxi runs from Anchorage to outlying villages and off-road destinations in the region begin at about $100 per person; generally speaking, you can figure on a dollar a mile as a standard going rate. Bush plane charters go by the hour, and can be much more expensive. Air-taxi and charter services are located at Merrill Field and at Lake Hood near Anchorage International Airport. The **Federal Aviation Administration,** Anchorage (907-271-2000), has a list of certified air-taxi operations throughout Alaska, including the Alaska Airlines commuter **PenAir** (800-448-4226; www.penair.com) which flies to Unalakleet, Dillingham, King Salmon, Dutch Harbor, Cold Bay, and the Pribilof Islands.

By Car

In peak season (June through August), rental car reservations should be made as much as two months in advance. All the major car rental companies (Avis, Budget, Hertz, National, et al.) operate from Anchorage and offer rates of about $50 per day with unlimited mileage. Local companies such as **Denali Rent a Car** (907-276-1230) usually charge less.

By Bus

The **Homer Stage Line** connects Anchorage and the Kenai peninsula. *907-235-2252; or 907-868-3914; www.homerstageline.com.*

By Ferry

Alaska's statewide ferry system offers scheduled service to many of the coastal towns in the South-Central area. Service in the summer season (May through September) is frequent, but ferries do not make daily stops at all ports; check your schedules carefully when planning your itinerary. Reservations for the state-run ferries are necessary on all routes, and may require up to six months' advance notice for summer travel with vehicles. For reservations call the main office in Juneau. *907-465-3941 or 800-642-0046; www.akmhs.com.*

Many privately owned tour companies service Prince William Sound and run boats between Whittier and Valdez, each offering varied tours, schedules, and accommodations. Some tour companies are listed by town on the following pages. Advertisements for tour companies abound throughout Alaska.

By Train

Alaska is not connected by rail to the Lower 48, but there is service within the state, and it takes passengers past breathtaking views, with vista dome cars on some of the routes. From mid-May to mid-September, there is daily service between Anchorage, Talkeetna, Denali National Park, and Fairbanks ($190 peak and $150 off-peak one way); between Anchorage and Seward ($130 round trip); and between Anchorage, Whittier, Portage, Spencer Glacier, and Grandview ($99 round trip). Off season, the 350-mile run between Anchorage and Fairbanks departs only once a week and costs $150 one way. Contact **Alaska Railroad** (907-265-2494 or 800-544-0552; www.akrr.com). For more luxurious train travel from Anchorage to Fairbanks, try the **Midnight Sun Express** (800-835-8907; www.midnightsunexpress.com).

■ CLIMATE

South-Central contains an enormous diversity of micro-climates: coastal islands under the mild maritime influence of the Japanese current (Montague Island holds the state record of the most rainfall in any one year, at 332 inches); abruptly rising coastal mountains where the rains become prodigious snows (Thompson Pass outside of Valdez holds the state's all-time snowfall record of some 975 inches in one year); and inland valleys lying in the precipitation shadow of the mountains but open to bitterly cold arctic winds during the winter (as represented by Glennallen, a crossroads in a valley beyond the Chugach Mountains north of Valdez).

SUNLIGHT

	SUNRISE	SUNSET	# OF HOURS
SUMMER MAXIMUM			
Anchorage	4:21 AM	11:42 PM	19:21
WINTER MINIMUM	SUNRISE	SUNSET	# OF HOURS
Anchorage	10:14 AM	3:42 PM	5:28

While visiting Anchorage, one may expect mild and sunny summers punctuated by periods of rain. The cold and snowy winter is from October through April and spring consists of a couple of weeks in May.

TEMPS (F°)	AVG. JAN. HIGH	LOW	AVG. APRIL HIGH	LOW	AVG. JULY HIGH	LOW	AVG. OCT. HIGH	LOW	RECORD HIGH	RECORD LOW
Anchorage	20	9	42	28	65	50	40	29	86	-38
Glennallen	-3	-28	43	17	70	42	35	12	90	-56
Homer	28	15	42	28	60	45	45	30	80	-21
Valdez	25	11	43	26	60	45	43	31	83	-24

PRECIPITATION (INCHES)	AVG. JAN.	AVG. APRIL	AVG. JULY	AVG. OCT.	ANNUAL RAIN	ANNUAL SNOW
Anchorage	0.8"	0.6"	1.9"	1.9"	16"	70"
Glennallen	0.3"	0.1"	1.5"	0.6"	9"	41"
Homer	1.7"	1.1"	1.7"	3.4"	23"	60"
Valdez	5.8"	3.0"	4.7"	8.0"	62"	245"

THE IDITAROD

The longest dogsled race in the world, the Iditarod begins in Anchorage and ends in Nome, 1,049 miles away. The trail follows an old dog-team mail route first blazed in 1910, and crosses two mountain ranges, then follows the Yukon River for 150 miles, passing bush villages and crossing frozen Norton Sound. The race itself, which officially began in 1974, was inspired by an event that took place in 1925. When a diphtheria epidemic broke out that year in Nome, teams of dogsledders relayed the serum that inoculated the town's children over a 674-mile segment of the trail over the course of six days. Two great sled dogs—the speed-racers Togo and Balto, who guided the final sled through a blizzard—became worldwide celebrities. (A statue of one of them, Balto, stands in Central Park in New York City, commemorating their achievement.)

Today's race has a first prize of roughly $70,000 plus a new truck, but the cost of launching a team can be twice as much as that. And today there are actually two different routes between the starting point and Nome, which alternate in even and odd years.

One passes through Ruby and Nulato, and the other takes a more southerly path through Iditarod and Anvik (more closely following the original route). Along the way, participants pass through 26 checkpoints in the wilderness. Big winners over the past twenty years have included Rick Swenson, Doug Swingley, Martin Buser, and Susan Butcher. The race begins on the first Saturday in March, and whereas in the 1970s it ended some 20 days later, the most recent winning times have been around nine days.

The Iditarod is an aerobic event for its athletes—the dogs.

■ FOOD, LODGING, & TOURS

RESTAURANT PRICES

Per person, without drinks, tax, or tip

$ = under $15   **$$** = $15–$25   **$$$** = over $25

ROOM RATES

Per room, per night, double occupancy

$ = under $70   **$$** = $70–$100   **$$$** = over $100

ANCHORAGE   *map page 144, A/B-3*

Population: 260,283
Visitors information: 907-276-4118; www.anchorage.net

◆ **RESTAURANTS**

Arctic Roadrunner. A no-frills, order-at-the-counter spot for beef and salmon burgers, french fries, and fixings. *2477 Arctic Boulevard; 907-279-7311, and 5300 Old Seward Highway; 907-561-1245.* **$**

Club Paris. Considered by locals the quintessential old-time Anchorage restaurant; serves steaks and seafood in the old-fashioned American way. Huge trophy fish mounted on dark wood walls beside fine old-time realist paintings by Byron Birdsall. *417 West Fifth Avenue; 907-277-6332; www.clubparisrestaurant.com.* **$$$**

Crow's Nest Restaurant. In the popular Captain Cook Hotel, this is considered by many to be the city's finest restaurant. The dining room is unexpectedly formal—white tablecloths, silver place settings—and has beautiful panoramic views. Menu features local seafood and changes seasonally. *Fourth Avenue and K Street; 907-276-6000 or 800-843-1950; www.captaincook.com.* **$$$**

Downtown Deli and Cafe. A downtown café convenient for tourists, as it's located across the street from the visitors center. Wholesome and simple sandwiches, seafood, fresh vegetables, bagels, and blintzes. *525 West Fourth Avenue; 907-276-7116.* **$–$$**

Glacier BrewHouse. Sprawling, open-beamed rustic atmosphere in a downtown location, specializing in wood-fired oven pizza, rotisserie chicken, steaks, and seafood. Fine microbrew selection, including house brands. *737 West 5th Avenue; 907-274-2739; www.glacierbrewhouse.com.* **$$–$$$**

Gwennie's Old Alaska Restaurant. Sourdough pancakes and reindeer sausage; breakfast served all day long. *4333 Spenard Road; 907-243-2090.* $

Hogg Brothers Cafe. Gigantic breakfasts; burgers. Very crowded on weekends. *1049 West Northern Lights Boulevard; 907-276-9649.* $

Humpy's Great Alaskan Alehouse. A favorite Anchorage hangout. Hearty food and beer in a loud, lively atmosphere. *610 West Sixth Avenue; 907-276-2337; www. humpys.com.* $

Jens' Restaurant. Don't let its strip-mall location turn you away. The innovative dishes, the conviviality of host Jens Hansen, and an excellent wine list make this the place for those in the know. After 10:00 P.M. or so, the wine bar can get quite lively. *701 West 36th Avenue; 907-561-5367; www.jensrestaurant.com.* $$$

La Cabaña. The oldest Mexican restaurant in Alaska. Good Americanized Mexican food and the best margaritas in town. *312 East Fourth Avenue; 907-272-0135.* $

L'Aroma. A first-rate Italian bakery and deli in the New Sagaya complex. Try one of the amazing little pizzas from a wood-burning oven. *3700 Old Seward Highway; 907-562-9797.* $

Marx Bros. Cafe. Intimate dining, lovely views, as well as exquisite food. Sets the culinary pace for Anchorage, with its original menus and local seafood and berries in unique combinations. The wine list is excellent. A favorite Anchorage restaurant. *627 West Third Avenue; 907-278-2133; www.marxcafe.com.* $$$

Moose's Tooth Pub and Pizzeria. Gourmet pizzas, hearty salads, and locally brewed beer. Arrive early to avoid a wait. *3300 Old Seward Highway.; 907-258-2537; www.moosestooth.net.* $-$$

Organic Oasis. Healthy, hearty fare for the hip. Limited menus but it's all good. Cafe ambiance. *2610 Spenard Road; 907-277-7882.* $–$$

Orso. Upscale nouveau Italian bistro with attentive service and an extensive wine list. *737 West 5th Avenue.; 907-222-3232.* $$-$$$

Qupqugiaq "Q" Cafe and Eatery. The conventional exterior disguises one of the marvels of Anchorage interior design. Sip a latte or eat satisfying panini or soup. *640 West 36th Avenue; 907-563-5633; www.qupq.com.* $

Sacks Cafe. Fresh, wholesome food. *328 G Street; 907-276-3546; www.sackscafe. com.* $

Simon & Seaforts Saloon and Grill. One of Anchorage's fine restaurants, where people come to celebrate a special event. Large and breezy with panoramic view of Cook Inlet, comfortable booths, and an air of elegance and sophistication. Fresh

Alaskan seafood and innovative game dishes, plus well-prepared steaks, pasta, and so on. Reservations recommended. *420 L Street; 907-274-3502.* $$-$$$

Snow City Café. One of the most popular (and best) breakfast and lunch spots in town. Informal, open, friendly dining in a deli-like downtown setting. *Fourth Avenue and L Street; 907-272-2489; www.snowcity.com.*

Sourdough Mining Company. Big, open, unfinished "miner" decor; this is the place for ribs, hushpuppies, and fried seafood. *5200 Juneau Street; 907-563-2272; www.alaskaone.com/aksourdough.* $

Thai Kitchen. There are several fine Thai restaurants in Anchorage, but poll after poll makes this one the clear winner. Go for the food or for take-out, not the atmosphere—it's located at the rear of a convenience store. *3405 East Tudor Road; 907-561-0082.* $-$$

Villa Nova. Dark, cozy Italian restaurant with real atmosphere and good pasta. *Corner of Arctic and International; 5121 Arctic Boulevard; 907-561-1660.*

◆ LODGING

Alaskan Frontier Gardens Bed & Breakfast. A lovely four-room B&B in a gorgeous wilderness setting overlooking Anchorage, 20 minutes by car from the heart of downtown, 10 minutes from the airport. The Ivory Suite has a fireplace, sauna, and jacuzzi. *7440 Alatna Avenue (corner of Alatna and Hillside Drive); 907-345-6556; www.alaskafrontiergardens.com.* $$$

Anchorage Hilton. This dark 22-story high rise dominates downtown Anchorage. Rooms have nice views of the city and Cook Inlet. There are stuffed brown bears and polar bears in the lobby, and a heated indoor pool is among the amenities. Rooms in peak season can cost $300 per night. *500 West Third Avenue; 907-272-7411; www.hiltonanchorage.com.* $$$

Anchorage Hotel. Established in 1916 and recently renovated; complimentary continental breakfast. *330 East Street; 907-272-4553 or 800-544-0988; www.historicanchoragehotel.com.* $$$

Anchorage Marriott Downtown. Newly built full-service hotel with 390 rooms. *820 West Seventh Avenue; 907-279-8000 or 800-228-9290.* $$$

Anchorage Sheraton. Towering above the Anchorage skyline, this hotel may be Alaska bland on the outside, but inside the lobby, with its marble murals and jade tiles, it's like a museum of Native Alaskan art. *401 East Sixth Avenue; 907-276-8700; www.sheratonanchoragehotel.com.* $$$

Anchorage International Hostel - Downtown. Open year-round; dormitory rooms with bunk beds, some private rooms, kitchen and laundry facilities, and common rooms. Fills up in the summer; reservations advised. *700 H Street; 907-276-3635.* $

Copper Whale Inn. Convenient location on west end of downtown coupled with superb mountain & inlet views. Fourteen guest rooms, lush summer garden, common area with stone fireplace. *440 L Street; 866-258-7999 or 907-258-7999; www.copperwhale.com.*

15 Chandeliers B&B Inn. Located in a gracious mansion 15 minutes from downtown. Theme-appointed rooms with four-poster beds, all with private baths. Beautiful landscaping with outside terrace. *14020 Sabine Street; 907-345-3032; www.alaska.net/~chndlr15.* $$$

Hotel Captain Cook. A landmark hotel formerly owned by well-known character and ex-governor Walter J. Hickel and now owned by his son. The spacious main floor, appointed in dark wood and oil paintings, houses restaurants and shops. Guest rooms are in the three gold towers, nicely decorated in muted tones, and supplied with all the amenities. The rooftop restaurant, Crow's Nest (see restaurants), is among the finest in Anchorage. *Fourth Avenue and K Street; 907-276-6000 or 800-843-1950; www.captaincook.com.* $$$

Merrill Field Inn. A mile east of downtown, this is a less expensive alternative to the high-rise hotels downtown and you can watch airplanes taking off and landing at nearby Merrill Field. A couple of good restaurants are within easy walking distance. *420 Sitka Street; 907-276-4547 or 800-898-4547; www.merrillfieldinn.com.* $$

Millennium Alaskan Hotel. A beautiful, popular luxury hotel (formerly known as the Regal Alaskan) situated against the backdrop of snow-covered mountains. A roaring fire in the lobby fireplace and a trail along Lake Spenard add to its pleasures. Sauna and exercise room. Excellent restaurant. Provides airport transportation and has views of the world's largest floatplane base. *4800 Spenard Road; 907-243-2300 or 800-544-0553; www.millennium-hotels.com/anchorage.* $$$

◆ WILDERNESS LODGES

Riversong Lodge. On Yentna River at Lake Creek (45 minutes by floatplane from Anchorage) and in a prime fishing area, the lodge has 10 cabins and a homey main building constructed of hand-hewn spruce logs and pine paneling. Fabulous gourmet meals are a trademark. Both fly-in day trips and overnight accommodations. *P.O. Box 19-1029, Anchorage, AK 99519; 907-733-2931; www.riversonglodge.com.*

◆ **TOURS**

Alaska Railroad. The state railroad, which serves Anchorage, Fairbanks, Seward, and points in between, offers scenic rail tour packages ranging from one or two nights to 10, in varying price ranges depending on hotel choices. There are a number of day tours as well. *907-265-2494 or 800-544-0552; www.akrr.com.*

Chugach Express Dog Sled Tours. Dogsled rides on a trail south of Anchorage in winter; on a glacier, via helicopter, in summer. Operator has extensive sled-dog experience, including nine Iditarod finishes. *Girdwood; summer: (Alpine Air) 907-783-2360; winter: 907-830-2738; home.gci.net/~alaskasnowdogs.*

Equinox Wilderness Expeditions. Based in Anchorage, this small, Alaska-owned and -operated company conducts guided canoe, kayak, and hiking expeditions across the state but specializes in the Arctic National Wildlife Refuge. Run by top river guide Karen Jettmar. *2440 East Tudor Road, #1102; 604-222-1219 or 604-765-3370 (cell); www.equinoxexpeditions.com.*

Era Aviation. Helicopter flightseeing tours in the Chugach Mountains and Turnagain Arm; also elsewhere in the state. *6160 South Airpark Drive (south side of Anchorage International Airport); 907-266-8450 or 800-866-8394; www.alaskaone.com/eracopters.*

Great Northern Air Guides. Located at Lake Hood and in the Anchorage International Airport; floatplane or wheel-plane trips available for fishing, hunting, and charters. *Box 91735, Anchorage, AK 99509; 907-243-1968 or 800-243-1968; www.gnair.com.*

Kenai Fjords Tours. A variety of cruises and overnight packages from Seward on the Kenai Peninsula through Resurrection Bay and Kenai Fjords National Park. The small, modern, comfortable ships have well-informed crews expert at wildlife viewing and natural history. Six-hour cruises start at roughly $130 per adult ($240 with round-trip rail or bus transportation from Anchorage to Seward). *907-265-4051 or 877-777-2805; www.kenaifjords.com.*

Major Marine Tours. Offers half- and full-day cruises out of Seward to Kenai Fjords National Park for wildlife viewing and up-close views of the many glaciers. Also a half-day glacier-viewing cruise of Prince William Sound departing from Whittier. Dinners are optional. *907-274-7300 or 800-764-7300; www.majormarine.com.*

Nova. Variety of rafting trips, flat to whitewater, plus glacier hikes. Trips depart from Chickaloon, about 1.5 hours north of Anchorage, or from Hope, 1.5 hours south of Anchorage. *P.O. Box 1129, Chickaloon, AK 99674; 800-746-5753; www.novalaska.com.*

Sport Fishing Alaska. Personalized fishing trips planned statewide. Run by former supervisor of Alaska State Fish & Game Department. *9310 Shorecrest Drive; 907-344-8674; www.alaskatripplanners.com.*

COOPER LANDING *map page 144, A/B-3*

Population: 369
Visitors information: 907-595-8888; www.cooperlandingchamber.com

◆ WILDERNESS LODGES

Gwin's Lodge. Modern cabins. Good place to headquarter a fishing operation—it's a stone's throw from the Kenai River and close to the Russian River as well. Restaurant, bar, and tackle shop. *Mile 52, 14865 Sterling Highway; 907-595-1266 or 866-282-7577; www.gwinslodge.com.* $$$

Hamilton's Place. Restaurant/bar/RV park with view of the beautiful Kenai River; general store, tackle shop, cabins, and camping area. Great place to hang out and talk to the fishing guides, most of whom will tell you their life story for a couple of beers. *Mile 48.5, 18280 Sterling Highway; 907-595-1260.* $$

Kenai Princess Wilderness Lodge. A sprawling, luxurious complex on a bluff overlooking the wild beauty of the Kenai River. Restaurant, exercise room, shuffleboard. *Mile 47.7, Sterling Highway; 800-426-0500; www.princessalaskalodges.com.* $$$

◆ CAMPGROUNDS

Chugach National Forest. The Forest Service operates several campgrounds along the Sterling Highway between Cooper Landing and Kenai. They tend to be full during fishing season, so reserve early. Also, more than 40 recreational cabins, rustic but comfortable, spread out across the vast Chugach National Forest for $25 to $45 a night. *For campground and cabin information relating to this area: 907-224-3374; www.fs.fed.us/r10/chugach. For reservations: 877-444-6777 or www.reserveusa.com.*

◆ TOURS

Alaska River Adventures. Half- and full-day fishing or scenic tours of the Upper Kenai Peninsula, and wilderness trips throughout Alaska. *907-595-2000 or 888-836-9027; www.alaskariveradventures.com.*

Alaska Wildland Adventures. Organizes full-day fishing trips and scenic floats on the Kenai River, as well as trips throughout Alaska. *907-783-2928 or 800-334-8730; www.alaskawildland.com.*

CORDOVA *map page 144, C-3*

Population: 2,580
Visitors information: 907-424-7260; www.cordovaalaska.com

◆ RESTAURANT
Killer Whale Cafe. This comfy breakfast and lunch spot, perched above a fun bookstore, serves great sandwiches and baked goods. Sit upstairs for a nice view of the harbor. *507 First Street, inside the Orca Book and Sound Co.; 907-424-7733.* $

◆ LODGING
Cordova Rose Lodge. This maritime-themed inn on a landlocked 1924 barge has five guest rooms (some with private baths). Full breakfast included. *1315 Whitshed Road; 907-424-7673; www.cordovarose.com.* $

HOMER *map page 144, A-4*

Population: 3,946
Visitors information: 907-235-7740; www.homeralaska.org

◆ RESTAURANTS
Café Cups. One of Homer's best restaurants. Come here for relief from the slabs of salmon and steak you've been eating for days, and enjoy innovative, interesting dishes. Desserts are elegant, microbrewery beer is on tap, and local artists' work decorates the walls. *162 West Pioneer Avenue; 907-235-8330.* $$
Chart Room Restaurant and Lounge. At the end of Homer Spit, this casual restaurant in Land's End Resort has tables both inside and on a wide wooden deck overlooking Kachemak Bay. The menu includes hamburgers, steaks, prime rib, and seafood. *4786 Homer Spit Road; 907-235-0406; www.lands-end-resort.com.* $$–$$$
Don Jose's Mexican Restaurant. Sturdy and predictable Mexican fare at reasonable prices. A local favorite. *127 West Pioneer Avenue; 907-235-7963.* $$
The Homestead. In a log building with pleasant ambience and a view of bay and spruce trees. Eight miles out of town , this is widely regarded as the finest dining

in the Homer area: seafood, steaks, etc. *Mile 8.2, East End Road; 907-235-8723.* $$$

The Saltry. Saltry's menu features Alaskan seafood prepared in exotic dishes, and accompanied by a great selection of imported beers. Wide open feeling, big windows, and glossy blond wood. To reach Halibut Cove, a small community across Kachemak Bay from Homer, take the *Danny J* ferry from the Homer harbor. *Halibut Cove; 907-296-2223.* $$–$$$

Samovar Café. A small, unique, and authentic Russian restaurant in the unincorporated Russian village of Nikolaevsk. It's 25 miles from Homer but worth the drive—especially if you crave piroshki, pelmini, or borsch straight from the old country. To reach it, drive back on the Sterling Highway toward Anchorage to Anchor Point, and follow the North Fork Road to the end of the pavement. Russian gift store as well, featuring traditional crafts, plus campground and B&B. *Village of Nikolaevsk; 907-235-6867; www.russiangiftsnina.com/cafe.* $-$$

Two Sisters Bakery. An endearing, funky breakfast-and-lunch café. The coffee is rich and the pastries fragrant and homemade. A longtime local favorite. Closes at 8:00 P.M. (Sundays at 4). *233 East Bunnell Avenue; 907-235-2280.* $

◆ Lodging

Beeson's on the Bay Bed and Breakfast. Six of the inn's eight guestrooms have views of the mountains and the bay. All rooms have private baths, including the cottage, which can sleep up to seven people. Hot tub. *1393 Bay Avenue; 907-235-3757 or 800-371-2095; www.beesons.com.* $$

Crane's Crest Bed & Breakfast. Panoramic view of Kachemak Bay. In season, sandhill cranes feed in the yard and entertain guests. *59830 Sanford Drive; 907-235-2969 or 800-613-2969; www.akms.com/cranes.* $–$$

Driftwood Inn. Three blocks from Bishop's Beach, this 21-room inn has standard hotel rooms as well as six "ships' quarters" rooms like those those on the Alaska State Ferry System—a double bed and a pull-down, Pullman-style single bed in each. Laundry, picnic facilities, and an adjacent RV park. *135 West Bunnell Street; 907-235-8019 or 800-478-8019; www.thedriftwoodinn.com.* $$–$$$

Lands End Resort. At the end of wide, windy, industrial Homer Spit, this motel/inn of 80 rooms faces a magnificent bay rimmed with snowcapped mountains. Bayside rooms have fabulous views; other rooms face a parking lot. For meals, there is the resort's own Chart Room Restaurant and Lounge. *4786 Homer Spit Road; 907-235-0040 or 800-478-0400; www.lands-end-resort.com.* $$$

Old Town Bed & Breakfast. Housed in the Old Inlet Trading Post, this wonderful B&B has three clean, airy rooms. Down the road is Bishop's Beach, a wild strand facing Cook Inlet, with a view of the Southwest Peninsula. *106 West Bunnell Street; 907-235-7558; www.oldtownbedandbreakfast.com.* $$

Seaside Farm. Five miles out East End Road, this farm includes a backpackers' hostel, some private rooms, housekeeping cabins, and tent campsites. *40904 Seaside Farm Road; 907-235-7850.* $

Shorebird Guesthouse. Private separate cottage with beach access and wildlife viewing (birds and seals). *4774 Kachemak Drive; 907-235-2107.* $$$

Skyview B&B and Vacation Rental. Two units with private bath and a bunkhouse sleeping six. *68056 W. Thomas St., Homer, AK; 907-235-3832.* $$

◆ **WILDERNESS LODGES**

Kachemak Bay Wilderness Lodge. The price at this luxurious property is per person for a five-day, four-night all-included package. Accommodations are in private cabins near wilderness hiking trails and waters for kayaking and canoeing; the main lodge has a piano, fireplace, and a dining area.. Staff naturalists lead guided hikes and boat trips across Kachemak Bay. Reservations: *P.O. 956, Homer, AK 99603; 907-235-8910; www.alaskawildernesslodge.com.* $$$

◆ **TOURS**

Alaska Wilderness 4-Wheeler Tours. Scenic hill country tours, wildlife viewing, beach tours, and clam digging. *4850 Spruce Lane; 907-235-8567.*

Bald Mountain Air Service. Alaska brown-bear viewing and photo safaris by floatplane. Day-long trips depart from June through September and visit various locations in Katmai National Park, depending on the month ($565 per person). Highly recommended, with expert guides and pilots. *907-235-7969 or 800-478-7969; www.baldmountainair.com.*

Center for Alaskan Coastal Studies. Day trips with a naturalist to tide pools and through forests by Peterson Bay and China Poot Bay. Trips leave daily from Memorial Day through Labor Day and can be combined with half-day kayak trips and overnight stays in yurts. Other, shorter tours visit the Carl E. Wynn Nature Center to view Alaskan native plants and wildflowers. *708 Smoky Bay Way, off Lake Street; 907-235-6667.*

Emerald AirService. Specializing in day-long, fly-out guided bear viewing on the Katmai Coast. $540 per person. Office on Homer Spit's fishing village boardwalk. *907-235-1971; www.emeraldairservice.com.*

Kachemak Bay Ferry. Summer only. Daily ferry service to Halibut Cove from Homer Spit. A popular tourist run, but just a sea-borne bus for residents. *907-235-7847.*

St. Augustine's Kayak and Tour. Kayak tours, for half-day or longer, in Katchemak Bay State Park. Bird watching, wildlife viewing, fishing with expert guides. *907-299-1894; www.homerkayaking.com.*

Rainbow Tours. Full-day whale-watching cruises, shuttles to Seldovia, and half-day halibut fishing charters. *907-235-7272; www.rainbowtours.net.*

Timberline Packers and Outfitters. Seven- to 12-day custom horseback adventures into remote parts of the Kenai National Wildlife Refuge. Hunting trips, too. *4151 West Hill Road; 907-235-2688.*

Trails End Horse Adventures. Guided horseback tours in the Homer hills or to the head of Kachemak Bay. *53435 (Mile 11.2) East End Road; 907-235-6393.*

True North Kayak Adventures. Sea kayaking on Kachemak Bay with wildlife viewing. Guided day trips out of a base camp on Yukon Island. Longer multi-day expeditions available. *907-235-0708; www.truenorthkayak.com.*

◆ FISHING CHARTERS.

There are about 60 fishing charters, most of which can be found on Homer Spit. They include: **Capt. Mike's Charters;** *907-235-8348; www.captmike.com*; **A-Ward Charters;** *907-235-7014 or 888-235-7014; www.awardcharters.com*; and **Thompson Halibut Charters;** *907-235-7222.*

KENAI *map page 144, A-3*

Population: 6,942
Visitors information: 907-283-1991

◆ TOURS

Fishing Tours. Numerous guides offer fishing tours for king salmon; try **Alaskan Adventure Charters** (907-262-7773; www.alaskancharters.com), or call visitors information (see above).

◆ WILDERNESS LODGES

Great Alaska Adventure Lodge. The lodge overlooks the confluence of the Kenai and Moose rivers and offers a variety of fishing options: driftboats, ocean cruisers, bush planes, and so on. Also bear-viewing trips and sightseeing. Reservations: (summer) *33881 Sterling Highway, Sterling, AK 99672; 800-544-2261*; (winter) *Box 2670, Poulsbo, WA 98370; 800-544-2261; www.greatalaska.com.* $$$

PALMER AREA   *map page 144, B-2/3*

Population: 4,533
Visitors information: 907-745-2880

Hatcher Pass Lodge. Four hours from Denali and two hours north of Anchorage. Besides nine private cabins, there are three rooms with mountain views in the lodge, an outdoor sauna, a restaurant serving lunch and dinner, and a bar. Nearby is a historic gold mining village. *Independence Mine State Historical Park, Mile 17, Willow-Fishhook Road; 907-745-5897; www.hatcherpasslodge.com.* **$$$**

Mat-Su Resort. Overlooking Wasilla Lake with floatplane and private boat dock. Lodge, and cabins with kitchenettes. Gourmet restaurant. *1850 Bogard Road, Wasilla; 907-376-3228.* **$$**

Motherlode Lodge. A B&B in a building dating from the 1940s. Eleven rooms (eight with private bath, three with shared bath). Fine dining by reservation. *Mile 14, Palmer Fishhook Road, Hatcher Pass; 907-746-1464 or 907-688-4055; www. motherlodelodge.com.* **$$**

Valley Hotel. Thirty-three rooms, 24-hour coffee shop, a liquor store, and lively lounge. *606 South Alaska Street; 907-745-3330; www.valleyhotelalaska.com.* **$$**

SELDOVIA   *map page 144, A-4*

Population: 286
Visitors information: 907-234-7612; www.seldovia.com

◆ **RESTAURANTS**

The Buzz. Home-style bakery. Breakfast and lunch and bike rentals. Open from March through September. *231 Main Street; 907-234-7479.* **$**

◆ **LODGING**

Alaska Dancing Eagles Bed & Breakfast. A homey place in a lovely waterfront spot. Besides B&B rooms in the lodge, there's a cabin for rent (two-night minimum). *907-234-7627 (summer), 907-360-6363 (winter); www.dancingeagles.com.* **$$**

Boardwalk Hotel. Modern, basic hotel with 14 guest rooms, all with bath. Overlooks harbor. *907-234-7816; www.alaskaone.com/boardwalkhotel.* **$$**

Seaport Cottages. Four one-bedroom cottages with kitchens. *313 Shoreline Drive; 907-234-7483; www.xyz.net/~chap.* **$$**

SEWARD   *map page 144, B-4*

Population: 2,830
Visitors information: 907-224-8051; www.sewardak.org

◆ RESTAURANTS

Apollo Restaurant. Eclectic menu includes Greek, Italian, and seafood dishes, as well as pizza. *229 Fourth Avenue; 907-224-3092.* $–$$

Chinook's Waterfront Restaurant. Fresh Alaskan seafood with a view of Seward and the harbor. *1404 Fourth Avenue, Small Boat Harbor; 907-224-2207.* $

Exit Glacier Salmon Bake Restaurant. Casual seafood restaurant and pub in secluded, wooded setting. Steaks & burgers too, plus microbrews on tap. *Exit Glacier Road; 907-224-2204.* $$

Ray's Waterfront. Serves large portions of excellent seafood; view of the harbor and the mountains beyond. Colorful bar. *1316 Fourth Avenue, Small Boat Harbor; 907-224-5606; www.alaskaone.com/waterfront.* $$–$$$

Resurrect Art Gallery and Coffee House. Featuring the work of local artists, this church-turned-café offers coffee, espresso drinks, and pastries. Live music most Tuesday nights. *320 Third Avenue; 907-224-7161.* $

◆ LODGING

Hotel Seward. Standard amenities amid colorful, gold-rush–themed decor. Near the waterfront and several restaurants. *221 Fifth Avenue; 907-224-2378 or 800-655-8785; www.hotelsewardalaska.com.* $$$

Marina Motel. Has 26 rooms, some with harbor view. At Mile 1 of the Seward Highway, within walking distance of the train station and waterfront. Clean and comfortable. *1603 Seward Highway; 907-224-5518; www.sewardmotel.com.* $$–$$$

Moby Dick Hostel and Lodging. Downtown, open in summer only, this hostel has both dorm rooms and private rooms. *432 Third Avenue; 907-224-7072; www.mobydickhostel.com.* $

Sea Treasures Inn. Downtown, with four rooms at the inn and a two-bedroom house at the same location. *236 Sixth Avenue, at Adams Street; 907-224-7667 or 866-872-2412.*

Snow River Hostel. Just off the end of Lost Lake Trail, 16 miles north of Seward, catering to hikers and those seeking an inexpensive, out-of-town experience; 14 beds, two baths, kitchen, and common room. *Reservations: No telephone, P.O. Box 425; Seward; AK 99664.* $

Summit Lake Lodge. Set in a beautiful area 46 miles north of Seward, near Moose Pass, this upscale roadhouse next to Tenderfoot Creek Campground has become quite popular. There are six guest rooms, a restaurant and bar in a separate building, and an espresso bar and gift shop in a third. *Mile 45.5 Seward Highway (coming from Seward, you'll go through Moose Pass before you reach the lodge); 907-244-2031; www.summitlakelodge.com* **$$**

Van Gilder Hotel. Built in 1916 and now listed on the National Register of Historic Places, this downtown hotel is furnished with antiques; some of the 24 rooms have views of the inlet. *308 Adams Street; 907-224-3079 or 800-204-6835.* **$$–$$$**

◆ CAMPGROUNDS

Waterfront Park and Resurrection Bay. A nice public campground run by the Seward Parks and Recreation Department, with picnic tables, on the water. *Ballaine Road and Madison Street; 907-224-3331; www.cityofseward.net/sprd.* **$**

◆ TOURS

Kenai Fjords Tours. Offers several options for wildlife and glacier tours in the Kenai Fjords area, from shorter day cruises to 2-day, 3-night stays at remote Fox Island Wilderness Lodge. Highly recommended. Excellent nature talks by the crew, lofty views, and a chance to see otters, eagles, sea lions, and orcas. *907-276-6249 or 800-468-8068; www.kenaifjords.com.*

Renown Charters and Tours. Year-round wildlife viewing cruises in Resurrection Bay, plus longer cruises to Kenai Fjords National Park in summer. *907-224-3806 or 888-514-8687; www.renowncharters.com.*

TALKEETNA   *map page 144, B-2*

Also see Denali National Park and Preserve, page 262
Population: 772
Visitors information: 907-733-2330; www.talkeetna-chamber.com.
Talkeetna/Denali Visitors Center. On highway at turnoff for Talkeetna is this excellent visitors center run by the Chamber of Commerce. Helpful staff will give you advice on accommodations, phone ahead for you, make plans for you to go river rafting or flightseeing, or take a horseback trip. *At the junction of the George Parks Highway and the Talkeetna Spur Road; 800-660-2688; www.alaskan.com/talkeetnadenali.*

◆ Restaurants

Talkeetna Roadhouse. Home-style country fare served in a rustic log-cabin setting. Popular with locals and climbers on their way to Mount McKinley. *Main Street; 907-733-1351; www.talkeetnaroadhouse.com.* $

◆ Lodging

Denali View B&B. Cedar-sided house in a wilderness setting overlooking valley with view of Denali. Three rooms. *15669 East Coffee Lane; 907-733-2778 or 877-533-2778; www.denaliviewraft.com.* $$

Fairview Inn. Six guest rooms with shared baths in a 1923 inn. Rowdy bar downstairs. *101 Main Street; 907-733-2423; www.denali-fairview.com.*

Forks Roadhouse. Rustic lodge with three cabins and 10 rooms (shared bath). Restaurant and bar. Open year round, with the main business during winter. *Mile 19, Petersville Road, Trapper Creek; 907-733-1851.* $$

Swiss-Alaska Inn. A family-run rustic inn with homey rooms and a restaurant. East Talkeetna by the boat launch; *907-733-2424; www.swissalaska.com.* $$

Talkeetna Motel, Restaurant, and Lounge. Roadside motel with restaurant, cocktail lounge; dancing. *Downtown Talkeetna; 907-733-2323.* $–$$

VALDEZ   *map page 144, C-3*

Population: 4,036
Visitors information: 907-835-4636 or 907-835-2984; www.valdezalaska.org

◆ Restaurants

Alaska's Bistro. Fine dining with a harbor view; known for excellent seafood and a long wine list. *In the Best Western Valdez Harbor Inn. 100 Fidalgo Drive; 907-835-5688.*

Mike's Palace. Italian and Greek specialties such as pizza and gyros, plus seafood. *201 North Harbor Drive; 907-835-2365.* $–$$

Pipeline Club. Lounge and restaurant featuring fine steaks and Alaska seafood. Favorite former hangout of Captain Joseph Hazelwood of *Exxon Valdez* infamy. Nightly entertainment. *112 Egan Drive; 907-835-4332.* $$–$$$

◆ Lodging

Best Western Valdez Harbor Inn. The most popular hotel in town has 88 rooms and fills up early in the summer, so reserve early. Located next to a small boat harbor. Adjoining bar and restaurant overlook the water and serve steaks and seafood.

100 Fidalgo Drive; 907-835-4391 or 888-222-3440; www.valdezharborinn.com.
$$–$$$

Valdez Hotel. Hotel with 103 rooms and suites, a pool, spa, exercise room, and other amenities. *Corner of Egan Drive and Meals Avenue; 907-835-4445 or 800-478-4445; www.aspenhotelsak.com.* **$$$**

◆ TOURS

Keystone Raft and Kayak Adventures. Raft trips down Keystone Canyon and the Tsaina, Tonsina, and Talkeetna rivers; 10-day kayaking and rafting excursions. Very reasonable prices. *Mile 16.5, Richardson Highway; 907-835-2606 or 800-328-8460; www.alaskawhitewater.com.*

Stan Stephens Glacier and Wildlife Cruises. Daylong cruises to Columbia and Meares glaciers in Prince William Sound. *907-835-4731 or 866-867-1297; www.stanstephenscruises.com*

WHITTIER *map page 144, B-3*

Population: 182
Visitors information: 907-472-2327; www.alaskaone.com/whittier

◆ LODGING

Inn At Whittier. This Victorian-style four-story structure, right on the water, has custom woodwork, including a knockout spiral staircase. The 25 rooms including two townhouse suites; ask for ocean views. Bar and restaurant. *P.O. Box 609, Whittier, AK 99693; 866-472-5757; www.innatwhittier.com.* **$$$**

◆ TOURS

For a complete list of the approximately 30 charter outfits offering boat tours out of Whittier into **Prince William Sound,** contact the City of Whittier Small Boat Harbor (907-472-2330). They include:

26 Glacier Cruise. Itinerary promises a view of 26 named glaciers. *907-276-8023 or 800-544-0529; www.26glaciers.com.*

Major Marine Tours. Half-day glacier-viewing cruises of Prince William Sound. *907-274-7300 or 800-764-7300; www.majormarine.com.*

Sound Eco Adventures. Gerry Sanger, former biologist, has been giving tours on his custom-built 31-foot boat in Prince William Sound since 1987. *907-472-2312 or 888-471-2312; www.soundecoadventure.com.*

WRANGELL–ST. ELIAS NATIONAL PARK AND PRESERVE
map page 144, D/E-3/4

Visitors information: 907-822-5234; www.wrangell.st.elias.national-park.com

◆ LODGING
Caribou Hotel. Rooms in the main building have private bath; rooms in the annex (formerly used to house workers building the Alaska pipeline) have shared bath. The **Caribou Restaurant** out front serves standard fare. *Mile 186.5 on Glenn Highway, Glennallen; 907-822-3302 or 800-478-3302; www.caribouhotel.com.* $$–$$$
McCarthy Lodge and Ma Johnson's Hotel. The lodge, built in 1916, used to take overnight guests. Now it is a dining room open for breakfast and dinner, and overnight guests stay across the street at Ma Johnson's, which has 20 rooms (shared baths) decorated with artifacts from McCarthy's copper mining days. *McCarthy; 907-554-4402; www.mccarthylodge.com.*

■ FESTIVALS AND EVENTS

■ JANUARY
Sled-Dog Racing, Anchorage. The season begins in mid-January and sprints are held every Saturday and Sunday until mid-February. *907-562-2235.*
Polar Bear Jump-Off, Seward. Only in Alaska—costumed participants jump into the frigid waters of Resurrection Bay. *907-224-5230.*

■ FEBRUARY
Fur Rendezvous, Anchorage. Probably the most popular festival in Anchorage, the so-called Fur Rondy includes more than 100 events—snowshoe softball, Eskimo blanket tosses, frostbite foot races, World Championship sled dog races, fireworks, and a parade. *907-274-1177; www.furrondy.net.*
Peninsula Winter Games, Soldotna. Festivities include the Alaska State Championship Sled Dog Races and Dog Weight Pull Contest, as well as ice sculpture contests, ice bowling, and snow volleyball. *907-262-5229; www. peninsulawintergames.com.*

■ MARCH
Iditarod Trail Sled Dog Race, Anchorage, Wasilla, and Nome. The most famous event in Alaska. Festivities include the actual race, a reindeer potluck and awards banquet. The colorful ceremonial start and most events are located in Anchorage;

the real race starts in Wasilla and finishes 1,049 miles later in Nome—where the party goes on for days. Connoisseurs often charter bush planes to one or more of the 26 isolated checkpoints to get the true flavor of this epic long-distance event. *907-376-5155; www.iditarod.com.*

Valdez Ice Climbing and Film Festival. World-class climbers compete on the many frozen waterfalls around Valdez; clinics, demos, and exhibitions also. *907-835-5182.*

■ MAY

Copper River Delta Shorebird Festival, Cordova. Celebrating the arrival of millions of migrating shorebirds. *907-424-7260.*

Kachemak Bay Shorebird Festival, Homer. Birding workshops, field trips, and other events to mark the arrival of migrating shorebirds. *907-235-7740.*

■ JULY

Moose Dropping Festival, Talkeetna. Parade, entertainment, food, and the famous moose dropping toss game. It's a fact that, a few years ago, an out-of-state animal rights group called and accused Alaskans of moose abuse by dropping them and demanded an end to it. *907-733-2330.*

Mount Marathon Race, Seward. A July 4 race up the 3,022-foot mountain behind the town. This is one of those uniquely Alaskan events that anyone can enter; participants range from world-class athletes to costumed crazies and local favorites who run both for fun and pride. *907-224-8051.*

■ AUGUST

Alaska State Fair, Palmer. Eleven-day event near Anchorage features agricultural exhibits from farms throughout Alaska, and is particularly noted for its oversized vegetables. Also rides, concerts, and food. *907-745-4827; www.alaskastatefair.org.*

Silver Salmon Derby, Seward. Begins the second Saturday of August and runs for nine to 14 days; local merchants sponsor big prizes for the largest salmon caught. (In 2004, the top prize for catching a tagged fish was $50,000.) *907-224-8051.*

Talkeetna Bluegrass and Music Festival. Four-day music festival with a down-home flavor. Billed as "Alaska's Greatest Campout," it's highly recommended by aficionados. *907-488-1372; www.talkeetnabluegrass.com.*

■ OCTOBER

Quyana Alaska Native Dance Festival, Anchorage. In celebration of Alaska's Native culture and held in conjunction with the annual Alaska Federation of Natives convention. *907-274-3611; www.nativefederation.org.*

INTERIOR

For many, the sprawling territory north of the Pacific Ocean and south of the land of the Eskimos is the real Alaska. It certainly is Alaska's "heart." And it is vast—larger than Texas and Oklahoma combined. To the south is the imposing Alaska Range. Mount McKinley—tallest mountain on the continent at 20,320 feet—can regularly be seen from Fairbanks 120 miles away. Several other peaks nearby are also in that range: Foraker, Deborah, and Hess. Surrounding Mount McKinley, or Denali, is Denali National Park and Preserve, where visitors can see, and hear, herds of caribou, colossal Alaskan moose, lumbering grizzlies, and wolves. To the north of Fairbanks is the Brooks Range, an immense protective barrier between the Arctic Ocean and the rest of the state. In the enormous sweep of land between the two mountain ranges are thousands of lakes, great rushing rivers, and vast expanses of taiga (spruce-birch woodlands). In the late spring, flocks of migratory waterfowl gather in such numbers that those viewing them feel as if they had stepped between the lines of the Book of Genesis and were witnessing the dawn of creation.

Along the river cutbanks of the Interior, the ivory tusks and skulls of mammoths are found each summer, as are the skeletons of steppe bison and other fauna of the Pleistocene. During the Ice Age, the Interior of Alaska was one of the few places of the far north not covered by glaciers. As a result, it became a refuge for the great mammals of the period, and part of an ice-free corridor, so the theory goes, leading toward the south.

Fairbanks is the central city of this region. From Fairbanks, it's possible to rent a car and drive south to Denali National Park, to set out east for Chena Hot Springs, or to range south on the Richardson Highway, which runs 366 miles to Valdez. In your own very-well-equipped car you might set out north along the Dalton Highway, heading for the Arctic Ocean. Or you can arrange for bush planes to take you to arctic villages and remote wilderness areas.

Temperatures range widely in the Interior. In the winter, temperatures of 50 below zero are not uncommon. In July, when the sun beats down for 22 hours a day, the temperature often rises to 90 degrees.

You can have a drink in an all-ice bar at the Aurora Ice Museum in Chena Hot Springs.

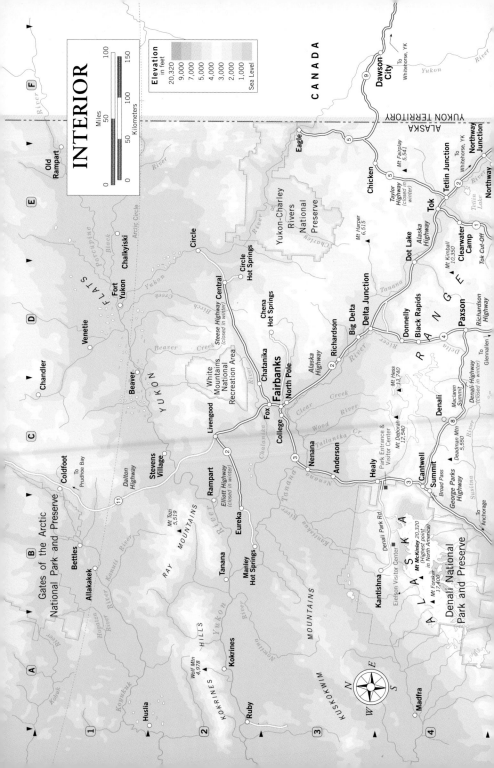

■ DENALI NATIONAL PARK AND PRESERVE
maps pages 210, 214, and 215

■ HISTORY

In 1794, Capt. George Vancouver, exploring the north Pacific inlet named for his former commander James Cook, took note of "distant stupendous mountains covered with snow." This glaciated white massif was what the ancient Athabaskans called Denali, "the high one." By the date of Vancouver's notation, the Spanish universities of Latin America had already been in existence for two centuries; calculus was being taught, as were human anatomy and physiology, the plays of Shakespeare, and the novels of Cervantes. Telescopes mapped the heavens. Despite these advances, the interior of Alaska—even its highest mountains—remained a question mark to most of the world.

Another century passed. Short arctic summers came, and long winters. And still Denali and its environs were the sole domain of caribou and moose, lynx and snowshoe hare, moccasined feet and wooden dogsleds. Then in 1896, a prospector named William Dickey, wandering near the headwaters of the Chulitna River, took out his transit and made some crude measurements. To his amazement, the peak in his viewfinder proved to be more than 20,000 feet high. That made Denali the highest mountain north of the Andes. As word of Dickey's measurement spread, excitement grew about the region. In a geological district of such stupendous vertical relief and uplift, might there be precious metals scattered near the surface and then exposed in stream and river beds? The answer to that question was yes, and in 1906 the Kantishna gold stampede brought more than 2,000 miners to the vicinity of Moose Creek and Wonder Lake.

When Charles Sheldon arrived by riverboat at Kantishna mining camp in 1906, he was already a self-made millionaire, having retired four years earlier at the age of 35 after making a fortune in a Mexican mining venture. A graduate of Yale University, a personal friend of President Theodore Roosevelt, and, like his friend, a lover of nature, Sheldon would devote the rest of his life to traveling, big-game hunting, writing, and conservation causes. As soon as he saw Denali and the spectacular countryside and wildlife surrounding the peak, Sheldon, now known as the "Father of Denali National Park," realized that the area should forever be withdrawn

(following pages) The classic view of Mount McKinley taken from the road to Wonder Lake.

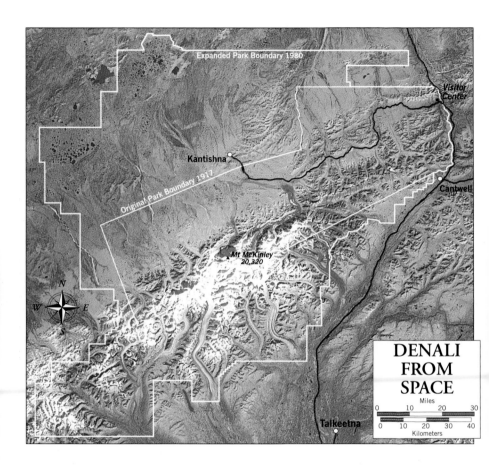

Miles
0   10   20   30
0   10   20   30   40
Kilometers

from private development and designated a national park. For the next 10 years he worked tirelessly toward that end, and in February 1917, as war ravaged Western Europe, President Woodrow Wilson signed the bill that established Mount McKinley National Park in the distant, little-known territory of Alaska.

By this time Mount McKinley had been climbed by two different parties of pioneering mountaineers. In the first attempt, which occurred in 1910, the four-member Sourdough Expedition made it to North Peak (19,470 feet), which they mistakenly believed was the summit. Interestingly enough, the Sourdoughs made their ascent with little more than doughnuts and thermoses of hot chocolate in

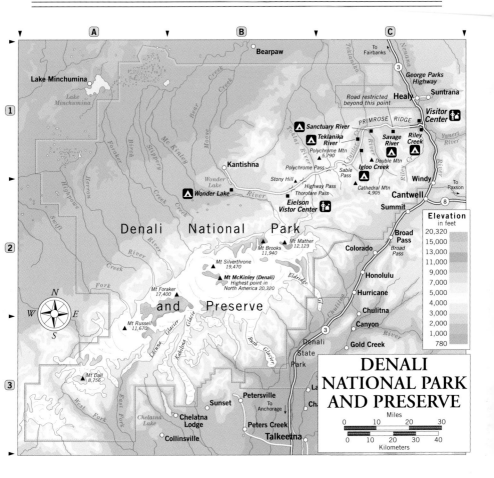

their packs—quite different from the elaborate supplies taken today. Three years later, Harry Karstens, Walter Harper, Robert Tatum, and Episcopalian minister Hudson Stuck apparently completed the first successful ascent of the South Peak (20,320 feet). While on the summit, they observed the 14-foot flagpole on the North Peak left by the previous expedition.

In the late 1930s, an intense controversy developed in the fledgling Mount McKinley National Park. Park officials believed that if the wolves were exterminated (as had already been accomplished in Yellowstone National Park), the numbers of ungulates—Dall sheep, moose, caribou—would naturally increase. Because tourists came to observe wildlife, wouldn't it make sense to provide them with more wildlife to see? Before implementing the plan, the park service brought in zoologist Adolph Murie, who had previously studied coyote predation in Yellowstone, to determine the relationship between wolf predation and ungulate populations, especially Dall sheep. Murie determined that the wolves had a "salutary effect" on populations, culling out the weak, infirm, and old individuals to the benefit of the whole population. Despite Murie's findings, however, the National Park Service practiced a wolf control program until 1992. Nowadays, Denali's wolf population ranges from 50 to 150 animals; its Dall sheep population is at 2,500 and its caribou population at 2,000.

The other major development in Denali's modern history was the 1980 Alaska National Interest Lands Conservation Act, which enlarged the boundaries of the park by nearly four million acres (to a total of six million acres). The act also changed the name of Mount McKinley National Park to Denali National Park and Preserve (Mount McKinley is still officially known as McKinley, though it is commonly referred to as Denali). Although hunting is prohibited in the central parklands, the surrounding newer parkland and preserve allow sport hunting as well as subsistence hunting by Native Americans.

■ APPROACHING DENALI

Most visitors to Denali come from far away—advancing slowly, over hundreds of miles, like one of Chaucer's pilgrims, with every third thought of that stupendous inspirational place over the horizon. At last, from a rail car traveling north from Anchorage or from an automobile heading south from Fairbanks, visitors spy an immense white mass. This enormous feature dominating the western sky is no cumulus cloud, no cloud of smoke from a burning forest, no hallucination. It is a mountain, a solid ancient block of rock and snow and ice that rises almost 4 miles above the level of the sea. Like a fortified castle of the Wagnerian gods, Denali stands alone, cold and aloof, remote and isolated, not married by ridge or range to other mountains. Crowned with snow and ice, it looms above a vast green sea of spruce and birch and meadow and slow subarctic river.

Seeing the peak itself depends on the weather—only one-third of visitors actually see it. Sometimes you can see it every day for two weeks. At other times, during the same season, it will rain every day for the same time span. Generally, if people plan to spend at least five days in the park, they have a good chance of seeing Denali, especially if they rise early before the clouds begin to form.

■ VISITING DENALI NATIONAL PARK AND PRESERVE

Park Entrance *map page 215, C-1*
The entrance to Denali National Park lies along the George Parks Highway (AK 3), 240 miles north of Anchorage and 120 miles south of Fairbanks. (If you're coming from Anchorage, also see the description of the town of Talkeetna, page 185.) At the entrance (and there's only one), you will be greeted by a sign informing all visitors that they must stop at the **Visitor Center** just up the road on the right. At this immense wood building you will obtain bus passes, backcountry camping permits, and road-accessed camping permits. There is also an auditorium, an information area, and a marvelous gift shop stocked with books, maps, postcards, posters, wildlife videotapes, and "Area Closed—Bear Danger" signs you can purchase and hang in your office back home. Here you can also pick up a copy of the park newspaper, which will tell you how to respond if you encounter a grizzly. *907-683-1266 in summer or 907-683-2294 year-round.*

Transportation
Entry into Denali from the Parks Highway is via the 91-mile Denali Park Road. Visitors may drive their own vehicles as far as Savage River, 15 miles into the park. After that point, the road is restricted to shuttle buses, tour buses, official park vehicles, and those with special-use permits (including those for the Teklanika River Campground; see page 220). Most people rely on a reasonably priced but sometimes crowded fleet of no-frills shuttle buses, run by a park concessionaire. These buses will drop off or pick up day hikers and campers anywhere along the road (except for restricted wildlife areas), make scheduled stops at rest or camping areas, and also serve as rolling wildlife tours. There is a steady stream of buses leaving from the visitors center every half hour or so from 5:30 A.M. throughout the day, so it's possible to get off one bus, go for a hike or picnic, then flag down the next bus with open seats traveling in either direction. It's worth consulting the exact schedule online (see below) to avoid surprises or disappointments. Drivers, many of whom pride themselves on their skills as entertainers and naturalists, conduct a narrative, answer questions, and brake for photo opportunities. If you arrive at peak season (mid-June through mid-August), you might encounter a delay of one or two days before you can obtain bus tickets—unless you make reservations in advance by calling 800-622-7275 or, in Anchorage, 907-272-7275. The same goes for camping sites and back-country travel. A convenient one-stop reservation service for both is available online at: www.nps.gov/dena.

THAT DENALI SHUTTLE BUS: *It Can Be the Worst ...*

Here's what a bad day is like:
A freezing rain pelts 35 people huddled in line at 7:00 A.M. before the Denali shuttle bus. Several people's shoes are soaked. The bus driver's glasses are steamed up, and by the time the bus is under way the bus windows are steamed up inside. The bus driver turns up the pace of his window wipers, and adjusts his receptionist-microphone. "Today, my job will be driving the bus," he says in a mechanical voice. "Your job will be looking for wildlife." Passengers in window seats turn sideways and try to open the steamed-up windows. "When you open a window on a day like this, the rain will blow onto the seat behind you. The rolls of paper towels on the overhead racks can be used to wipe the steam off the windows. This is what we call a three-roll day." He laughs a mirthless laugh, then resumes his sing-song. "We often see moose in this area. Moose live in the forest here."

An hour passes and no one sees an animal. "If it weren't for the clouds," says the driver, "you'd see Mount McKinley from the road." Another hour passes. "Dall sheep are probably up there on the slopes, behind those clouds."

More time passes. "It's important to stay seated on Polychrome Pass because there's a thousand-foot drop off. It will be especially important on a day like this when there is no visibility and buses are coming in both directions. When it rains hard the road sometimes washes out."

A blonde woman pulls eyeshades and earplugs from her purse. Everyone under the age of 20 is asleep. Everyone else is fretting.

Several hours later, the bus has turned around and is heading back. If anyone has seen an animal, they haven't mentioned it. The driver feels he should respond to the increasing air of dissatisfaction. "Many people come to Denali hoping to see the grizzly bears, and they are not visible every day. We have many other animals here. Ground squirrels are abundant. "

"I didn't come here to see ground squirrels," says one man loudly.

"You want to see grizzlies?" says his companion. "Wrap yourself in bacon and get out at Mile 38." The two men glower at one another.

Eight hours after they began that morning, 35 passengers, none of whom have seen ground squirrels, arrive back at the visitors center, exhausted. They'll remember this day and bring it up whenever someone mentions Alaska.

...or the Best of Experiences....

Here's what a great day is like:

It's 7:00 A.M. and 35 people dressed in REI jackets and walking shoes climb aboard a green school bus that will travel through Denali National Park. The driver says his name is John, not Driver, so anyone who wants to ask him a question should ask for John.

He's hardly pulled the bus out of the parking lot when a teenage girl cries, "Moose!" Every day passengers shout at John: "Moose!" and every day he pulls over the bus, his eyes riveted with apparent excitement on the forest. Binoculars are focused, light meters consulted. People are generous to strangers. "Here, take my seat. Can you see him there at 11 o'clock?"

During the next hour, the shuttle passes three bull caribou with 40-pound antlers, standing silhouetted against the sky on the top of a ridge. Then the clouds open wide, sunlight comes streaming across the vast landscape. "That's Denali!" cries the driver. "Mount McKinley! Only 30 percent of those who come here see it!"

The bus continues to the Toklat River, and soon the driver is choking with excitement. "Look down . . . that's fantastic . . . a grizzly is chasing wolves away from a kill!" Thirty-three human beings strain out the bus windows, snapping pictures. The other two passengers tell the driver they'd like to get out here to hike. Get *out*? Here? Surely the driver will refuse to let them, but he opens the door and says, "Have fun."

The bus continues. At a rest stop everyone sees a sow grizzly cross a wide gravel bar, jump into a rushing glacial river, swim across, get out, and shake herself. Her two cubs are scared to jump in. They race back and forth on the bank, then take the plunge. Caught in the current, they flail around. The mother is not trying to save them. She seems to be saying: You want to be a bear? You swim rivers. The cubs make it.

Three and a half hours after it left the visitors center, the bus turns around at Eielson. Heading home, more caribou appear, and a fox runs along the road. Dall sheep appear on a far hillside, and Mount McKinley shows itself three times. The light on the snowy peaks is a brilliant, burnished silver. All the way home, there's laughter. A German family is speaking in broken English about the wonders of America, pleasing everyone. The couple who got off to hike appear on the road and get on again, uneaten. A magical feeling drifts over the crowd. It's been one of the best days of their lives. One of the days they'll bring up again and again whenever someone mentions Alaska.

A Denali National Park shuttle bus encounters caribou along the park road.

Note that riding deep into the park is an all-day, unhurried proposition, and you need to arrive with weather-appropriate clothing (plan for wetter and colder than you think) as well as your own food and drink, binoculars, and camera. If the weather is rainy, consider not going—condensation makes it almost impossible to see from the windows. Another option for park travel is provided by private tour buses: they're generally more expensive and comfortable, but tend to be less flexible about pick-up and drop-off services; inquire beforehand.

Campgrounds

Near the park entrance, **Riley Creek Campground** has 100 spaces, with facilities for campers, trailers, and tents, as well as flush toilets and tap water available. This is the only campground open year round. **Savage River Campground,** at Mile 13 on the park road, is a popular overnight facility with 33 spaces and the same set-up as Riley Creek. There are some nice views from Savage. **Teklanika River Campground,** at Mile 29 on the park road just before the Savage River Check Station, has 53 spaces and is the only other campground accessible to vehicles. There are excellent hiking possibilities in the countryside around Savage and

Teklanika, and wildlife abounds near both. In recent years, wolf sightings have been increasingly common along the road in this area.

Sanctuary River (seven sites) at Mile 22, **Igloo Creek** (seven sites) at Mile 34, and **Wonder Lake** (28 sites) at Mile 85—are accessed only by park bus, which means you must obtain a bus ticket at the same time you secure a camping permit, and you must carry all your gear with you on the bus.

In the event camping sites are closed for a couple of days, don't worry—private campgrounds are located at Lynx Creek, about a mile north of the park turnoff on the George Parks Highway, and at Healy, about 10 miles north of the park turnoff on the Parks Highway. There are also facilities just to the south on the Parks Highway at Grizzly Creek.

■ THE ROAD TO WONDER LAKE

Park Entrance to Mile 10.5   *map page 215, C-1*

Moose are often seen browsing among the trees in the forested areas close to the center. Birding can be good in the early summer (June through early July). About seven miles up the road, which climbs steadily up from the Nenana River valley, you leave the spruce forest and enter the tundra, where there are few if any upright trees. At about Mile 9.5 (if the clouds lift) you will have a good view of Mount McKinley to the southwest. There are numerous pull-outs where you can photograph the peak, and shuttle bus drivers will pull over if the view is good. One of the best views is near Mile 10.5, where McKinley is flanked by Double Mountain and Sable Mountain.

Savage River Area   *map page 215, C-1*

Past the Savage River Check Station there is excellent hiking on undeveloped trails. The canyon behind the station is narrow and beautiful, with wildflowers and caribou tracks along the river bank. You can hike along the broad braided portion of the Savage River, across the road, as well in the highlands to the north. Several important words of caution: first, the glacial water, especially during the run-off, is freezing cold and deadly swift (keep children at your side at all times); second, grizzlies can be encountered anywhere and are unpredictable animals; third, if you are climbing on Primrose Ridge just to the west, be aware that storms can develop quickly and create dangerous "white-out" conditions.

(following pages) Biking is one way to see Denali National Park.

Wildlife photographers track huge Dall sheep rams in the Savage River canyon and surrounding uplands both early and late in the season (they migrate south to the big peaks in the summer). From the bus you'll see them as specks of white high against brown-ochre cliffs, and you might see a wildlife photographer as a blue speck. He's been lying on his stomach in his blue parka in the rain for hours; and now he's focusing his telescopic lens on a ram, hoping it will shift position slightly, so he can take a picture unlike anything you've ever seen before. Don't pass up the chance to get off the shuttle bus and bushwhack up the mountain (whistling now and then to warn grizzlies) and take out a pair of binoculars, to see a ram up close.

Primrose Ridge *map page 215, C-1*
For the first few miles past the Savage River bridge, the road parallels Primrose Ridge, a 4,500-foot tundra range that in a good year can have some pretty nice wildflower displays around the summer solstice in late June. The ridge can also be very beautiful in September, when the tundra foliage turns brilliant colors of red and orange, yellow and purple. Caribou and sheep are often seen on Primrose Ridge. Grizzlies will appear, more often than not, as light brown or sunbleached "honeybee-like" shapes lumbering among the berry patches, often with cubs.

Sanctuary River Area *map page 215, C-1*
At about Mile 23 there is an old-fashioned ranger cabin just south of the road. This is the tiny Sanctuary River Campground (accessible only by bus), one of the best campgrounds in the park. When Adolph Murie made his study of park wolves in 1939, he stayed for a time in the Sanctuary ranger cabin.

The road soon crosses the beautiful Sanctuary River—a good place to look for moose, especially cow moose. To the southwest you will see Double Mountain, which is best photographed late in the day, as the sun streams in from the west and brings out all the fine detail and shadowing in the mountain. Past Sanctuary River the road climbs a ridge (good place to look for caribou in the autumn), and then descends into the valley of the Teklanika River.

Teklanika River *map page 215, C-1*
Teklanika River Campground is reached at about Mile 29. This is the second-largest campground in Denali National Park, though one of the most difficult to obtain permits for, because of its popularity. A little farther on, the road crosses the Teklanika River. Moose are frequently seen in the bed of the river, as are wolves,

which den in the closed area upstream (closed meaning no one can hike there—be certain to consult park orientation maps). The road proceeds through a spruce forest that's dense for the subarctic—though elsewhere the trees would be considered few in number and small in size.

Igloo Ranger Cabin and Cathedral Mountain *map page 215, C-1/2*
At Mile 34, just past the Igloo Ranger Cabin and Igloo Creek Campground, the really good country for grizzly-watching begins. Just past the cabin and to the south, on the flanks of Cathedral Mountain, I once observed and photographed a pair of mating grizzlies—an extremely rare sighting even by Denali standards. At about Mile 36 there is a soapberry patch due south of the road in which grizzlies can be seen feeding every August. Once past the Igloo Creek Campground, you are in prime grizzly country and should always proceed, even if walking on the road, with extreme caution—make a lot of noise and travel in groups.

Tattler Creek *map page 215, C-1*
Tattler Creek is often recommended for hiking by rangers (but be sure to ask again for advice if you decide to go there). After you bushwhack up the creek a ways, a shoulder of tundra opens up between two steep mountainsides. This is a lovely place to wander about for a few hours, picking blueberries and daydreaming. Grizzly tracks will probably be visible in the mud, and on the precipitous cliffs of the mountain you'll see the narrow, inaccessible footpaths of Dall sheep.

Sable Pass *map page 215, C-1/2*
Beyond Tattler Creek—at Mile 38.3—all travel off the road is prohibited for five miles. This is known as the Sable Pass Critical Habitat Wildlife Closure Area, and is heavily used by grizzlies. If you walk here, don't even think of leaving the road.

The East Fork of the Toklat River is a good place to take a photograph of the Alaska Range, which is upstream and is especially striking early in the morning or in the evening. The cabin visible a mile to the south is Murie Cabin, where Adolph Murie and his family lived for about two years while he was undertaking his historic wolf study. At that time the Dall sheep population had declined drastically. The National Park Service assumed this was due to their major predator, wolves, which they proposed to eliminate. Murie established that the sheep population had declined due to six winters of exceptionally heavy snow.

Today, wolves den on the tundra to the south of the cabin—in an area closed to hiking. Past the East Fork, the road climbs toward Polychrome Pass (3,700 feet).

Polychrome Pass and Toklat River *map page 215, B/C-1/2*

The summit of Polychrome Pass (where buses make a rest stop) offers a command-ing view of the Plains of Murie (named for Adolph Murie) and the Alaska Range. This is an excellent location to look for wildlife, particularly caribou, wolves, and grizzly bear. Because there are no trees and the view encompasses dozens of square miles, animals are easily spotted. Behind the road, on the grassy ridges of Polychrome Mountain, Dall sheep are also visible, often quite near and even on the road. Marmots and pikas are also commonly seen near the rest area. Wolves hunt on this mountain, especially in the evening hours.

The road descends Polychrome Mountain by some tortured switchbacks and steep inclines, and then crosses wide swaths of tundra country on its way to the Toklat River, which is reached at Mile 53.1. Just downstream is a wolf denning area closed to hiking and the remnants of the cabin where naturalist Charles Sheldon spent one long, lonely winter early in the 20th century. Another rest stop is made at Toklat, and some buses turn back at this point. If your ticket is for the Eielson Visitor Center or for Wonder Lake, your bus will proceed.

Highway Pass and Stony Hill *map page 215, B-2*

The road past Toklat climbs toward Highway Pass, another famous location for wildlife photographers, where anything from grizzly bears to ground squirrels can be seen at any time. Keep your eyes open. At Mile 60.5, the road crosses Stony Creek, and then climbs up Stony Hill, where some of the finest wildflower displays in the park can be seen around the summer solstice. This is also an excellent area to see grizzly bears. Some buses park at the top of Stony Hill, where there is a sublime view of Mount McKinley, or Denali, to the west.

Thorofare Pass and Eielson Visitor Center *map page 215, B-2*

Thorofare Pass, about 4 miles farther up the road, affords another excellent view of the great peak, as well as opportunities to view caribou and, believe it or not, a small colony of gulls that make this area home every summer. Also, be on the look-out for long-tailed jaegers—scissor-tailed birds that nest on the tundra and are sometimes seen fighting off hawks, eagles, and foxes. Finally, at Mile 66, is Eielson Visitor Center, named for a pioneering aviator who landed his plane on the gravel bar of the McKinley River at the bottom of the hill. Ninety-five percent of all visitors

Tundra vegetation can be surprisingly green, turning in autumn to brilliant reds and yellows.

go no farther, because the bus trip to this point and back (*sans* hiking excursions) is seven hours long. The views of Mount McKinley from Eielson can be spectacular—I have spent many an hour in the middle of the arctic summer "night" waiting for the sun to rise (around 2:50 a.m.) to obtain a photograph of Denali from this vantage.

Wonder Lake *map page 215, B-2*

The road winds the remaining miles toward Kantishna. This portion of the road passes through magnificent rolling tundra, with scattered lakes and groves of spruce. Keep those binoculars close at hand—you're apt to see moose and grizzly bears lumbering about on the moist terrain. At Mile 83.5 you will have your first view of Wonder Lake and Wonder Lake Campground (one of the most popular campgrounds in the entire national park system—good luck in obtaining a camping permit). If you've come this far, you'll be eager to get off the bus and walk around. The views here may be the finest on the planet. On a rare and beautiful day you might see a bull moose feeding on water lilies beneath a long forested ridge, with Denali towering in the background. This is where Ansel Adams took his two famous pictures of the peak in June 1947. (He set up his tripod on the ridge above the Wonder Lake ranger cabin.)

Kantishna *map page 215, B-1*

Beyond the old park boundary now stretches the vast Denali Preserve, a buffer of protected land created by the Alaska National Interest Lands Conservation Act of 1980. The town of Kantishna is a private inholding. The growth in this area is nothing short of astonishing—wilderness lodges, restaurants, overnight cabins, private tour buses. The Alaska congressional delegation has for years lobbied for the park road to loop through Kantishna and double back east another 90 miles to the George Parks Highway, making an immense circle through the last great wilderness. There has even been talk of a rail line from Healy to Kantishna. In any event, if you have traveled the road to Wonder Lake, and made the journey on a clear day, you may count yourself lucky. Private tour buses and air charters serve Kantishna, where there are private campgrounds, the historic Kantishna Roadhouse (see page 264) and other upscale lodges nearby, some accessible only by air. These places (see pages 263–264) offer rustic-flavored deluxe accommodations at premium prices—with

The original Kantishna Roadhouse on the grounds of the modern lodge by the same name.

KANTISHNA
ROADHOUSE
CIRCA 1919

hot tubs, saunas, excellent food, guided day hikes by trained naturalists, fishing excursions, and wildlife viewing tours both inside and outside Denali National Park.

■ ACTIVITIES IN AND AROUND DENALI NATIONAL PARK AND PRESERVE

Hiking

If you must stay outside the park for a few days, there are still dozens of things to do. There are a number of good **hiking trails** in the vicinity of the park entrance, and at the visitors center you can obtain maps and up-to-date information about each of them. These include the popular **Horseshoe Lake Trail,** which is accessed by a trailhead 1 mile west of the park turn-off from the George Parks Highway, and just before the railroad tracks. The trail leads north about three-quarters of a

Wonder Lake, with the Alaska Range in the background, Denali National Park and Preserve.

mile to a beautiful lake in the valley of the Nenana River. Moose are often seen here, especially in the morning and evening. As with all park trails, be aware that grizzly bears can be encountered at any time.

Another good trail in this area is the 5-mile (round trip) **Mount Healy Overlook Trail**. A third easily accessed trail near the park entrance is the **Triple Lakes Trail,** which leads south from the George Parks Highway 3 miles to some picturesque lakes near the Riley Creek drainage. Good USGS topographic maps for all three trails are available at the visitors center, as well as more specific guidance from rangers. Park rangers also lead fascinating nature hikes into the backcountry every day. These "discovery hikes" can range from 2 to 5 or more miles, and normally include talks on such topics as wildflowers, geology, glaciers, and wildlife.

Dogsledding

A **dogsledding demonstration** is given every day at the kennels housing Denali's sled dogs, located near park headquarters. In the wintertime rangers patrol the park by dogsled, going from cabin to cabin on a well-established route. At that time the ground is covered with snow and the temperatures are cold, optimum conditions for these dogs. In summer, the dogs are biding their time, waiting for the weather to improve and get colder, but three times a day they pull a ranger around a mud track on a big, old-fashioned sled. The moment the dogs see the rangers getting a team ready, they go wild, leaping up on their kennel houses, racing around trying to be noticed, yelping and yipping, and generally displaying that they are 100 percent worthy of being chosen. Those that are, from the lead dog to the two on the wheel, go joyfully into their harnesses. Those not chosen look like children left behind on picnic day, woofing around in their pens, or sitting down on their haunches with downcast eyes.

As there's no parking by the kennels you must walk there or catch a bus for the short trip from either the visitors center or the Riley Creek Campground. Check departure and show times when you arrive.

Rafting

Rafting the **Nenana River** near the park entrance is popular. Several licensed concessionaires operate from highly visible sites just off the George Parks Highway in the vicinity of the Lynx Creek shopping and hotel area. Be forewarned—this is a potentially dangerous activity, with Class III and Class IV rapids on an extremely swift and cold glacier-fed river (dry suits are provided). A more secure but still invigorating alternative is a ride in one of a number of large jet boats that ply their trade in the same general area.

Flightseeing

Park visitors often take **flightseeing tours**, either by helicopter or fixed-wing aircraft. These businesses operate near the park entrance (an airfield is located directly behind the Denali National Park rail stop) as well as from airstrips in nearby towns such as Talkeetna and Healy. Such scenic trips provide a unique view of the park, especially of its dramatic geology. Opportunities for aerial landscape photography on a clear day are boundless. If you've been in the area for days, and the weather hasn't cleared, this may be one way to get up above the clouds and see the mountain.

Bicycling

Bicycling is increasingly popular in the park, with bicycle rentals available both in the park area and in Talkeetna. One of the advantages of bicycling is that you do not have to wait for a bus ticket to travel on the closed portion of the park road. The disadvantages include exposure to the subarctic environment (there can be snow on any day of the year), a rough gravel road with buses flinging sharp pieces of gravel unpredictably, and a possible encounter with grizzlies, which can run faster than you can pedal. That said, worry more about the buses.

■ DENALI HIGHWAY   *map page 210, B to D-4*

The largely unpaved Denali Highway runs parallel to the Alaska Range for 135 miles, between Cantwell and the George Parks Highway on the west and Paxson and the Richardson Highway on the east. Along the way there are developed trails, canoe routes, campgrounds, and several roadhouses providing food, lodging, and sometimes gasoline. Because the road is not surfaced, travel proceeds at a slow and civilized pace, enabling visitors to pull off and take photographs of the scenery or wildlife, have a long relaxed picnic, observe the interesting geological features (cirque basins, glacial moraines, kettle lakes), or stretch their legs. This freedom of activity stands in marked contrast to Denali National Park just down the road, where travelers are confined to often uncomfortable park buses (the park buses serve as school buses from September through May and are designed more for children on short rides to school than for adults on 12-hour jaunts to and from Wonder Lake).

The night sky over Chena.

The Denali Highway also offers visitors an opportunity to see the Alaska Range without the many restrictions encountered in Denali National Park. There are no park entrance fees, park bus tickets, campground permits, restricted hiking zones, patrolling park rangers, or prohibitions on big-game hunting or fishing (other than applicable state regulations).

The Denali Highway opened in 1957, providing road access to (then) Mount McKinley National Park from the Richardson Highway. After the George Parks Highway was completed in 1972, enabling folks to drive directly from Anchorage to the park, fewer people drove the Denali Highway. Today it is one of the nicest "back roads" in the state.

For many, the ability to enjoy the Alaska wilderness at their own pace is quite refreshing. Visitors can see the same wildlife as in Denali National Park—caribou, moose, Dall sheep, grizzlies, black bears, wolves, fox, coyotes, lynx, golden eagles, ptarmigan, and so forth—and, with the exception of Denali itself, the subarctic scenery is virtually identical to that within the park. Much of the area along the road is managed by the Bureau of Land Management, which has a multiple-use philosophy of land use (as opposed to the mindset within the national park system, which works to preserve land and wildlife by minimizing interference from humankind). Thus along the Denali Highway you will see off-road vehicle trails, snowmobile use areas, well-marked canoe routes, fishing camps, and, in the spring and fall, big-game hunting camps (the road is closed in winter).

Paxson to Tangle Lakes *map page 210, C/D-4*
Most visitors begin their trip down the Denali Highway at the tiny village of **Paxson** (pop. 43), on the Richardson Highway. For the first 20 miles the road climbs steadily from the Summit Pass area past Sevenmile Lake (Mile 6.8) toward **Tangle Lakes,** which are encountered at Mile 20. There are several hundred archaeological sites in the Tangle Lakes area, and summer off-road vehicle use is restricted to signed trails. Visitors will also find two BLM campgrounds with toilets and boat launch (lake trout fishing is good). Visitors often see caribou, moose, and grizzlies at Tangle Lakes. In the fall it is a very popular area with guides, outfitters, and hunters.

Canoe Trails

The 35-mile **Delta River Canoe Trail** begins at the Tangle Lakes BLM campground just north of the Denali Highway, with a take-out near Mile 212 of the Richardson Highway. The Delta River drains north into the Tanana, which ultimately discharges into the Yukon River, which in turn winds its way to the Bering Sea. A shorter boating excursion can be found on the **Upper Tangle Lakes Canoe Trail,** which involves portages through the Tangle Lakes to Dickey Lake and ultimately the Middle Fork of the Gulkana River, with a take-out near the Richardson Highway (this route involves potentially dangerous rapids). Both canoe trails are managed by the Bureau of Land Management.

Maclaren Summit   *map page 210, C-4*

The next major feature on the Denali Highway is **Maclaren Summit** (4,086 feet) at Mile 35.2, which provides travelers with a commanding view of Mount Deborah, Maclaren Glacier, and Mount Hayes to the north. These are the highest mountains before the Denali massif—on a clear day they are visible from downtown Fairbanks (70 miles north of the Alaska Range). A good hiking trail from the parking lot leads over the tundra to the north nearly three miles.

After Maclaren Summit, the Denali Highway descends to cross the Maclaren River (caribou are often seen in this region) and, once past a series of ridges, Clearwater Creek.

Susitna River   *map page 210, C-4*

Draining south from two enormous glaciers—West Fork and Susitna—is the enormous **Susitna River,** crossed at Mile 79 on a 1,036-foot bridge. From here to its termination at the George Parks Highway the Denali Highway has good populations of moose, bear, and caribou. Beaver are often seen on the smaller side streams that are free of the glacial till brought down on the major river. Fishing for salmon, trout, and arctic grayling can also be good at various times of the year. Once you reach the George Parks Highway (always nice to be on a paved road again) it is only 27.5 miles north to Denali National Park and Preserve's entrance area. Fairbanks is about a two-hour drive to the north, and Anchorage is a good four- to five-hour drive to the south.

■ FAIRBANKS   *map page 210, C-3*

My memories of Fairbanks are primarily of the winters, which begin with snc
September, reach a nadir in January with daily highs of 45 below zero, and !
in terms of freezing temperatures and persistent snow drifts, through April.
remember frozen car batteries, car tires flattened and frozen solid to the ground;
alternator belts and coolant hoses shattered by the cold; my hand literally frozen to
the door knob of the house (and my wife unfreezing it with a pan of warm water);
and a pan of water thrown into the yard that froze with a musical tinkling sound
before it reached the ground. There have been December "days" that consisted of
five hours of twilight, ice fog so thick that aircraft (including U.S. mail and Fed-Ex
planes) could not land for a week, furnaces that died when the phone lines were
down, frozen pipes and backed-up water in the house, starving moose eating campus shrubbery on the first day of spring, wolves that devoured pet dogs at suburban homes, caribou driven out of the mountains by snow and found wandering
around town, people with dry coughs that lasted all winter, light planes that simply

Icefog on an average January day in Fairbanks.

CARIBOU FOG

The temperature dropped steadily as we left the foothills and started into the high country.... As the sun rose briefly above the mountain tops, the thin air seemed to be filled with iridescent frost spangles, brilliant crimson and blue and green as they flashed in the sun's rays. Frank nudged me and pointed. A low bank of fog seemed to be drifting slowly over the frozen river.

"Caribou," Frank explained. "When it gets this cold, their breath and body heat form a cloud of steam big enough to hide them." As I watched, the cloud parted for a moment, and I saw a herd of fifty caribou climb the far bank and trot into the spruces.

—Klondy Nelson with Corey Ford, *Daughter of the Gold Rush,* 1958

disappeared on winter flights (never to be found), violent drunken fights reported nightly in the wild frontier bars along First Avenue, and some amazingly rancorous political battles. No doubt about it, winter life in Fairbanks—about 100 miles south of the Arctic Circle—can be an ordeal.

In the summer, though, Fairbanks (pop. 30,224) changes into a friendly and interesting town, with some unusual sites and activities found nowhere else in North America. At midnight on the summer solstice you can observe people golfing or playing baseball; at the annual Tanana Valley State Fair in mid-August, you can see vegetables—pumpkins, squash, carrots, zucchini, lettuce, cucumbers—of truly prodigious size, all grown under the continual bath of sunlight. Try putting children to bed at 10:00 or 11:00 P.M., with the sun still high in the sky, and you may find your persuasive abilities sorely tested!

■ **UNIVERSITY OF ALASKA FAIRBANKS** *map page 238, A-1*
Chief among the attractions in Fairbanks is the campus of the **University of Alaska Fairbanks** (907-474-7211). The school is located on a wooded hill on the west end of town, and is easily reached via University Avenue or Farmer's Loop Road. The school was originally established by the territorial legislature in 1917 as the Alaska Agricultural College and School of Mines. Among its first graduates was Margaret Murie, who was instrumental, with Supreme Court Justice William O. Douglas, in the formation of the Arctic National Wildlife Range in 1960. Murie later authored such classic works as *Two in the Far North* and *Wapiti Wilderness.*

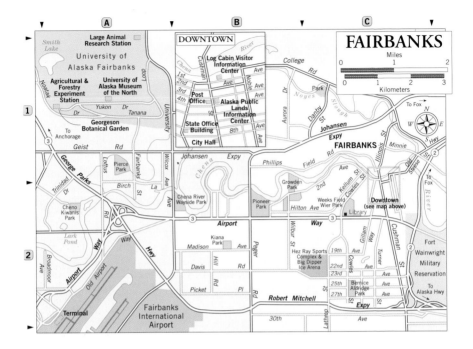

Today the Fairbanks campus is home to more than 10,000 students, many from Asian countries on the Pacific Rim, and supports more than 160 undergraduate and graduate degree programs, including degrees in geophysics (in which students investigate greenhouse gases, global warming, plate tectonics, and the northern lights, among other topics), anthropology (Alaska's a perfect place to study indigenous cultures), and oceanography (this department should be near salt water, but universities are not always known for their common sense). UAF also owns the distinction of being the only university in the world with its own rocket-launching facility: Poker Flats, as it is called, is located north of town (not open to the public) and is used for studies of atmospheric physics.

Constitution Hall (just off Tanana Drive in the center of the campus) is where the original Alaskan constitution was signed. Also here is the superb campus bookstore, which has Alaska's best collection of books on Alaska. It's a short walk across campus (or a ride on the free shuttle bus) to the **University of Alaska Museum of the North**. This state-of-the art facility is one of the "top 10" tourist sites in Alaska. Inside you will see such treats as Oscar, an enormous stuffed Kodiak bear (one of the largest ever shot) that greets you at the door; Blue Babe, an incredibly well-preserved 35,000-year-old mummified steppe bison; a pair of fossilized ivory mammoth tusks; various Eskimo artifacts; photographic and painting exhibits; and dioramas featuring wolves and other Alaskan fauna. The new Rose Berry Alaska Art Gallery displays a collection of Alaskan art objects, many of which, for lack of space, languished for years in storage. The gift shop is worth a lingering visit, with books, cards, calendars, jewelry, musk ox fur, caribou antler artifacts, and some one-of-a-kind Alaskan posters. *907 Yukon Drive; 907-474-7505.*

Down the hill from the museum is the **Agricultural and Forestry Experiment Station,** where researchers conduct experiments with high-latitude barley and wheat, as well as flowers, vegetables, and trees. There are also some reindeer (domesticated caribou) that may be viewed in their pens. The station is open to the public for informal, walk-through tours. The attached **Georgeson Botanical Garden** (117 West Tanana Drive; 907-474-6921) is open for guided, informative one-hour tours—a must for the horticulturally-inclined, from May through September. A short drive away via Miller Hill and Yankovich roads is the university's **Large Animal Research Station** (2220 Yankovich Road; 907-474-7207), also known as the Musk Ox Farm, which has large outdoor enclosures with musk oxen and caribou. If you visit between Memorial Day and Labor Day, take the hour-long guided tour.

■ OTHER FAIRBANKS ATTRACTIONS

Pioneer Park   *map page 238, B-2*

Back toward town along Airport Way, visitors often stop at **Pioneer Park** (formerly Alaskaland, and still known to locals by its old name)—a modest frontier theme park with a number of exhibits open to the public free of charge. Included are full-size walk-through replicas of a gold rush town, an Indian village, and a turn-of-the-century gold mining operation. The beached riverboat Nenana serves as a visitors center, and a narrow-gauge train circles the 44-acre park. The Pioneer Aviation Museum (housed in a dome designed by famed architect Buckminster Fuller) and former President Warren Harding's personal railroad car are also attractions. There is a sizeable cluster of gift shops and Alaska artisans selling their wares, as well as a popular all-you-can-eat, very reasonably priced salmon bake. *Airport Way and Peger Road; 907-459-1087.*

Pike's Landing is a popular Fairbanks restaurant situated on the banks of the Chena River.

Information Centers *map page 238, B-1*
Sites to visit downtown include the interagency **Alaska Public Lands Information Center** (250 Cushman Street; 907-456-0527), with maps and books galore, at the corner of Cushman and Third Avenue; the many gift shops and art galleries selling arts and crafts along Cushman; and the Fairbanks Convention and Visitors Bureau **Log Cabin Visitor Information Center** (550 First Avenue; 907-456-5774 or 800-327-5774), located along the Chena River just east of the Cushman Bridge. The friendly personnel have an encyclopedic knowledge of the recreational opportunities available in the Interior.

Chena River
No trip to Fairbanks is complete without a half-day voyage down the Chena River on the wooden paddleboats *Discovery II* or *Discovery III*. Both are operated by the Binkley family, which has been in the steamboat business for 105 years. Their 3.5-hour narrated tour packs in the Alaskana—everything from a sled dog demonstration to a guided cultural tour of an Athabaskan Indian village and a bush pilot skills exhibition. One of the six Captains Binkley will also take you to the

Replica of a gold rush town in Pioneer Park, Fairbanks.

confluence of the Chena and the Tanana rivers, where you can watch the relatively clear waters of the snow-fed Chena mix with the turbid, glacially fed waters of the mighty Tanana. *1975 Discovery Drive; 907-479-6673 or 866-479-6673; www.riverboatdiscovery.com.*

Flightseeing

You might also investigate taking a short flightseeing trip to give yourself a bird's-eye view of the Interior landscape. Many of these affordable trips land on a remote lake where you can fish for northern pike, salmon, or rainbow trout. You can also catch scheduled mail planes for day trips to Fort Yukon, Arctic Village, Anaktuvuk Pass, and Bettles. Most of the small charter companies are located on the southern end of the Fairbanks airport, where there is also a water runway for floatplanes.

■ NORTH AND EAST OF FAIRBANKS

Just north and east of town are a number of places worth investigating. At **Gold Dredge Number 8 Historic Site** (1755 Old Steese Highway; 907-457-6058 or 800-544-2206), on the Old Steese Highway (a remnant cutoff that parallels the

modern Steese Expressway, both of which merge at the town of Fox to become the Steese Highway—less confusing than it sounds), visitors pan for gold with metal pans and sometimes find small nuggets. You can also pan for gold at **FE Gold** (907-389-2414; *www.fegoldcamp.com*), Mile 27.5 on the Steese Highway.

■ CHENA HOT SPRINGS   *map page 210, D-2/3*
The 57-mile Chena Hot Springs Road, reached via the Steese Highway at Mile 4.9, is a pleasant and scenic drive that bisects the 254,000-acre **Chena River State Recreation Area.** This is one of the most likely places in the state to view moose from the roadway as they graze in the numerous sloughs, ponds, and meadows. Hiking and fishing opportunities abound, with a number of trailheads, camp-grounds, and river access points. At the end of this paved, all-weather road is the town of Chena Hot Springs, which provides a partial sense of the casual lifestyle of rural Alaska. Here you can also soak in warm geothermal springs at the **Chena Hot Springs Resort** (907-451-8104 or 800-478-4681). There are cabins here, a

Panning for gold at Gold Dredge Number 8 (left). Another form of gold wrested from the landscape is birch syrup. Michael East at Kahiltua Birchworks boils the valuable sap down into a sugary refinement (above).

SOURDOUGH'S WEATHER BUREAU

We had no thermometers in Circle City that would fit the case [reach low enough], until Jack McQuesten invented one of his own. This consisted of a set of vials fitted into a rack, one containing quicksilver, one of the best whiskey in the country, one kerosene, and one Perry Davis's Pain-Killer. These congealed in the order mentioned, and a man starting on a journey started with a smile at frozen quicksilver, still went at whiskey, hesitated at the kerosene, and dived back into his cabin when the Pain-Killer lay down.

–Recorded by William Bronson, *The Last Grand Adventure,*
describing late 1890s in Alaska

---

bar, a restaurant, an airfield, and a variety of recreational possibilities, including fishing, ATV tours, and gold panning; winter options include aurora viewing, dog sled rides, and cross-country-skiing.

■ **NORTH POLE** *map page 210, C-3*

The town of North Pole, a 14-mile drive southeast of Fairbanks on the Richardson Highway, serves the army and air force bases in the area. The **Santa Claus House** (907-488-2200 or 800-588-4078)—filled with Christmas accouterments and, naturally, toys—is a favorite with children. Each December, thousands of letters from around the world arrive in North Pole—which, aside from the name, has nothing to do with that geographic location much farther north.

■ **CIRCLE** *map page 210, D/E-2*

One of the most popular short drives from Fairbanks runs over the largely gravel Steese Highway through the scenic White Mountains to the town of Circle. Along the way are ample opportunities for hiking, berry-picking in season, wildlife viewing, and fishing. The vistas at Twelvemile Summit and Eagle Summit are spectacular, especially in late August and early September, when the tundra begins to turn colors. You also get to see the Yukon River up close.

Circle (at Mile 162) offers an easily accessible "bush-like" environment for those who cannot make a trip deeper into the Interior. The town holds a pioneer cemetery, a trading post, a museum, old-time miners' cabins, antique dog-freight rigs, a café, bar, and motel. Nearby is the Arctic Circle Hot Springs Resort. (See page 261.)

■ BUSH VILLAGES

Few Interior villages can be reached by road; most are visited via airplane or river-boat. In these villages time seems to move very slowly. The movement of the sun across the sky each day, the phases of the moon (especially to hunters and trap-pers), and the seasons are more important than calendars and clocks. In the remote villages, wild land is still seen as a physical home, while in the road-accessible vil-lages, the "western" view of land as property predominates. In either case, the bush community is isolated for much of the year and develops a unique culture. Some people live close to the land—hunting, fishing, gardening, foraging for berries, and making their own winter clothes from the skins of wild animals. Others have adopted a more modern lifestyle, which includes computers, video games, junk food, and 100-mph snowmobiles.

■ FORT YUKON *map page 210, D-1*

People either love or hate Fort Yukon, a village set near the confluence of the Yukon and Porcupine rivers. Those who love the place enjoy solitude, blueberry- and cranberry-picking, salmon- or pike-fishing, and wildlife-viewing. Those who hate it chafe at the isolation and the low, swampy terrain—busy with mosquitoes in the summer and deadly cold in the winter. For hundreds of miles in every direc-tion from Fort Yukon are myriad sloughs, ox-bows, lakes, ponds, bogs, rivers, forests, and meadows. Historically this was excellent trapping country, and the town was formed by a field agent for the Hudson's Bay Company in 1847.

Fort Yukon is a short (less than one hour), relatively inexpensive plane flight from Fairbanks, with daily service from several commuter airlines. There are two small hotels in town, a general store, and a restaurant. The local inhabitants are Athabaskan and are related linguistically to the Navajos and Apaches of Arizona and New Mexico. Today many Athabaskans pursue a modified subsistence lifestyle, which includes maintaining fishing wheels for salmon in the summer, picking berries and hunting moose in the autumn, fur-trapping in the winter, and hunting waterfowl in the spring. Although snowmobiles have largely replaced the dogsleds of old, some people still raise, train, and race their dogs in the snowy months.

■ MANLEY HOT SPRINGS *map page 210, B-2*

This small community lies north and west of Fairbanks at the end of the Elliot Highway. Besides a campground, it has the historic Manley Roadhouse, an excellent place to have a beer and meet the people of the bush—a colorful group that includes professional fur trappers, mushers, gold and silver prospectors, hard-rock miners, and commercial and subsistence fisherman. The area produces an abundance of vegetables, due to the warm soil and long summer days.

The hot springs in Manley are superb and non-sulphurous, and visitors can enjoy the soothing waters in a large pool. Tours may be arranged to local gold mines and fishing camps.

■ RUBY   *map page 210, A-2*

Ruby is located on the Yukon River more than 200 miles west of Fairbanks. Founded in 1907 during the gold rush, the town is one of the main checkpoints on the annual Iditarod Trail Sled Dog Race. There is a roadhouse here, and you can charter aircraft to take you to remote lakes, mountaintops, and stretches of river. A stay here offers visitors a look at the bush lifestyle, which includes commercial and subsistence fishing for salmon, trapping, logging, and winter dogsledding.

Most bush villages are accessible only by plane. Here Michael East unloads supplies from a Super Cub at Quiet Lake.

Dangerous Dan McGrew

A bunch of boys were whooping it up in the Malamute saloon
The kid that handles the music-box was hitting a jag-time tune;
Back of the bar, in a solo game, sat Dangerous Dan McGrew,
And watching his luck was his light-o'-love, the lady that's known as Lou.
When out of the night, which was fifty below, and into the din and the glare
There stumbled a miner fresh from the creeks, dog-dirty, and loaded for bear.
He looked like a man with a foot in the grave and scarcely the strength of a louse,
Yet he tilted a poke of dust on the bar, and he called for drinks for the house.
There was none could place the stranger's face, though we searched ourselves for a clue;
But we drank his health, and the last to drink was Dangerous Dan McGrew.

–Robert Service, *The Shooting of Dan McGrew,* 1907

■ From the Canadian Border to Fairbanks

The Alaska Highway has changed substantially since it was constructed during World War II. Where it once was little more than a crude track in the wilderness, it is now a true paved highway over its entire length, easily traveled by a standard passenger car in good shape. Many visitors to Alaska make the long trek up through Canada via the highway, which begins at Dawson Creek in eastern British Columbia near Alberta and ends in Fairbanks. The entire trip is an adventure in itself, and should be enjoyed as such. Slow down and take in the landscape; stop to take day hikes or picnic. Buy a copy of *The Milepost* (800-726-4707) and study it.

■ Northway *map page 210, E-4*

On the south side of the Alaska Highway, just west of the Canadian border, is the 730,000-acre **Tetlin National Wildlife Refuge,** an important summer habitat area for hundreds of thousands of ducks, geese, cranes, and other waterfowl. At about Mile 1264 is Northway Junction, the turnoff for the village of Northway—the village's former leader, Chief Northway, lived to be 114 and was annually featured on his birthday by Willard Scott of NBC's "Today" show. Even in his 90s, Chief Northway worked every summer in the tribal fishing camp, where salmon are still caught in fishing wheels and prepared for winter use as human and as sled-dog food.

A. A. Bennett of Fairbanks was one of the state's early bush-pilot heroes. Here he poses in front of his Swallow biplane in 1927. The photograph is from the collection of the Alaska Aviation Heritage Museum in Anchorage, an unusual museum that displays vintage aircraft and chronicles the exploits of the pilots who linked the rural communities of Alaska's interior to the larger cities.

■ **TOK** *map page 210, E-4*

The first major town encountered on the Alaska Highway as you drive from Canada northwest into Alaska is **Tok,** located at the junction of the Alaska Highway and the Tok cutoff to the Glenn Highway. You may notice some old burn areas on the nearby hillside. A major fire in the summer of 1991 nearly destroyed the town, and wasn't finally put out until the first fall snowstorms. Tok has an excellent **Alaska Public Lands Information Center** (907-883-5667), which has an incredible quantity of excellent, free information—maps, brochures, handouts—and superb front-desk staff.

■ **DELTA JUNCTION** *map page 210, D-3*

While driving north on the Alaska Highway toward Delta Junction, keep your eyes open for bison on or near the roadway. At Mile 1422, you enter Delta Junction, a sizeable town (pop. 840) at the junction of two important roads—the Alaska Highway and the Richardson Highway (which leads south to Valdez). Delta

Junction provides road travelers with their first view of the **trans-Alaska pipeline,** which stretches from the oil fields of Prudhoe Bay on the Arctic Ocean 800 miles south to the port of Valdez. The pipeline is best seen north of town, where it crosses the Tanana River on a bridge. This region has a number of year-round natural springs and better than average subarctic soil that supports potatoes, wheat, barley, oats, and hay.

On the final approach to Fairbanks you will encounter ever-increasing evidence of civilization—an air force base, the town of North Pole, housing developments, and shopping malls. Finally, at Mile 1520, your journey is over. The Alaska Highway is behind you, and Alaska's vast Interior is before you. You can turn north and drive all the way to the Arctic Ocean on the Dalton Highway (see the Arctic Alaska section) or turn south toward Denali National Park, Anchorage, the Kenai Peninsula, and the Pacific Ocean.

■ TAYLOR HIGHWAY   *map page 210, E-4*

The Taylor Highway begins at Tetlin Junction on the Alaska Highway, about 79 miles west of the Canadian border. It leads 161 miles north to the village of Eagle on the Yukon River, with a cut-off east to Dawson City in the Yukon Territory. The Taylor also provides access to the Fortymile National Wild and Scenic River, popular with river rafters, and the Yukon-Charley National Preserve, a 2.2 million-acre area administered by the National Park Service, which maintains an office in Eagle. Like the Denali Highway between Paxson and Cantwell, the Taylor Highway between Tetlin Junction and Eagle enables travelers to get off into the real backcountry of Alaska.

The Taylor Highway (more like an improved logging road) heads north from Tetlin Junction through the **Tanana Valley State Forest,** a scenic area of spruce and birch forest and grassy meadowlands. Look for moose and black bear in this area, especially in the morning and evening hours. At about Mile 35 **Mount Fairplay** (5,541 feet) is visible just to the east—there is a nice turnout where you can stop and take photographs. In days gone by, caribou were plentiful in the Interior and summered on the tundra of Mount Fairplay and other alpine peaks. Their decline was probably due to overhunting.

The once bustling mining town of **Chicken** (pop. 17) is at Mile 64. If you are passing through in the morning, stop in for a hot cinnamon roll and a friendly tour of the ghost town, whose 13 original log buildings include the 1905 schoolhouse.

At Mile 95.7 there is a turnoff to the right for the Canadian border, and the historic town of **Dawson City**. If you continue north, the road steadily climbs toward some beautiful alpine mountains, reaching an altitude of nearly 4,000 feet. Caribou, moose, bear, and Dall sheep can be hunted to the west on **Walcutt Mountain,** an area where all motorized vehicles (off-road vehicles, planes) are prohibited. Past the Walcutt Mountain area, the road more or less plunges down American Creek to Eagle, on the banks of the mighty Yukon River.

■ EAGLE *map page 210, F-3*

Eagle (pop. 129) is an interesting place—a look at the Alaskan bush life in one of the few small communities accessible by road. The accouterments of civilization exist here—gas stations, restaurants, a post office, various stores, a laundromat and shower, motels, cabins, and campgrounds. If the summer mosquitoes were not so bad, and the winters not so cold, dark and interminable, it would probably be a town of 20,000. But this is Alaska, and so the community consists of miners, trappers, dog mushers, and other bush types—some of whom were semi-immortalized by writer John McPhee in his 1972 Alaska classic, *Coming into the Country.* There is much to do here, from fishing and hunting to river-rafting, hiking, and simple sightseeing around town. The **Eagle Historical Society** (907-547-2325) offers a guided walking tour of several of the town's historic buildings, departing from the courthouse every morning at 9 from Memorial Day through Labor Day. One nice trip is a ride on the *Yukon Queen II* riverboat, which goes 100 miles between Dawson City and Eagle (run by Gray Line of Alaska; book in advance by calling 800-544-2206 or, in Alaska, through Gray Line's Anchorage or Fairbanks offices, 907-277-5581 or 907-451-6835 respectively). Planes can be chartered here, as well as rafts. The folks at the Yukon-Charley Rivers National Preserve office (907-547-2233) in Eagle will be happy to show you a video on the preserve, and to recommend activities. The noted nature writer Barry Lopez once visited the Yukon-Charley Rivers Preserve, and wrote a wonderful essay ("Yukon-Charley: The Shape of Wilderness") about his experience in the wild backcountry. Lopez wrote that he was surprised to find no rangers, no trails, no signs of development—only the pure and natural surface of the earth.

Enormous vegetables such as these cabbages grow in the Interior valleys during the summer, aided by warm temperatures and endless daylight.

CLIMBING MCKINLEY

R. D. Caughron was one of America's premier mountaineers, having ascended dozens of major peaks on four continents. Included in his many accomplishments was an international expedition in 1996 to K2 from China. He died in April 2002 at the 7,200-meter mark of Makalu in Nepal, and was buried there, on one of the many mountains he loved. His story of Mount McKinley describes a climb he made in 1980 with two friends, Gerry Dienel and Dean Rau.

From Wonder Lake we're taking stock up to the base of the Muldrow Glacier, or at least as far as the horses and pack animals will go. In my mind, I'm going through the checklist of everything we brought, and our plan—which is to climb the mountain on the north side and go down it on the West Buttress side.

We come to the McKinley River. It's very wide, running fast, and you can't see into it at all. Gerry, my partner from Pennsylvania, heroically makes the first move with his pack unbuckled at the waist loop. Three seconds later, I'm stunned to see Gerry swept away downstream. He's paddling like crazy. Can he make it with his pack? Barely. He clings to the other side about 100 yards downstream. "Come on across!" he shouts. My legs tremble. Dean, our third partner, gives a shout. Here's our two packers. Say, do you mind if we catch a lift across the river? Thank goodness. Now it starts to rain, big time, and the river behind us is rising fast. Oh well, these conditions are what those sourdoughs who did the first ascent of McKinley's north peak from a bar in Fairbanks must have been comfortable with. Right. Gerry's okay, but now several miles farther toward McKinley, we're all equally wet. This is real.

We camp part way to the Muldrow Glacier. It's a beautiful campsite. Green all around. The sun even starts to show itself. Must be around 10 P.M., but who knows in the partial light? Bugs. Everywhere. Biting bugs. Up goes the tent and the bug net. You just have to love this stuff. Spirits are high. What was that for dinner now? Hamburger Helper with what?

DAWN

Dawn looks just like dark. We're up early. Sort of a gobble breakfast. Cold grains and coffee. We go by the packers still encamped, but they pass us by mid-morning. When we get to the moraine our stuff is all out on the ground. Thanks, Curly. See ya. We start to organize our loads. We'll have to make several carries up to where we can go down on the ice and use our sleds. First a cup of coffee. What's that? The stove doesn't work? I pump until the gas can't take any more pressure. Anyone got a match? It still doesn't work. What's that, a leak around the base of the burner? We jump back just in time to watch our stove explode about 30 feet into the air, spinning as it goes. Expletives. We tried both stoves in Anchorage and they worked just fine. Hell, we haven't even gotten to the glacier yet. Can it be fixed? One medical doctor, one Ph.D. in biochemistry, and one M.S. in mechanical engineering, and we give up after five minutes. The stove is absolutely repair proof. Whose idea was it to bring that latest and greatest piece of junk anyway?

We bury the stove. Nothing else to do. We now have one stove, and since our water depends on melting snow, that stove is a critical item in our kit. We cross our fingers. Time to go anyway.

TO THE GLACIER

It's at least a mile and a half to the glacier. We make the trip three times apiece. At last we get all our gear to the overlook. The scenery is awesome. Bright sunny rays through the clouds, highlighting embedded rocks and gravel in the glacier's blue and black ice. Up above you can't see a thing. Cloud. Low hanging cloud at that. It's slippery but we get down to the glacier. It's so wide here, miles and you can see forever. What's this? It's a cache of ski gear left by some Japanese. Just junk, but historical junk. We're awed. I wonder if they made it.

Onward and upward. We come to the first crevasse. Who knows how deep it goes. Don't want to fall in. We rope up. Party of three for the Muldrow Glacier. Looks like we've reserved the entire route. No one, no where. An occasional bird flies overhead. Looks like a vulture. Great, but not really.

We're getting along well. Only one argument settled by an arm wrestling contest, which I lost. Didn't know an orthopedic surgeon could be so strong. Maybe I wasn't trying hard enough? Time to eat something. What was that again, with the Hamburger Helper? Tea. Great.

The weather remains cloudy, but as we head up, hauling our sleds behind us with about 100 pounds each of personal and group equipment, McKinley's sculpted ridges start to emerge through the mist. Wow, it's clearing. My goodness there's our route, all the way to Brown's Tower. Looks like a long way. Looks pretty level, through the ice field. We'll have to switch sides as we head up, but doesn't look like a problem as long as we don't fall into something.

ASCENT

We've come to the up part. A steep slope requires some ice climbing, and a rope. Ever hauled a 50-pound orange plastic sled dangling from a line, up on ice and snow? Great fun. Well, we did it. We even recovered our ice screws we used to protect our ascent. The idea with the sleds is very simple. When the terrain is flatter, or gradual, the weight goes into the sled. When the terrain steepens, the load goes on your back.

What is this? Looks like a big snow cavern. Someone has been here before. We clear enough room to be comfortable. Guess we'll sleep here: What's that smell? Gas fumes. It's our stove. Well, at this altitude the gas doesn't burn completely. But we've no choice. We've only got one small stove, and that's all we've got to make water, which is what we really need desperately. Orange Tang and hot chocolate, that's what we all like best. Looks like we've got about five pounds of drink and 30 pounds of Hamburger Helper. Hum.

Good thing we brought that shovel. Better to have the restroom outside than in the cave. But it's steep around here. Don't slip now. Early morning, for the big push up to Brown's Tower. It's a humper. All the weight is on my back. We move slowly. It

Traversing a Mount McKinley ice field.

takes forever to gain elevation, but we're finally almost there. We round the corner. The scenery is gorgeous. Views as far as the eye can see. A sculpted ice ridge makes me think this is the Himalayas.

Dean, in charge of our orthopedic surgery department, is having a hell of a time with headache. It's the dreaded altitude sickness. Will Dean recover? Will we have to go down fast to save his life? I listen to his chest. No gurgling. Pass the Hamburger Helper. A day passes, and now Dean starts to feel better. Whew!

STORM AND COLD

As we're heading up a large snow valley between the north summit and the true south summit, the wind picks up. It doesn't look good back down the valley toward Talkeetna. Right. Let's build a snowblock cave.

Very nice. Nothing for *Architectural Digest,* but good enough. And the wind does start to howl. The next day (actually it is pretty difficult to tell time here), we decide to keep going up. Big mistake. As we inch our way up this valley in snowshoes, whiteout to whiteout, we're literally pinned down by the wind. We dig in again. This time just enough time to dig a trench and pitch our tent. How many times did we have to get out and shovel snow from around our tent during the storm? Too many times to remember.

We survive. The storm clears, but now there's three feet of powder to navigate through, and the temperature has really dropped. Decision time. It's clear but cold. Really cold. Numbing cold. We inch forward making Windy Gap at 18,000 feet around 11 A.M. What should we do? We look over to see some lumps in the snow. I guess those are the bodies of the German couple that died here and haven't been evacuated yet. Tough to get a helicopter to 18,000 feet I guess. We shiver and move on.

The idea is to stash our stuff and mark the stash with wands so we can find it upon our return. We're going for the top today, tonight, whenever we get there. We move out. No wind. It feels really strange. So cold and clear. A jet, a big commercial passenger liner zooms overhead about 1,000 feet up. That must be a thrill.

THE SUMMIT

It's deep snow. Not hard crust. We plough our way around the 18,000-foot corner. We're laboring really hard, and all three of us have headaches now. It takes forever. We reach the last rise. Looks like a 50-meter slope up to the summit ridge. We're 20 meters up the slope. One of our members announces he's finished and can't make it any farther. The other two of us just bend over and stare at the snow. We insist he go

On the summit of Mount McKinley.

on, and we're pretty emphatic. Either you go up to the top, or we'll carry you up. No way any one of us turning around now. Slowly, painstakingly slowly we reach the summit ridge. Only 75 meters horizontal to go. It's so cold a large ice crystal is hanging from my nose, and I look at Gerry to see rime all around his face. I've got on every piece of clothing I brought with me, including the balaclava I found at Windy Gap, and I'm FREEZING. We're finally there. Hello. Goodbye.

A miniature Czech flag is flying on top of the summit of Mount McKinley. Picture time. Hugs all around. Two minutes go by. We've got the panorama recorded. We turn around and go down the direction we've come. Must be round 5 P.M. The snow is loose and light. It's still a chore to move. We inch forward. A long line appears in the distance. It's a guided party coming up from the West Buttress. Just about the time our paths intersect, we have to turn to head back to our cache. We're freezing. The arctic air mass coming in from over the Pole is about 40 below. The Himalayas are warmer. We've only got about half the oxygen to breathe that one has at sea level, and our heat metabolism is about 50 percent of that at sea level too. This is going to be a struggle.

DESCENT

We do it. We reach our cache. There are those bodies again. Dreadful. Up goes our little tent. Our stove hums away for one cup of water, and after remembering to turn the stove off, we all fall into a deep sleep.

Our route plan is pretty simple. Head down the west side of the mountain to the 17,000-foot-level camp. Down some very steep slopes, windswept and crusty. The going is treacherous, awkward, and we're exhausted. At last, we're on the level above the rocky West Buttress. The slope appears very avalanche prone.

We're greeted as heroes by the climbers in the 14,000-foot camp. All those tents and smiles seem like a return to civilization to us.

Another day. Farewell to our new friends in camp, around Windy Corner and heading down toward the Kahiltna airstrip. As we descend, the view of Mount Foraker is awesome. Mount Hunter and Huntington equally so. The scenery goes on forever. I can see green some 12,000 feet below. Gorgeous. Paradise. We arrive at the Kahiltna Glacier late in the day. I will never eat Hamburger Helper or use snowshoes again in my life! Another group flies in and we fly back to Talkeetna.

After spending days in the numbing whiteness of snow and ice, the valleys never looked so green and inviting.

■ TRAVEL INFORMATION

■ GETTING THERE

The hub of this area is Fairbanks, which is serviced by major air carriers. To reach Fairbanks by car from the Lower 48 via the Alaska Highway, a trip of several thousand miles, see page 187. If you fly into Anchorage, you can reach Fairbanks by driving north on the scenic George Parks Highway, or by taking the train.

■ GETTING AROUND

By Car

Major car-rental companies operate from Fairbanks; rates start around $50 per day, and most offer unlimited mileage. The 358-mile scenic **George Parks Highway** connects Anchorage and Fairbanks and provides access to Denali National Park and Preserve. The **Dalton Highway,** a 400-mile-plus limited-access gravel road from near Fairbanks to Prudhoe Bay, is technically off limits for most rental cars, but a few companies will rent four-wheel drives that are Dalton-approved. For highway snow conditions call the **State Department of Transportation in Fairbanks;** *907-456-7623; www.dot.state.ak.us.*

By Train

From mid-May through mid-September, there is daily passenger service between Anchorage and Fairbanks by way of Talkeetna and Denali National Park (one way $190 peak and $150 off-peak). Off season, the 350-mile run between Anchorage and Fairbanks departs only once a week and costs $140 one-way.

Sunflowers border the road near the town of North Pole, southeast of Fairbanks.

Contact **Alaska Railroad** (907-456-4155 or 800-544-0552; www.akrr.com). The **Midnight Sun Express** (800-426-0500; www.midnightsunexpress.com) is a more luxurious way to take the train from Anchorage to Fairbanks.

By Plane

From Fairbanks it is possible to travel to rural towns and scenic areas by commuter carriers offering intrastate scheduled air service, or by chartered air service provided by local pilots. The Federal Aviation Administration in Anchorage (907-271-2000) has a list of certified air-taxi operations throughout Alaska. The following serve this area:

Frontier Flying Service flies between Anchorage and Fairbanks and more than 30 Interior and Arctic villages. *907-450-7200 or 800-478-6779; www.frontierflying. com.*

Larry's Flying Service flies from Fairbanks to Anaktuvuk Pass, Bettles, Fort Yukon, and a dozen other villages. *907-474-9169; www.larrysflying.com.*

Warbelow's Air Ventures offers service to more than 25 Interior villages, bush mail-plane trips, Arctic Circle tours, hot-springs fly-ins, and sightseeing charters. *907-474-0518 or 800-478-0812; www.warbelows.com.*

Bus Tours

Bus tours of the Interior include excursions to Circle Hot Springs and into the Yukon Territory. Another popular package is a bus excursion into the Arctic following the Dalton Highway from Fairbanks to Deadhorse and crossing the Yukon River, the Arctic Circle, and the Brooks Range en route, then returning to Fairbanks by air.

Alaska Trails. Offering shuttle connections to any point between Anchorage, Denali National Park, Talkeetna, and Fairbanks; pick-up and drop-off privileges go with any ticket. Also same-day travel between Seward and Denali National Park, and travel to Canadian parks. *800-770-2267 or 800-770-7275; www. alaskashuttle.com.*

Gray Line of Alaska. Offerings range from one-day sightseeing to multi-day excursions throughout Alaska and include numerous Denali Sampler packages of varying duration. *907-456-7741 or 888-452-1737; www.graylinealaska.com.*

Northern Alaska Tour Company. Fairbanks-based tour operator offers winter and summer one- to three-day packages to the Arctic, traveling by van or combining van and air, plus an 8-day winter Aurora Adventure and numerous other packages. *Fairbanks, 907-474-8600 or 800-474-1986; www.northernalaska.com.*

■ CLIMATE

Only the Siberian heartland has a more extreme climate than that of the interior valleys of Alaska. In the winter the cold air settles as in a bowl, and week-long spells of 40 or even 50 below zero are not uncommon. When the temperature rises (above 0°) it snows. Spring and fall last about a week in May and September, respectively. July brings warm, even hot, temperatures and occasional thunderstorms.

SUNLIGHT

SUMMER MAXIMUM	SUNRISE	SUNSET	# OF HOURS
Fairbanks	2:59 AM	12:48 AM	21:49
WINTER MINIMUM	SUNRISE	SUNSET	# OF HOURS
Fairbanks	10:59 AM	2:41 PM	3:42

TEMPS (F°)	AVG. JAN. HIGH	LOW	AVG. APRIL HIGH	LOW	AVG. JULY HIGH	LOW	AVG. OCT. HIGH	LOW	RECORD HIGH	RECORD LOW
Denali N.P.	10	-8	38	15	67	42	32	13	94	-60
Fairbanks	-2	-20	40	19	72	52	36	19	99	-66
Fort Yukon	-13	-31	38	17	75	53	33	10	100	-78

PRECIPITATION (INCHES)	AVG. JAN.	AVG. APRIL	AVG. JULY	AVG. OCT.	ANNUAL RAIN	ANNUAL SNOW
Denali N.P.	0.7"	0.4"	3.2"	1.1"	16"	80"
Fairbanks	0.5"	0.3"	2.0"	0.8"	11"	67"
Fort Yukon	0.4"	0.3"	1.1"	0.6"	7"	41"

■ Food, Lodging, & Tours

RESTAURANT PRICES
Per person, without drinks, tax, or tip
$ = under $15 $$ = $15–$25 $$$ = over $25
ROOM RATES
Per room, per night, double occupancy
$ = under $70 $$ = $70–$100 $$$ = over $100

CIRCLE *map page 210, D/E-2*

Population: 100

◆ Lodging

Arctic Circle Hot Springs Resort. Family resort some 135 miles northeast of Fairbanks with an Olympic-size swimming pool, bubbling with hot spring water. Guests can choose from lodge rooms, furnished cabins, or hostel-type (bring your sleeping bag) accommodations. Campers and RVs welcome. Winter activities include cross-country skiing, dogsled rides, and watching the aurora borealis. Small plane landing strip, ice cream parlor, saloon, and restaurant. *Eight miles south of Central, which is at Mile 127.5 of the Steese Highway; 907-520-5113.* **$–$$**

DELTA JUNCTION *map page 210, D-3*

Population: 840
Visitors information: 907-895-5068; 877-895-5068 www.deltachamber.org

◆ Restaurants

Pizza Bella. A taste of Italy, American-style, in the tundra. *Mile 265, Richardson Highway, across from the visitors center; 907-895-4841.* **$**

Rika's Roadhouse. Historic landmark; homemade soups and sandwiches served cafeteria-style. Open only until 5 P.M.; closed mid-September to mid-May. *Mile 275, Richardson Highway; 907-895-4938.* **$**

◆ LODGING

Kelly's Alaska Country Inn. A downtown motel, with clean, modern rooms; kitchenettes available. *1616 Richardson Highway; 907-895-4667; www. kellysalaskacountryinn.com.* $$

DENALI NATIONAL PARK AND PRESERVE *map page 210, A/B-4*

Also see Talkeetna, page 203
Population: 171
Visitors information: 907-683-1266 in summer or 907-683-2294 year-round; www.nps.gov/dena

Talkeetna/Denali Visitors Center. If you're traveling to Denali from Anchorage, this visitors center is an excellent place to make reservations and plans. The helpful staff will show you pictures of accommodations, call ahead and make reservations, and give you practical advice. *At the junction of the George Parks Highway and the Talkeetna Spur Road; 800-660-2688; www.alaskan.com/talkeetnadenali.*

◆ RESTAURANTS

Lynx Creek Pizza. American-style tomato, cheese, and meat pizza. Thick bean and meat (no veggies or rice) burritos. Beer. Checkered tablecloths. Informal and convivial. One mile north of the park entrance. *Mile 238.6, George Parks Highway; 907-683-2547.* $–$$

The Perch. Breakfast, dinner, and packed box lunches are available, all served with home-baked breads and desserts. Many consider this the best restaurant in the area, with large portions and great value for your money. Located 11 miles south of the park entrance, the Perch Resort also has cabins to rent. *Mile 224, George Parks Highway; 907-683-2523 or 888-322-2523; www.denaliperchresort.com.* $–$$

◆ LODGING

Carlo Heights Bed and Breakfast. An appealing modern wood cabin on a hill overlooking a river valley. Comfortable and private. Located 11 miles south of the park entrance. *On private road one mile off Mile 224 of George Parks Highway; P.O. Box 86, Denali, AK 99755; 907-683-1615.* $$

Denali Dome Home Bed & Breakfast. A beautiful, clean home on four levels, open and airy, with a big living room and fireplace. Full breakfast. Jacuzzi and sauna. Open year round. Located 12 miles north of the park entrance, just off the

George Parks Highway at Mile 248.8. *137 Healy Spur Road; 907-683-1239 or 800-683-1239; www.denalidome home.com.* **$$$**

Denali Princess Wilderness Lodge. Overlooking the Nenana River with 440 rooms; shuttle service to park and railroad station; spa, restaurant, and a gift shop on premises. Located a mile from the park entrance, and despite its suggestive name, not exactly a wilderness lodge; it's connected by a long driveway to the main road. *Mile 238.5, George Parks Highway; 907-683-2282 or 800-426-0500; www. denaliprincesslodge.com.* **$$$**

Denali River Cabins and Cedars Lodge. Lovely location on the Nenana River, 54 wood cabins, hot tub, and riverside sauna; 48 standard hotel rooms in the lodge. Located six miles south of the park entrance. *Mile 231.1, George Parks Highway; 800-230-7275; www.denalirivercabins.com.* **$$$**

Healy Heights Family Cabins. Cedar cabins, some with full kitchens, some with fridge, coffeemaker, and microwave. On 12 wooded acres, 12 miles north of the park entrance. Mountain views, serene setting, and outside decks. *Turn at mile 247, George Parks Highway; 907-683-2639; www.healycabins.com.* **$$–$$$**

McKinley Chalet Resort. Most of the 345 rooms are mini-suites. Amenities include restaurants, a bar, the Cabin Dinner Theater, wildlife and natural history tours, and rafting. One mile north of the park entrance. *Mile 239, George Parks Highway; 907-683-8200 or 800-276-7234; www.denaliparkresorts.com.* **$$$**

Perch Resort. Attractive modern cabins off the highway in the forest. Private and shared baths. The resort, 11 miles south of the park entrance, also has a good restaurant. *Mile 224, George Parks Highway; 907-683-2523 or 888-322-2523; www.denaliperchresort.com.* **$$–$$$**

◆ WILDERNESS LODGES

Camp Denali. Log-cabin enclave in the heart of the park, near the end of the park road. Noted for rustic charm, it offers home-cooked meals and spectacular views of Mount McKinley. Resort emphasis is on natural history, education and tranquility. Expert naturalists on staff, leading guided hikes and evening programs. *90 miles west of the George Parks Highway on a private parcel within the park. P.O. Box 67, Denali National Park, AK 99755; 907-683-2290; www.campdenali.com.* **$$$**

Denali Backcountry Lodge. Deep within the park, at the end of the park road in the community of Kantishna. Stays in the 30 cabins (with private baths) include meals as well as activities such as guided hiking trips, wildlife viewing, bicycling, photography, and natural history programs. *Reservations: 410 Denali Street,*

Anchorage, AK 99501; 907-376-1992 or 877-233-6254; www.denalilodge.com. $$$

Denali West Lodge. Spectacular Mount McKinley view, with private log cabins, on Lake Minchumina, just outside the western border of the park. Mush your own dogsled team; trek upland forest and alpine tundra; paddle creeks, rivers and wetland marshes; or photograph wildlife. Package prices include lodging, meals and activities (and winter clothing in winter). *P.O. Box 40AC, Lake Minchumina, AK 99757; 907-674-3112 or 888-607-5566; www.denaliwest.com.* $$$

Kantishna Roadhouse. One of the oldest roadhouses in Alaska, located within the park at the end of the park road. You'll find 30-plus modern cabins, good food three times daily, day hikes with trained naturalists, interpretive evening programs, fishing, wildlife-viewing, and gold panning. *90 miles west of the George Parks Highway on a private parcel within the park. P.O. Box 130, Denali National Park, AK 99755; 907-459-2120 or 800-942-7420; www.kantishnaroadhouse.com.* $$$

North Face Lodge. Comfortable rooms in a modern lodge; North Face is run by the same people who run Camp Denali and located a mile away from it in the heart of the park, 90 miles west of the George Parks Highway. Hiking, canoeing, and fishing all nearby. Flightseeing trips also available, as well as nature walks with a naturalist. Stunning views of Mount McKinley. *P.; www.campdenali.com.* $$$

◆ CAMPGROUNDS

Denali Grizzly Bear Cabins and Campground. Old Alaskan establishment offering tent cabins, hookups, tent sites, and RV hookups, propane, as well as a grocery store and a gift shop. A 6-mile drive to the park entrance. Make reservations early. *Mile 231.1 George Parks Highway; 907-683-2696 or 866-583-2696; www.denaligrizzlybear.com.* $–$$$

McKinley RV Park Campground. True, the campground is right on the busy highway, but it is convenient—both to the park entrance (11.5 miles to the north) and to the adjacent restaurant, gas station and store. *Mile 248.5, George Parks Highway; 907-683-2379 or 800-478-2562.* $

◆ TOURS

Nenana Raft Adventures. Three- to four-hour scenic and whitewater floats on the Nenana River, plus all-day and overnight trips elsewhere in the state. *907-683-7238 or 800-789-7238; www.raftdenali.com.*

FAIRBANKS *map page 210, C-3*

Population: 30,224
Visitors information: 907-456-5774 or 800-327-5774; www.explorefairbanks.com

◆ **Restaurants**

Alaska Salmon Bake. This is a great deal—a huge outdoor barbecue every day in the summer; buffet with grilled halibut, salmon, ribs, baked beans, potato salad, garden and caesar salad, sourdough rolls, blueberry cake, iced tea, lemonade, and other hearty foodstuffs. Everybody stops here at least once, and many people park their RVs overnight in the parking lot nearby. Located inside Pioneer Park (the former Alaskaland), which has a gold rush ambience and an old-fashioned carousel. *Airport Way and Peger Road; 907-452-7274 or 800-354-7274; www. akvisit.com.* **$**

Castle Restaurant. Restaurant, bar, and night club. Dinner only, featuring steak and seafood, a billiard room, and live music after nine. *4510 Airport Road; 907-474-2165.* **$$–$$$**

Chena's. Bar and restaurant with pleasant outside deck, featuring smoked ribs and chicken, top steaks, and Alaska seafood. *4200 Boat Street; 907-474-3644.* **$$–$$$**

Ester Gold Camp Dining Hall. Nightly dinner buffet, including all-you-can-eat crab; lots of food at reasonable prices. Across the parking lot, the immortal Malamute Saloon provides nightly live performances (songs, dance, stories, Robert Service poems). Touristy, but still fun. Open from Memorial Day to Labor Day. Five miles south of Fairbanks at Ester Gold Camp. *Main Street, Ester; 907-479-2500; www.akvisit.com.* **$$**

Gambardella's Pasta Bella. Good Italian food, though often crowded at lunch hour. This eatery at the corner of Second Avenue and Barnette Street downtown has a garden patio in summer and a cozy fireside in winter. *706 Second Avenue; 907-457-4992; www.gambardellas.com.* **$–$$**

Hot Licks Ice Cream. Where college students hang out; serves homemade ice cream, gourmet coffee. *3453 College Road; 907-479-7813; www.hotlicks.net.* **$**

Pike's Landing. Diners can sit on a large deck overlooking the Chena River, in an elegant dining room, or in a casual sports bar. Open for breakfast, lunch, and dinner. *4438 Airport Way; 907-479-7113; www.pikeslodge.com.* **$$–$$$**

Pump House Restaurant. The Pump House is perhaps the in-town restaurant most favored by Fairbanks locals. A great place to hang out in the evening. *Mile 1.3 Chena Pump Road; 907-479-8452; www.pumphouse.com.* **$$–$$$**

Sam's Sourdough Cafe. Excellent breakfasts and hearty lunches and dinners. *3702 Cameron Street; 907-479-0523.* $

Two Rivers Lodge. Probably the best food around Fairbanks—plus a nice folksy atmosphere. A trout lake out in front. *Mile 16, Chena Hot Springs Road; 907-488-6815; tworiverslodge.com.* $$$

◆ LODGING

Captain Bartlett Inn. This midsize hotel with 200 nicely appointed rooms is across the street from Pioneer Park (formerly Alaskaland). Also houses the Dogsled Saloon. *1411 Airport Way; 907-452-1888 or 800-478-7900 inside Alaska, 800-544-7528 outside Alaska; www.captainbartlettinn.com.* $$$

Cloudberry Lookout Bed & Breakfast. An extraordinary log-and-glass structure set on 60 wooded acres just outside Fairbanks; it's a seven-minute drive from the University of Alaska. The four guest rooms are furnished with family heirloom antiques, and each has a private bath. An extensive trail system adjoins the property. Watchtower for superb viewing of the northern lights when visible. Kitchen and laundry facilities available. Rates include full breakfast. *310 Yana; 907-479-7334; www.mosquitonet.com/~cloudberry.* $$

College Inn. Across from the University of Alaska. Nothing fancy, but great prices ($59 single, $69 double, $269 weekly) for clean, no-frills rooms. Friendly local ambience. *700 Fairbanks Street; 907-474-3666.* $$

Fairbanks Princess Riverside Lodge. Located out by the airport, conveniently close to Pike's Landing, a popular watering hole and restaurant. *4477 Pike's Landing Road; 907-455-4477 or 800-426-0500; www.princesslodges.com.* $$–$$$

Seven Gables Inn and Suites. Pleasant accommodations close to the airport, the university campus, and several small shopping centers. The inn has many nice touches, including Jacuzzi baths and delicious breakfasts. *4312 Birch Lane; 907-479-0751; www.7gablesinn.com.* $–$$

◆ WILDERNESS LODGES

Chena Hot Springs Resort. Spa offers winter aurora borealis–watching accommodations and activities that include full-body massages, cross-country skiing, ice fishing, ice skating, and dogsledding. Summer guests can enjoy the endless daylight with camping, picnicking, hiking, horseback riding. The resort also has a restaurant. *65 miles northeast of Fairbanks, at the end of a long paved road bearing the same name; 907-451-8104 or 800-478-4681; http://chena-hotsprings.h993011. serverkompetenz.net.* $$–$$$

◆ **Campgrounds**

Ester Gold Camp. Private campground five miles south of Fairbanks, with clean, comfortable sites to park your RV or set up your tent. At the same location is the Ester Gold Camp Hotel, with rooms for $60 and up. *Main Street, Ester, .5 mile from Mile 351 of the George Parks Highway; 907-452-7274 or 800-354-7274; www.akvisit.com.* **$**

◆ **TOURS**

Arctic Outfitters. Car rentals for the Dalton Highway; caters to independent travelers. During the summer, also operates Dalton Shuttles, scheduled van service between Fairbanks and Prudhoe Bay, which will drop you off at the Arctic National Wildlife Refuge, the Gates of the Arctic National Park, and other destinations. *3820 University Avenue South, Fairbanks; 907-474-3530; www.arctic-outfitters.com.*

Northern Alaska Tour Company. A variety of one-day or multi-day trips, by van or air or a combination, to the Arctic (Prudhoe Bay, Barrow, Nome) and the Brooks Range, depart from Fairbanks. *907-474-8600 or 800-474-1986; www. northernalaska.com.*

Riverboat Discovery. Half-day river cruise; includes tour of an Indian village and mushing demonstration by a sled-dog team. *1975 Discover Drive; 907-479-6673 or 866-479-6673; www.riverboatdiscovery.com.*

KANTISHNA

See Denali National Park, page 262.

TOK & VICINITY *map page 210, E-4*

Population: 1,393
Visitors information: 907-883-5775 summer; 907-883-5887 winter;
www.tokalaskainfo.com

◆ **RESTAURANTS**

Fast Eddy's Restaurant. Good American food—fresh halibut, steaks and potatoes, pizza. *Mile 1313, Alaska Highway; 907-883-4411.* **$**

◆ **LODGING**

Cleft of the Rock Bed & Breakfast. Three rooms in-house and, from mid-May through September, five cabins, set in grove of white spruce. Car battery plug-ins for winter visitors. Warm Christian hospitality. *122 Sundog Trail; 907-883-4219 or 800-478-5646; www.cleftoftherock.net.* **$$–$$$**

Golden Bear Motel & RV Park. The motel has 60 modern rooms with standard amenities; laundry facilities and restaurant on premises. RV park as well. Nothing fancy, but reasonable and convenient. Mile *124.3, Tok Cutoff Highway; 907-883-2561 or 866-883-2561.* **$$-$$$**

■ FESTIVALS AND EVENTS

■ FEBRUARY

Festival of Native Arts, Fairbanks. Native dance groups and artisans come from across Alaska to the University of Alaska Fairbanks for this three-day event; usually held in the latter part of the month. *907-474-6889; www.geocities.com/festivalofnativearts.*

Yukon Quest. Top mushers compete in a 1,000-mile sled-dog race between Fairbanks and Whitehorse (the race starts in Fairbanks in even years, in Whitehorse in odd years). *907-452-7954; www.yukonquest.com.*

■ MARCH

Iditarod Trail Sled Dog Race. Dogs and mushers cross 1,049 miles of tundra, rivers, mountains, and ice-locked sea coast to reach Nome 11 to 15 days later. Festivities include a reindeer potluck and the Iditarod awards banquet at the finish. *Wasilla, Iditarod Trail Headquarters; 907-376-5155; www.Iditarod.com.*

Winter Carnival, North Pole. Events include craft bazaars, music and dancing, a parade, and ice sculptures. *907-488-2242.*

World Ice Art Championships, Fairbanks. Ice carvers from around the world complete in the world's biggest ice-sculpting contest. Watch them work for the first 11 days of the event, then admire the results for the rest of the month. *907-451-8250; www.icealaska.com.*

■ APRIL

Arctic Man Ski & Sno Go Classic, Fairbanks. Competitors ski down a mountain and then are pulled up a neighboring hill by their partners on snowmachines. Even crazier than it sounds, and high-speed wipe-outs are common. *907-456-2626; www.arcticman.com.*

Nenana Ice Classic. Highlight is a lottery where people pay $2 to guess the time the ice breaks (to the day and minute). First prize is a share of the pot—$301,000 in 2004! *970-832-5446; www.nenanaakiceclassic.com.*

■ JUNE

Midnight Sun Baseball Game, Fairbanks. Late-night game played in late June in celebration of the summer solstice, the longest day of the year. *907-451-0095; www.goldpanners.com.*

■ JULY

Fairbanks Summer Arts Festival. Running from late July into early August, this annual festival features music, dance, theater, opera, ice-skating, and various lectures and workshops dedicated to the arts. *907-474-8869; www.fsaf.org.*

Golden Days, Fairbanks. Reenactment of gold being found near Fairbanks in 1902. Five days of fun include Alaska's biggest parade, contests, flower show, the Rubber Duckie Race, and other races. *907-452-1105.*

World Eskimo-Indian Olympics, Fairbanks. Participants compete in a variety of events including the knuckle hop, blanket toss, and ear pulling. *907-452-6646; www.weio.org.*

■ OCTOBER

Oktoberfest, Fairbanks. Held in late September, early October. Not a huge shindig, but fun. Features German food and polka dancing. *907-479-5531.*

■ NOVEMBER

Athabascan Old-Time Fiddling Festival, Fairbanks. Features traditional Native fiddling music, which incorporates Cajun, Scottish, and Appalachian techniques brought by white gold miners. This is the real thing, not a tourist show, with lots of Native villagers in attendance. *907-452-1105.*

THE ARCTIC

The chief quality of the Alaskan Arctic is space. This becomes most evident when you enter the region by air—as most visitors do. Your plane lifts off from a village airstrip that is itself remote. Gradually, you reach cruising altitude, navigating around hills, climbing to thread through passes, descending to cruise above river valleys, all the time advancing over a landscape that has no work of man on it. To the north is the Arctic Ocean; to the west, the Bering Sea and Siberia. The Brooks Range forms the Arctic's southern flank, and what stretches before you as you travel north is spruce taiga, then treeless tundra, and finally, snow- and ice-filled seas.

For most of your flight, as you look down below, you see no cabins, no tents, no boat docks, not so much as one smoke plume from one campfire. Occasionally you will see animals—a black bear feeding on some blueberries beside a lake, looking up annoyed at this buzzing overhead; a great bull moose on a bed of sphagnum moss; a herd of caribou running free and wild over a rolling tundra dome. If it is autumn, the colors will amaze you—the salmon leaves of the blueberry patches, the purple of the spent fireweed, the orange of the dwarf birch, and the yellow of the alpine willow. If it is summer, you will see a thousand variations on the color green. But rarely in your travels in arctic Alaska will you see anything that is connected with the human race.

One road leads into the Arctic from the Interior, and that is the Dalton Highway, which follows the Alaska pipeline north from Fairbanks (see page 276, following). Other roads in the region radiate out several miles from small towns before ending in the bush.

Most of the parks described in this chapter are reached by bush plane. They are, for the most part, without roads, campsites, or visitors centers. Several small arctic towns are worth a visit, if only for the purpose of absorbing their austere isolation. From Nome it's possible to visit and stay overnight in several Eskimo villages, and even to fly over the Bering Strait to spend the night in Siberia.

For listings of airplane companies, wilderness lodges, and accommodations in Arctic towns, see page 307, following.

Lichens, bearberry, and other low plants typical of dry, or alpine tundra.

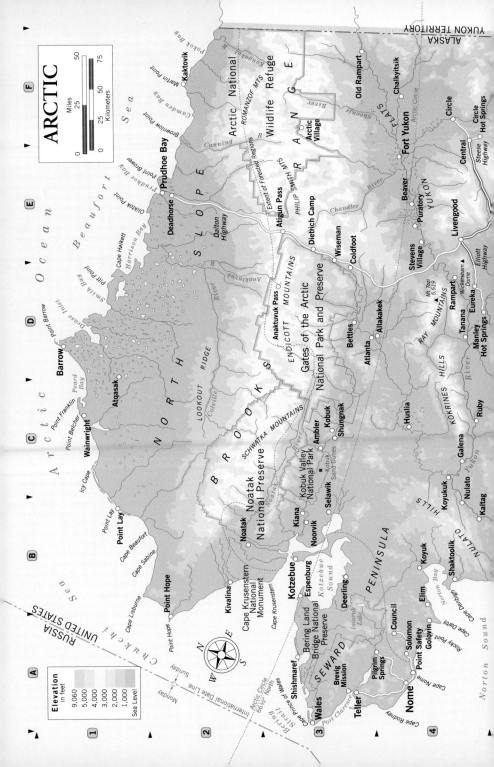

■ LIFE IN THE ARCTIC WILD

Life is difficult for both plants and animals in arctic Alaska. Summer is painfully brief, and winter is triple its length in much of the Lower 48. Everywhere life clings to a tiny foothold, defending that niche with passion and cleverness—from the alpine forget-me-not growing in the lee of a solitary rock that breaks the wind to the grizzly bear retiring to its den every October, fattened by a summer of feeding. People live along rivers and along the coasts, relying on the fish and the animals drawn to water. Vast areas have no people in them at all. There is much nobility and mystery here: in the way an arctic blossom courageously blooms, despite being half-buried in an early snow; in the hair-raising howl of the wolf down the valley, letting you know it has smelled your campfire; and in the delicate play of the northern lights among the stars of the constellation we call Ursa Major.

One place to hide out in during the long, cold Arctic nights is the local saloon.

ARCTIC SEASONS

Nick Jans is a writer who spent 20 years in Ambler, an Inupiat Eskimo village of 350 people located 50 miles north of the Arctic Circle and 200 miles from the nearest road.

It's not much—a single willow leaf, yellow, curled at the edges. The early August sun rests warm on my back as I work outside the cabin, and white-crowned sparrows flicker through the trees. Forty miles to the east, a thunderhead billows against the dreamwashed bulk of Old Man Mountain. But the leaf knows the truth, and so do I. Summer's over.

It's hard to believe, looking at this vibrant green landscape, that it will burn bright, fade, and drift into snow, all in just three weeks. Arctic seasons blow open and shut like doors in the wind; the change is startling, something I've never gotten used to. There's often a single week you can point to, sometimes a day, that marks an edge.

Still, the old joke about the two Arctic seasons, winter and fall, is off base. Ambler may be among Alaska's cold spots (four winters ago, we held between 40 and 70 below zero for 21 days straight), but you'd never guess that from the almost tropical intensity of a midsummer day. From late May to early August, the sun hardly sets, carving an elliptical path above the horizon. Frost can hit on the Fourth of July—

A yellow birch leaf rests on a bed of bearberry leaves (red), lingonberry leaves (green broadleaf), and the pine-like leaves of crowberry that carpet the Arctic landscape.

this is, after all, the Arctic—but eighty degrees on a cloudless day isn't unusual, and 90s aren't out of the question.

Then there are the manic extremes of light: near total darkness to unending day in just six months, then back again. The whole damn village goes haywire in late spring. Friends drop in to visit at midnight; second graders stagger into school bleary-eyed, bragging they "never sleep yet." You can't blame me, a few years ago, for shooting my alarm clock full of holes.

After the frantic bustle of spring, summer life in Ambler turns languid. High schoolers play basketball outside at 2 A.M.; the women pick berries; men set out at midnight to hook sheefish. The only ones exerting much energy are the kids. Sunbrowned and wearing shorts, they ride bikes, play games, and cool off in the Kobuk's bone-chilling waters.

But from the heady week of solstice, when the sun never sets, the light keeps falling away. At first it's just a minute a day, but the pace quickens, the midnight twilights deepen. Winter's coming, though the sun burns down and fireweed blooms.

By mid-August, night is dark enough for stars, and the morning tundra creaks with frost. "Falltime," people say. "Time to get busy." The men set out hunting for caribou and bear. The women fish in earnest, endless cycles of checking net, cutting and drying. It's time, too, to gather cranberries, wild rhubarb, and masru, Eskimo potato. In the still, luminous days between the first cold rains, the cry of wild geese echoes down the sky.

Meanwhile, school's started. Trapped inside, I can't help staring out across the flats, where each leaf blazes red and gold. To the west, snow squalls pile against the Jades, then clear in brilliant rifts of blue.

I rush home, throw my gear together, and head out on the river. If anyone asks why, I don't have a good reason. Sometimes I run downstream a few miles and sit on a high bank, listening to the river, facing into the sun. I know it's only winter coming, but I find myself saying goodbye to all the bright things of this world, to the time that, just a month ago, seemed to last forever.

Leaves fade and fall; shelf ice reaches out into the current, sealing away the water into hard silence, more each day as the river cools, until, sometime in October, only a few steaming runs remain. I watch them close one by one, and feel myself settling with the land, drifting down into the cold, white dream. Far to the south, the sun leans against the Waring Mountains. I open my hand and let it go.

–Nick Jans, *A Place Beyond,* 1996

■ FAIRBANKS TO ARCTIC OCEAN: DALTON HIGHWAY

The Dalton Highway officially begins north of Fairbanks at Mile 73.1 of the Elliott Highway and continues over 414 miles of unpaved road to Deadhorse, near Prudhoe Bay on the Arctic Ocean. It is a true adventure, a pilgrimage of continual discovery through the last really wild corner of the United States.

■ PREPARING FOR THE JOURNEY

Before you get started, be sure to stop at the **Bureau of Land Management** (1150 University Avenue; 907-474-2200 or 800-437-7021) office in Fairbanks to obtain the latest information on the road—forest fires, truck or bus accidents, pipeline problems, avalanches, inclement weather, and mud slides can close the road for days. The **Alaska Public Lands Information Center** (250 Cushman Street; 907-456-0527) is another good stop for information. If you are interested—as many are—in fishing and hunting along the Dalton Highway, also make a stop at the **Alaska Department of Fish & Game** (1300 College Road; 907-459-7213) or at any sporting goods store for the necessary licenses; you can also dial 907-459-7385 for some friendly recorded advice on hot spots. North of the Yukon River, only bow-and-arrow hunting is permitted within five miles of the Dalton Highway, a fact that has created a game-rich corridor (bow-hunter certification card necessary).

When I made my trip up the Dalton Highway, I took all of the ordinary precautions. In the back of my Subaru station wagon, I packed as many tools and spare parts as I could, from crescent wrenches to needle-nosed pliers, battery-operated tire pumps to reinforced tow-straps, fuses to air hoses, alternator belts to spark plugs. There were also two full-sized, wheel-mounted spare tires (the Dalton has few services and you are practically guaranteed at least one flat tire) and four five-gallon gas containers, as well as enough food and bottled water for two weeks—not to mention hip-waders, shovels, winter clothing, spare cameras, and enough ammunition to bring meat into camp for years, if necessary. Most rental contracts specify the

Coldfoot road sign speaks for itself.

The Dalton Highway follows the trans-Alaska pipeline for much of the distance from Fairbanks to Prudhoe Bay.

vehicle cannot be taken off the paved road, and the Dalton currently is not paved, but a few rental agencies (Hertz, for instance, and Arctic Outfitters) will rent four-wheel drives specifically for the Dalton Highway. Always drive slowly and always pull over for trucks (to save your windshield). Expect snow at any time of the year and carry tire chains.

■ ALONG THE PIPELINE
For much of its length, the Dalton Highway runs parallel to the trans-Alaska pipeline, which is owned and operated by the Alyeska Pipeline Service Company. The Dalton, originally known as the "Haul Road," was built, as the name suggests, to haul construction materials for the pipeline and the massive Prudhoe Bay oil fields. Construction began in 1974, and for the next two decades it was a private road, closed to the public. A bitter lawsuit, fought all the way to the Supreme Court, opened it for general use in 1994; it then officially became the Dalton, part of the Alaska highway system, although many Alaskans still use the original name. As you drive, you'll notice the pipeline is elevated on metal support structures—

this keeps the pipe from making contact with the permafrost, the permanently frozen ground that is synonymous with arctic Alaska. If the permafrost were to melt, pipeline supports could shift and 30-inch pipes might suddenly start spewing their hot contents on the pristine arctic tundra. Fortunately, spills have occurred only a few times—and each time the mess has been quickly cleaned up.

■ **FAIRBANKS TO THE YUKON RIVER** *map page 272, D-4*

For the first 55 miles, from Fairbanks to the Yukon River, the Elliott Highway (which connects to the Dalton) traverses gentle hill-and-valley country, densely forested with white spruce, quaking aspen, and paper birch. Only occasionally will you see evidence of human civilization—normally related to gold dredging and mining operations, some historic, some still active. Note that access to any of the active mines is considered trespassing.

More and more, you are leaving civilization behind. On Wickersham Dome (Mile 29.7) —many of these gently rounded, glacier-sculpted mountains are known as "domes"—there is a pullout and several nice trails on the tundra (with good blueberry picking each August). You can often spot black bears and moose in this area near dawn and dusk, as well as the occasional coyote, fox, grizzly, or wolf.

A pullout above the **Yukon River Bridge** (Mile 56) is a nice place to stop, stretch your legs, and meditate on one of the world's great rivers. The Yukon is Alaska's largest and oldest river, the fifth-longest on the continent, and the 20th-longest on the planet. King, silver, and chum salmon arrive here in July to spawn where they themselves were born, after having traveled here from the Bering Sea, 1,000 river miles away. During the most recent ice age, the Yukon's valley was an ice-free refuge and a travel corridor for early man as well as many species of plants and animals. The turbid, roiling river drains an immense area; when you look at that 2,300-foot-long steel girder bridge, you comprehend something of the huge volume of water traveling beneath it toward the Bering Sea. Prior to the bridge's construction—which was an expensive and major obstacle on the Dalton Highway—earth-moving equipment and supply trucks had to be ferried across the Yukon River in hovercraft.

The gas station and tire repair shop on the north side of the Yukon bridge is one of the last on the highway—be forewarned. Also available at the crossing are a restaurant, motel, phone, and emergency communications; east of the highway, there's a campground. The **Yukon Crossing Visitor Contact Station** here is operated seven days a week, June through August.

A vivid Arctic sunset illuminates the fall sky.

■ NORTH OF THE YUKON RIVER *map page 272, D/E-3*

After crossing the Yukon, the Dalton Highway climbs through more tumbled hill-and-valley country—similar to that on the southern approach—until, gradually, forests give way to grassy meadowlands and tundra.

At Mile 98 you pass by **Finger Mountain,** which is distinguished by its many exposed rock escarpments, or tors. Nearby are thermokarst lakes (meltwater pooled over permanent ice fields) as well as soft mounds in which tundra vegetation covers glacial sand, old dune fields, or ice blocks. Ten or 12 thousand years ago, this landscape would have had woolly mammoths and steppe bison on it. Forty million years earlier Alaska was closer to the equator, and dinosaurs roamed the valley. Fossils from both periods abound in the area.

■ CROSSING THE ARCTIC CIRCLE *map page 272, D-3*

According to an old Alaska saying, "There's no law above the Yukon River, and no God above the Arctic Circle." The Arctic Circle is crossed at Mile 115.3. There is a pullout here and a campsite (many people stop to photograph the nice view to the west)—but to my way of thinking, the Arctic does not truly begin until you leave behind the last upright tree, and that does not occur until you reach the Chandalar Shelf at about Mile 236.

By about Mile 166, you are driving in the valley of the **Middle Fork of the Koyukuk River.** This is historic country, scattered with deserted gold claims and cabins from the 1900s; many of the area's residents are descendants of these early settlers and local Natives. Famed outdoorsman Robert Marshall, founder of the Wilderness Society, explored this country in the 1930s and 1940s, later writing his influential books *Arctic Village* and *Alaskan Wilderness.*

Coldfoot, a village with a 3,500-foot airstrip, is at Mile 175. This is the last place before the Arctic coast where you can take on fuel or get some hot food not cooked over a campfire. Its amenities include several motels, a 24-hour restaurant, a store, trading post, launderette, gas station, emergency medical service, and the most northerly saloon in North America. The **Arctic Interagency Visitor Center** (907-678-5209) in Coldfoot, run jointly by the National Park Service, the BLM,

Beyond the Arctic Circle, a trackless expanse of snow-white snow—the quintessential Arctic landscape.

and the U.S. Fish and Wildlife Service—basically everything to the west for 400 miles is national park or preserve—is open from June through Labor Day to answer travelers' questions; it also has permanent exhibits on the Arctic landscape and offers evening slide programs.

Wiseman is passed at Mile 188.6. Robert Marshall spent some time here living among and writing about the lives of its inhabitants. Today, about 25 people live year-round in the Wiseman area.

Once past the Chandalar Shelf, you are really in arctic country. From Mile 194 is a view to the north of Sukakpak Mountain, the traditional boundary between Inupiat Eskimo and Athabaskan Indian territories. At Mile 236.8 you pass the last white spruce. The tree is less than six inches wide a foot from the ground, and yet is several hundred years old—slow growing this far north. The climb up through the Brooks Range to Atigun Pass (Mile 244.7) is long, arduous, and potentially dangerous. Keep your eyes open for oncoming trucks, which may, if their brakes give out on the far side, need quite a bit of road in order to navigate a tight turn. And remember, all this is on loose gravel, which has a way of lengthening braking distances. On top of Atigun Pass you can expect to see Dall sheep right by the road.

In summer, **Atigun Valley** is covered in varying shades of green, opening to the wide expanse of the arctic coastal plain beyond. You can spot Dall sheep here, and, if the migration coincides with your visit, hundreds, even thousands, of barren-ground caribou, as well as the occasional grizzly bear or wolf. It's difficult to believe, but true, that for more than 10,000 years people have made their living in this land, which has no upright trees or natural shelter from the elements.

The rest of the journey features an enormous tundra plain with gorgeous skies and limitless vistas. Try doing as local animals do, and travel in the bright summer evenings. The light can be magical. If it is early summer, you will encounter more and more caribou as you approach the coast. This is their summer range, and they prefer to be as close to the water as possible. For insect relief they actually stand in rivers. If you forget your insect repellent, you may be inclined to join them. You will also encounter large numbers of songbirds and waterfowl who happily devour the same insects that mammals are trying to escape from. The road ends at Mile 414. You are in the vicinity of Deadhorse, which is associated with the Prudhoe Bay operation. (For more on facilities here, see page 312.) The best thing about turning around at this point is that you get to see it all again.

■ GATES OF THE ARCTIC NATIONAL PARK
AND PRESERVE *map page 272, D-3*

For quite a stretch on the Dalton Highway north of Wiseman, the Gates of the Arctic National Park is only 5 miles west of the road. But for the foreseeable future, that is as close as you can get by car to this 8 million-acre national park. For the most part, travel into the park is limited to bush plane charters, most commonly out of Bettles or Kotzebue (see page 307). Catching a bush mail plane from Fairbanks to the Eskimo village of Anaktuvuk Pass will also put you in the center of some breathtaking country. Popular drop-off points include Wild Lake and near the headwaters of any of six National Wild Rivers that course through the park— the Alatna, John, Kobuk, Noatak, North Fork of the Koyukuk, and the Tinayguk. The number of possible hiking or float trips is close to infinite. Inflatable rafts, collapsible kayaks, or pack canoes (all of which can be carried inside aircraft) are the choices of most experienced travelers. A typical scenario involves being flown to the upper stretches of a river and traveling downstream anywhere from 50 to several hundred miles, taking side hikes or backpacking excursions as opportunities present themselves. It's often possible to take out at a downstream village and catch a mail plane, thereby saving the considerable cost of a pick-up charter.

Probably the biggest attraction in the park, other than the actual Gates of the Arctic between Frigid Crags and Boreal Mountain (names supplied by the intrepid, tireless, and sometimes melodramatically inclined Robert Marshall), are the **Arrigetch Peaks,** reached via a floatplane trip to Circle Lake west of Bettles. These abrupt granite spires lure a few mountain- and rock-climbers. To the north are lovely mountain lakes, scattered cottonwoods, and a vast wilderness of pale-green tundra.

My sole excursion into Gates of the Arctic National Park occurred just south of Atigun Pass on the Dalton Highway and consisted of a long pack over **Oolah Pass,** a popular cross-country walk en route to the park. If you've ever hiked on tundra overlying permafrost, you can picture the following scenario—a man and woman, each with an 80-pound pack, surrounded by a cloud of mosquitoes, trying to hike on a moving waterbed (water-logged tundra is anything but stable) while keeping an eye out for tussocks (grass clumps that can pitch you to the ground) and grizzly bears. The scenery may be out of this world, but the going is rough, and only for the hardy, experienced, and well-equipped.

A landscape typical of Gates of the Arctic National Park. Here a crystal-clear river cuts through the Schwatka Mountains.

■ ARCTIC NATIONAL WILDLIFE REFUGE
map page 272, F-2/3

Rivers run clear and cold over smooth beds of cobblestone, with even the deepest pools as transparent as glass. Wildflower beds extend for miles toward glaciers, glacial lakes, and quiet bogs of sphagnum moss. Birds fly across the tundra in massive flocks like something out of the dawn of creation. Caribou and wolves wander, and brilliant green northern lights flicker over a snow-covered valley. This is the Arctic National Wildlife Refuge, the largest wildlife refuge in the world, which extends from the Canadian border more than 250 miles west to the Dalton Highway and south from the Arctic Ocean hundreds of miles to the foothills above the Yukon River. Notably moved by his visit here, Edward Abbey wrote:

> Well, I'm thinking, now I'm satisfied. Now I've seen it, the secret of
> the riddle of the Spirit of the Arctic—the flowering of life, of life
> wild, free and abundant, in the midst of the hardest, cruelest land on
> the northern half of Earth.

Moose cow and calf, common sights in this part of the world.

Most visitors enter ANWR by air charter via Fort Yukon, Bettles, or Kaktovik on Barter Island. Such trips are expensive and often delayed because of weather problems. My own introduction to ANWR occurred rather unexpectedly, when one of my graduate students invited me on a hunting trip. We flew together to Fort Yukon on a commercial prop plane, then transferred our gear to a bush plane, a two-seat Piper Super Cub. One at a time, we were ferried north a hundred miles to the mountains west of the Sheenjek River. The pilot landed quite literally on top of a nameless mountain in a maneuver I will never forget—a controlled crash, throttle just above stall. At the last minute, I muttered some sort of quick prayer in which I made a number of heartfelt promises about being a good person in the service of noble causes. We came to a halt, wings bobbing back and forth and caribou scattering out of the way. (Our widely respected pilot died at the controls of his plane two months later in the Yukon Flats National Wildlife Refuge, as did a U.S. Fish and Wildlife Service biologist riding in the back seat.)

We spent five days hunting there. It rained the whole time (thank God it didn't snow), and I must say the trip was unlike anything else in my experience. Images

Migrating caribou in the Arctic region.

BUSH ETIQUETTE

Bush residents are generally helpful and friendly, but may seem distant in dealing with an outsider. Being relaxed, smiling, and polite goes a long way. Being overly loud or inquisitive is frowned on by many Native people; long comfortable silences often punctuate everyday conversation. By no means brag of your own recent exploits; listen instead. Always ask permission before pointing a camera at someone or exploring an apparently deserted cabin or fish camp. If you find yourself in the presence of people who make it clear they resent outsiders, withdraw as gracefully as possible and move on to the next experience. Be aware that some Native villages actively encourage visitors, while some just as actively discourage them. Most are somewhere in the middle. Ask around in advance.

Out on the river, approaching a Native camp with a friendly wave and a smile can often lead to an invitation to stop for coffee or a shared meal—and a truly memorable experience. People who sometimes won't give you the time of day in town are often expansive hosts to fellow travelers, in the best bush tradition. But if things seem busy or you feel ignored, take the hint. Subsistence fishing or hunting is serious work, and folks may not have time to chat with strangers.

Lower sections of the Kobuk, Noatak, and Koyukuk rivers sometimes are quite busy with local motorboat traffic and camps. Accept the occasional floating Pepsi can as part of the reality in modern bush Alaska. While it may seem wilderness to you, the rivers are the local highways between villages. Relax and enjoy the traffic as part of the local ambiance. If it's a more remote, secluded experience you seek, spend as much time as possible off the main rivers, backpacking or floating one of the many remote tributary valleys.

–Nick Jans

of that trip will always linger—the rock ptarmigan huddling in the lee of a wind-flagged spruce at timberline, the river otter that wandered into camp one day, the grizzly I encountered as I was packing the caribou meat from the kill site to camp. The bear approached at a leisurely but determined walk to a distance of about 30 yards. I took off my pack and fired one round into the tundra in front of it, and it ambled off at the same measured, dignified pace in the other direction. After all, there was a steaming pile of viscera to be had for free back at the kill site.

My second visit to ANWR was less exciting, but no less spectacular in terms of the scenery. I simply walked east from the Dalton Highway in the vicinity of the lower Atigun Canyon. This little adventure gave me a vivid sense of the arctic coastal environment and of the foothills that are so important to wildlife in the area, especially caribou. More than 130,000 caribou comprise the Porcupine Caribou Herd, which has been at the center of a long-running debate over oil and gas exploration and development on the coastal plain.

■ BROOKS RANGE COMMUNITIES

North of the Arctic Circle, villages are few and far between. They are extremely important to the wilderness traveler, for they provide airstrips, river access, last-minute supplies, and reliable communications in the event of an emergency. As in other bush areas of Alaska, life proceeds at a slow and relaxed pace in these remote villages, a laid-back ambience that can come as quite a shock to the visitor. In the bush, appearances are considered far less important than function. Today's oil drum is tomorrow's wood stove—a sort of philosophy that pervades the lives of most residents, Native and non-Native alike.

■ AMBLER   *map page 272, C-3*
This Inupiat village of 309 on the upper Kobuk offers a small, comfortable (if expensive) lodge and restaurant, well-stocked village stores, and an expertly run flying service connecting to neighboring villages as well as Fairbanks. Ambler and its sister village upriver, Shungnak, are famous for their hand-crafted birch-bark baskets. It's often possible to arrange in both places for fish trips, drop-offs, or boat rides on the main Kobuk River, though regular guided services are nonexistent.

■ ANAKTUVUK PASS   *map page 272, D-3*
Anaktuvuk Pass has the most beautiful setting of any bush village in Alaska. Located 260 miles northwest of Fairbanks in the central Brooks Range, it sits on a broad divide between the John River, which drains south, and the Anaktuvuk River, which drains north. The last remaining settlement of the Nunamuit or inland Inupiat Eskimo, Anaktuvuk Pass is an area of unusual historic importance to the Inupiat. For untold ages, the arctic caribou have used the wide pass in their

Anaktuvuk Pass, nestled in the heart of the Brooks Range some 260 miles northwest of Fairbanks, has one of the most beautiful settings of any bush village in Alaska.

annual migrations, and it is here the Eskimo once waited for their prey. Even today, the Natives use the area for subsistence hunting, though they have set their nomadic traditions aside for village life. Direct scheduled airline flights from Fairbanks to Anaktuvuk are available on a regular basis, which makes the village one of the most accessible in Arctic Alaska. The Gates of the Arctic National Park and Preserve's **Anaktuvuk Pass Ranger Station** (907-661-3520) is in the village, as are a restaurant and a no-frills public campground.

■ ARCTIC VILLAGE   *map page 272, F-3*
Arctic Village is located about 100 miles northwest of Fort Yukon and provides a jumping-off point for explorations of the central Brooks Range; popular destinations include the Wind River, the Philip Smith Mountains, and the headwaters of the Sheenjek River. A direct air charter to Arctic Village can be obtained from Fairbanks, about 300 miles to the south; mail plane service is generally cheaper

unless you're loaded with gear. The village maintains a cabin for overnight visitors and offers guided one-day tours by prior arrangement, but little else in the way of facilities is available. Unless you're part of a tour, staying here is not recommended. The village maintains jurisdiction over a 1.4 million-acre reservation, where hunting and fishing can be pursued only with a tribal permit, which is rarely granted to outsiders; inquire in advance. (See page 309.)

■ **BETTLES** *map page 272, D-3*
Located nearly 200 air miles northwest of Fairbanks, Bettles is best known as the main jumping-off point for the 7.9 million-acre Gates of the Arctic National Park and Preserve to the north. Visitors also use the town as a base of operations for summer fishing and autumn hunting trips, as well as for winter dogsled excursions. There are a number of large national wildlife refuges nearby (Kanuti, Yukon Flats, Nowitna, Koyukuk, and Selawik), as well the Kobuk Valley National Park to the west. Overnight accommodations are available in Bettles, and there are state and federal offices representing wildlife and land management agencies. A number of outfitters operate out of Bettles. Regular air service to Bettles is offered from Fairbanks.

■ **KIANA** *map page 272, B-3*
This Eskimo village on the middle Kobuk, once a gold mining camp, offers a picturesque mountain setting at the mouth of the Squirrel River. Facilities include two well-stocked stores; a local flying service; two Native-run guiding operations offering riverboat trips, fishing, and wildlife viewing; and a lodge a few miles east of town.

■ **SHUNGNAK AND KOBUK** *map page 272, C-3*
These two Eskimo villages on the upper Kobuk River, just eight river miles apart, are common take-out places for float trips on the upper Kobuk. Below Kobuk, the current slows and motor skiff and low-flying aircraft traffic can be heavy at times. Both villages offer small stores and gasoline sales. Overnight accommodations are available by prior arrangement in Shungnak, as are informally arranged boat rides, drop-offs, and fishing trips. Inquire at the City Office, at stores, or along the waterfront.

■ ARCTIC COAST COMMUNITIES

■ BARROW   *map page 272, D-1*

Asking a resident of Anchorage if he's ever been to Barrow is like asking a resident of Santiago, Chile, if he's been to the South Pole. The setting in which Barrow (pop. 4,581) goes about its business is austere, to say the least: vast, treeless, bushless tundra near a gravel beach at the edge of the Arctic Ocean. The ground is usually frozen and covered with snow, or, if the permafrost melts, slushy. Author Annie Dillard, in her essay "An Expedition to the Pole," described the surrounding Arctic Coast as a land of icebergs and water and cold blue sky. Winter is almost a fulltime season here, and the brief green of summer is an anomaly in an otherwise cold and dark landscape.

Eighty years ago, Barrow was a traditional Eskimo settlement; 30 years ago it was traditional and poor but modernizing, with few outsiders. Twenty years ago revenues from the trans-Alaska pipeline began flowing into the coffers of the governing borough, itself the center of Inupiat business and government for a huge section of the Arctic. Traditional Eskimo life has diminished since, and tribal members now receive shares of oil revenues, though most still hunt and fish. There's a bleak, wind-blasted rawness to the place—a sprawl of prefabricated buildings, with yards dominated by drying caribou hides and machinery in every state of repair. There is also a beautiful, modern school that—as in most bush communities—has become the center of community life. People are often pointedly unwelcoming of outsiders, but the cachet of visiting the northernmost community in the Western Hemisphere still brings a steady flow of visitors—and it *is* a unique experience. Where else can you see polar bears roaming the edge of town, scavenging whale carcasses? Hunting of the endangered bowhead whale, carefully monitored, is an ancient and ongoing tradition that the local people fiercely defend.

An ongoing source of public debate is whether or not Barrow will remain "damp" (no alcohol sold locally) or become "wet," as it once was. Critics point out that there has been little actual reduction in the availability of booze, thanks to local bootleggers. Every few years petitions are circulated by pro-alcohol forces and brought to a public vote; so far the consensus has been to retain the "damp" status. If you want a drink, you'd better bring it with you.

A more recent and far more volatile issue concerns the plans of oil companies to develop the vast NPRA (National Petroleum Reserve-Alaska). As the Prudhoe Bay fields continue to decline, the pressure to open new areas to exploration and drilling has continued to build. Unfortunately, some of the choice areas for such industrial activity are centered on the Barrow people's ancient hunting, fishing, and subsistence-gathering sites, such as Teshukpuk Lake, where many residents hunt caribou. Permits are now in place to explore for oil offshore, which raises for some the specter of a disastrous spill in the shifting pack ice of the Arctic Ocean. The people of Barrow, who have benefited for so long from oil drawn from distant wells, are now facing the very real possibility of having drilling pads almost literally in their back yards—on land that is their ancestral domain and yet technically under the jurisdiction of the federal government.

Scheduled and extremely expensive daily jet airline service to Barrow is available from Fairbanks, and a taxi driver (probably an immigrant who can't wait to get

The treeless city of Barrow, which lies haphazardly along the shores of the Arctic Ocean.

A whalebone arch (top) designates Point Barrow, the northernmost point of the United States. The Inupiat blanket toss (above), now a ritual presentation, formerly was employed to enable hunters to spot game above the flat and desolate landscape. Ceremonial drummers perform in Barrow (right).

home again) can take you from Barrow Airport to the Top of the World Hotel. If you come in summer, bring eyeshades and earplugs, so you can get to sleep. Otherwise, you'll be kept awake by children playing, ATVs roaring around, and dogs barking outside in the sunlight of midnight. There are several restaurants in Barrow (see page 310), and those are invariably the northernmost places in America where you can eat or drink whatever you are eating or drinking there (for example, the Mexican cuisine at the venerable Pepe's North of the Border). A tour company will take you down to the beach in a four-wheel-drive vehicle to see the Arctic Ocean, possibly a polar bear, and a monument to humorist Will Rogers and aviation pioneer Wiley Post, who both died here in an airplane accident in 1935.

■ **PRUDHOE BAY** *map page 272, E-2*
Prudhoe Bay is the center of operations of the Alyeska Pipeline Service Company, which sends the oil drilled here south via the trans-Alaska pipeline to the coastal town of Valdez, where the crude is then piped onto oil tankers. In his book *Arctic Dreams,* Barry Lopez writes about his journey to this stark landscape, now tamed by the region's major industry:

> I look up at Pump Station #1, past the cyclone fencing and barbed wire. The slogging pumps sequestered within insulated buildings on the tundra, the fields of pipe, the roughshod trucks, all the muscular engineering, the Viking bellows that draws and gathers and directs— that it all runs to the head of this seemingly innocent pipe, lined out like a stainless-steel thread toward the indifferent Brooks Range, that it is all reduced to the southward journey of this 48-inch pipe, seems impossible.
>
> No toil, no wildness shows. It could not seem to the chaperoned visitor more composed, inoffensive, or civilized.

Public access to the Prudhoe Bay oil fields is limited. In recent years a number of tour companies have offered packaged bus tours via the Dalton Highway. Accommodations are available in Deadhorse (see page 312).

A tundra pond near Kotzebue ringed by cotton grass in bloom. Its root clumps produce unstable tussocks, dreaded by hikers.

■ SEWARD PENINSULA COMMUNITIES

■ KOTZEBUE   *map page 272, B-3*

The Eskimo community of Kotzebue, located 26 miles above the Arctic Circle on Kotzebue Sound, north of the Seward Peninsula, is an important regional town providing access to the Kobuk Valley National Park, Bering Land Bridge National Preserve, Cape Krusenstern National Monument, Noatak National Preserve, and the western sections of Gates of the Arctic National Park and Preserve. The National Park Service maintains an office (907-442-3760 for visitor information in summer; 907-442-3890 at other times) in Kotzebue, and park managers will assist travelers in planning a journey in the parklands. Kotzebue is serviced by jet from Nome and Anchorage; a number of bush flying services offer transportation to the vast, lightly traveled wilderness areas that make up virtually the entire surrounding landscape.

Kotzebue is a town of roughly 3,500 people (with another 4,200 living in nearby villages). Though the vast majority of the population consider themselves Inupiat Eskimo, it is, like most larger Alaska bush communities, a cultural melting

SMALL ADVENTURES

And I think over again
My small adventures
When from a shore wind I drifted out
In my kayak
And thought I was in danger.
My fears,
Those small ones
That I thought so big,
For all the vital things
I had to get and to reach.
And yet, there is only
One great thing,
The only thing:
To live to see in huts and on journeys
The great day that dawns
And the light that fills the world.

–Kitlinguiharmiut, or Copper Eskimo, song,
recorded and translated by Knud Rasmussen, *The Report of the Fifth Thule
Expedition, 1921–1924, the Danish Expedition to Arctic North America*

pot in the throes of modernization. The town itself is a hodge-podge of prefab steel buildings, cookie-cutter houses, and plywood shacks, all circled by the trappings of 21st-century subsistence lifestyle: snowmobiles, boats, sleds (both current and yesteryear's forgotten models), and animal parts in various stages of decomposition. While traditional Inupiat ways are still practiced by some, the affectations of hip-hop culture and the NBA are often equally visible. Thirty years ago, this was a sprawling Native village with at best two or three pickup trucks in town; now there are dozens of vehicles and even occasional traffic jams. The rutted, dusty, muddy, icy trails that passed on the map for avenues are being paved one by one, and the town's first traffic signal was recently erected. Compared with Nome, Kotzebue feels more like a large village than a small city: there's a rough, untrammeled atmosphere to the place, and like Barrow, it is unarguably unique. Although it's not a tourist destination in the usual sense of the word, just being here informs the mind and senses; visitors will find many of the amenities of town life, including a modern hotel, restaurants, stores, and a bank. During the summer the sun does not set for 36 continuous days.

■ **NOME**   *map page 272, A-4*

Surrounded by treeless arctic tundra, Nome is located on the southeastern corner of the Seward Peninsula north of Norton Sound. Nome supposedly got its name when an early cartographer, unsure what to call this remote spot, wrote on an early map: "NAME?" Later a draftsman copied this out as "Nome." Today the city's motto is, "There's No Place Like Nome."

Nome (pop. 3,505) has long been a major town in this area, beginning origi-

What remains of the Council City and Solomon Railroad near Nome.
(following pages) The lights of the aurora borealis, which band the sky about 200 nights of the year in central and northern Alaska, are one of the natural wonders of the northern skies.

Gold Dust Soup

Everybody in Nome was prospering in those days.... Gold was flowing freely, and a platter of ham-and-eggs cost four dollars. Even the stew bums in Nome were getting their share. The swamper in the Northern Saloon offered to polish the brass spittoons for nothing, in exchange for the privilege of panning the sawdust in the front of the bar, where patrons paying for drinks spilled gold dust on the floor. In the Arctic Restaurant on Front Street the cook kept a pot of soup bubbling on the stove all winter, using the greasy wooden spoon to measure out a customer's dust. He rinsed the spoon in the soup. By winter's end he had amassed a comfortable stake at the bottom of the pot, and went back to the States in the spring.

—Klondy Nelson with Corey Ford, *Daughter of the Gold Rush,* 1958

Up to 20,000 gold prospectors flooded into Nome in 1899 and 1900, creating massive tent cities. Here, a woman and young boy use a rocker to help separate pay dirt from plain dirt.

nally as a mining camp in 1898 and at one time serving as home to more than 20,000 gold prospectors. Those days are gone now—thankfully—and Nome has evolved into the business and governmental hub for this part of arctic Alaska. It's remote: 539 miles northwest of Anchorage and 165 miles from the coast of Siberia. It's decidedly more of a real city than similar-sized hub towns like Kotzebue and Barrow, with paved streets and sidewalks. Weathered wooden houses, low commercial buildings, and saloons curve about a stony and treeless shore. The largest buildings in town are the modern high school and the headquarters of the Sitnasuak Native Corporation, which owns and operates a gas station, a parts store, apartments, and a combined hardware and grocery store. The rubble of century-old gold mining operations, including pieces of machinery and a large gold dredge, lie about on the outskirts of town.

This is a friendly, close-knit town, where locals don't lock their houses or cars—though the blight of petty crime is changing that. The architecture is typical rural Alaskan—low cinderblock or prefabricated buildings—but some new structures have copied gold rush–era architecture. Fast-food restaurants and stores offer many of the items that you can get in the Lower 48. Drinking is a problem here, as it is elsewhere in the Arctic.

Nome is noted for being at the finish line of the 1,049-mile Iditarod Trail Sled Dog Race, which begins in Anchorage the first Saturday in March. Twenty years ago it took mushers 20 days to complete this trip. In the past few years, the winning time has been shortened to just under nine days, and stragglers take an additional week. First prize? Roughly $70,000, plus a new truck. Nome celebrates Memorial Day with a "Polar Bear Swim" in 35-degree Fahrenheit water.

Several longish gravel roads (up to 80 miles) originating in Nome lead into the backcountry of the Seward Peninsula. Roughly 180 species of birds are seen here, and the tundra in the summertime is quite beautiful. It's also the only place in Alaska where you can count on seeing wild musk oxen from the road; the local population of these prehistoric-looking members of the goat family is the largest in the state. One can drive and hike to good stream fishing for grayling and (in season) several species of salmon. You can also fly on Bering Air to Siberia and stay in the home of a Russian family (see pages 307 and 314). The **Nome Convention and Visitors Bureau** (301 Front Street; 907-443-6624) provides a walking tour map of the town and information on activities.

■ **KOBUK VALLEY NATIONAL PARK**   *map page 272, B/C-3*

In 1980, just as he was leaving office, President Jimmy Carter signed the bill that made this 1.7 million-acre area a national park. One of the prettiest areas in Alaska, it is replete with clear running streams and rivers, the northernmost sand dune field in the hemisphere, ancient archaeological sites, and all of the diverse fauna and flora typical of a vast province of the Brooks Range. Depending on the season, Kobuk Valley, like other parks of northwestern Alaska, sees light to moderately heavy traffic along the main river corridor.

One of the most fascinating areas of the park is the **Onion Portage** site, on a looping bend of the Kobuk River. This is considered one of the most important archaeological sites in North America, and has been studied by archaeologists since its 1940 discovery by anthropologist Louis Giddings. He and his successors have found chiseled stone spear points and tools, ancient hearthbeds, Siberian-style pit houses, and other artifacts. Data suggest that Native people used this game-rich area continuously for at least 12,000 years, attracted by the annual caribou migrations that usually pass

Fall colors (above) in Kobuk Valley National Park. The park's sand dunes (right), encompassing more than 25 square miles, rise as high as 100 feet in places.

through here, and the layering of so many successive cultures is what makes this site unique. Currently the archaeological digs are not being worked, and are off-limits to visitors. Still, a walk along the beach and up the spruce- and aspen-crowned knoll to Giddings's cabin (now used as a seasonal ranger station by the National Park Service) puts visitors in the footsteps of ancient arctic man—and offers gorgeous views of the surrounding tundra and the Jade Mountains beyond.

The other main attraction of the Kobuk Valley National Park is the 25-square-mile **Kobuk Sand Dunes,** some of which rise to more than 100 feet in height. *907-442-3760 for visitor information in summer; 907-442-3890 at other times.*

■ BERING LAND BRIDGE NATIONAL PRESERVE
map page 272, A-3

The Seward Peninsula reaches far from the mass of the North American continent, and of Alaska—straining, it would seem, to join up with the nearby coast of Asia. Between the extreme point of this peninsula, near Cape Prince of Wales, and the extreme point of Russia's Chukchi Peninsula, Cape Dezhnev, is the shallow Bering Strait: the 53-mile wide, notoriously treacherous, current-swept body of water that is the demarcation point between the Bering and Chukchi seas. During past glacial epochs, when sea levels dropped hundreds of feet, the two continents were sporadically joined; it was over this exposed sea bed that Siberian immigrants ventured eastward into the New World. According to one theory, these people walked, canoed, rafted, and kayaked deeper into the continent, ultimately reaching the tip of South America. If there is ever an epic poem written of the Americas, it will begin here, with the first Asians walking into the Great Land, amazed at the abundance of wildlife and at the complete absence of human life.

A large portion of the northern Seward Peninsula has been designated as Bering Land Bridge National Preserve. In the preserve are thousands of lakes, several hot springs, ancient lava flows, extinct volcanoes, beautiful Imuruk Lake, prehistoric camping sites, Jurassic fossil sites, active Eskimo villages and reindeer herding camps, 3,000-foot mountains, and subsistence fishing sites. Wildlife includes everything from grizzly bears, wolves, and caribou to bearded seals, walrus, and bowhead whales offshore. The reintroduced musk ox is also found in the preserve. Bering Land Bridge National Preserve lies just below the Arctic Circle, with access from Kotzebue and Nome. The Taylor Highway reaches within 20 miles of the preserve. *907-443-2522 for visitor information.*

■ Cape Krusenstern National Monument

map page 272, B-2/3

Cape Krusenstern is among the least visited, distant outposts of the National Park System. Access is by air charter from Kotzebue, possibly by boat, or by snowmobile in winter. The monument is not particularly large—66,000 acres—but the wildlife and plant associations found here are unique, the windswept coastline starkly spectacular. Along the coast are ancient archaeological sites and a scattering of modern subsistence camps, most of them occupied only seasonally. When you visit Cape Krusenstern, you're decidedly on your own; National Monument or not, there is no ranger station and no trails. The coastal weather is notoriously unstable and windy. Relatively nearby villages include Noatak (30 miles inland) and Kivalina (on the coast). There are no accommodations or restaurants outside of Kotzebue.

It is also a country inhabited by that ubiquitous symbol of the far north—the grizzly bear. One of my former graduate students once spent a summer conducting research at Cape Krusenstern National Monument with her husband, a University of Alaska biologist, and she reported an amazing observation. The local grizzly bears would boldly climb down the steep cliffs where the seabirds lived in order to rob the eggs and hatchlings from the seabird nests. I must confess I was somewhat skeptical until shown a sheet of 35-mm color slides clearly demonstrating this behavior. *907-442-3760 for visitor information in summer; 907-442-3890 at other times.*

While the terrestrial interior of Cape Krusenstern is not exactly an oasis of life—it supports a few moose, musk oxen, foxes, and brown bears, plus seasonally migrating caribou—the coastline is rich. Bearded seals, beluga whales, and seabirds are abundant in summer, and occasionally walrus or bowhead whales wander close to shore. When sea mammal carcasses wash ashore, they draw sizeable congregations of scavenging bears and foxes. Fishing in the various coastal lagoons and spring-fed streams can be excellent for pike and sea-run Dolly Varden, known to the Natives as "trout."

The coastal region of the monument contains a wealth of prehistoric sites, as this area was used intensely during the Bering Land Bridge period, and subsequently by Eskimo people attracted to the rich marine resources. Eskimos still maintain hunting and fishing camps here. Seals are particularly valued, providing meat, oil, and skins, as are the chum salmon available in local waters. Access is, by arctic Alaska standards, relatively easy, with daily jet service to Kotzebue from both Fairbanks and Anchorage, and then charter aircraft available for the 20-minute flight north to Cape Krusenstern. The major negative factor at Cape Krusenstern is the weather, which is like coastal seaside weather anywhere in the northern latitudes—heavy on the rain and fog and quite unpredictable. All visitors should be prepared for total self-sufficiency, and for the distinct possibility that weather may extend the visit many days beyond any scheduled departure time.

■ NOATAK NATIONAL PRESERVE   *map page 272, B/C-2/3*

The 6.5 million-acre Noatak National Preserve is part of an integrated complex of parklands including the Kobuk Valley National Park and Gates of the Arctic National Park. Together, these three immense parks protect the entire central and western Brooks Range west of Atigun Pass and the Dalton Highway. If you started walking west at Atigun Pass, you could trek continuously on national park land for nearly 500 miles. What you would notice on such a journey is that, as you advance westward, the fauna, flora, and even geographic features become increasingly like those of northern Asia. In fact, the wild Noatak River basin is rich in anthropological and fossil evidence of the interplay between the North American and Asian continents. Over these lands traveled plants, animals, and people—not only in an easterly direction, but also westward, cross-fertilizing life in Asia as well.

The Noatak National Preserve is remote—more than 350 air miles north and west of Fairbanks. To get there you'll have to catch a mail plane from Fairbanks to Bettles, where bush plane charters are available. Many visitors also use Kotzebue as a jumping-off point; the park staff there will be happy to help you plan your journey. (Visitors should research prices for travel via Bettles and via Kotzebue once they have their destination in hand; the difference could be quite large.) The Noatak River itself is 450 miles long and drains almost due west from the Schwatka Mountains to Kotzebue Sound on the Chukchi Sea, which is south of the Arctic Ocean.

A trip down the Noatak will lead you through jagged peaks, rolling tundra plains, canyons, a few rapids, quiet pools, and, in the lower reaches, spruce forests. It's considered one of the finest wild rivers in the world. You may see many other travelers or you may have long stretches virtually to yourself, depending on the season. Wildlife, though often spread thin, can be highly visible to a keen observer. Dall sheep, moose, caribou, swans, falcons, eagles, foxes, and grizzlies are fairly common, and you might just glimpse a wolf. The Noatak also offers fine fishing for grayling, chum salmon, and Dolly Varden. Take out at a Noatak village, or paddle all the way to Kotzebue. Note: Exercise extreme caution crossing Hotham Inlet. *907-442-3760 for information in summer; 907-442-3890 at other times.*

■ TRAVEL INFORMATION

The Alaskan Arctic, characterized by its vast, frozen, sparsely populated tundra, is largely inaccessible by road. Aside from the lone Dalton Highway (a 414-mile-long, limited-access gravel road connecting Fairbanks to Prudhoe Bay), the Arctic has no major thoroughfares. Air travel is the lifeline to the north and the domain of the Alaskan bush pilot.

The major airlines have established routes and offer package deals—such as a one- or two-day trip to Barrow from Fairbanks with a guided bus tour—but these trips are of short duration and fairly limited in scope. Independent travelers may prefer the customized arrangements of a smaller tour company, making use of the air services of experienced bush pilots and guaranteeing a room at the end of the flight. Reservations made at least six months to a year in advance are recommended for travel during the peak season (late May through early September).

Tour operators and air taxi services do exist in the Arctic. A few of them are listed below.

Alaska Airlines. Air travel to Barrow, Nome, and Kotzebue; local arrangements are handled by Native ground operators. *800-468-2248; www.alaskaair.com.*

Ambler Air Service. Regular air service and charters between upper Kobuk villages and Fairbanks. *Ambler; 907-445-2121 or 907-458-8100.*

Arctic Air Guides Flying Service. Air-taxi and flightseeing tours of the Arctic region, wheels and floats. *Kotzebue; 907-442-3030.*

Bering Air. With hubs in Nome, Kotzebue, and Unalakleet, Bering offers scheduled service to 32 villages in western Alaska; also flightseeing tours. *Nome; 907-443-5464 or 800-478-5422 (within Alaska); www.beringair.com.*

Brooks Range Aviation. Serves entire Brooks Range and the Arctic National Wildlife Refuge with both floatplanes and wheels. *Bettles; 907-692-5444 or 800-692-5443; www.brooksrange.com.*

Frontier Flying Service. Serves Nome and Kotzebue and numerous other Arctic towns. *Fairbanks; 907-450-7200 or 800-478-6779; www.frontierflying.com.*

Gray Line of Alaska. Four-day Prudhoe Bay North Slope Explorer package tour travels up the Dalton Highway between Fairbanks and Deadhorse by coach, then returns south by air. *907-451-6835 or 800-544-2206; www.graylinealaska.com.*

Lee's Sea Air. Locally operated bush air charters in Kobuk Valley area; airport landings only. *Kiana; 907-475-2101.*

Warbelow's Air Ventures. Scheduled and chartered flights throughout the upper Yukon and other interior villages. Brooks Range bush tours. *Fairbanks; 907-474-0518 or 800-478-0812; www.warbelows.com.*

Wright Air Service. Scheduled and chartered flights to the upper Yukon and the central and eastern Brooks Range. *Fairbanks; 907-474-0502 or 800-478-0502 (within Alaska); www.wrightair.net.*

■ CLIMATE

This region, much of it north of the Arctic Circle, marks the northern extent of Alaska's great forests and the beginning of the dry tundra zone that extends to the shores of the Arctic Sea. This is the driest region of the state, with precipitation comparable to the driest areas of the American Southwest, such as Yuma and Death Valley. It is cold but dry year-round north of the Brooks Range. Inland areas, to the south of the Baird and Schwatka mountains (as represented by Kobuk Valley National Park), have warmer summers and in some years quite heavy precipitation. Nome, on the Seward Peninsula, has a climate moderated by its proximity to the Bering Sea. This entire region undergoes periods of 15 or more hours of darkness daily from November through January and non-stop daylight from May through July. Temperatures in July may exceed 90° F and fall in January to –60° F.

SUNLIGHT

SUMMER MAXIMUM	SUNRISE	SUNSET	# OF HOURS
Barrow	84 DAYS OF CONTINUOUS DAYLIGHT		
WINTER MINIMUM	SUNRISE	SUNSET	# OF HOURS
Barrow	67 DAYS OF CONTINUOUS DAYLIGHT		

TEMPS (F°)	AVG. JAN.		AVG. APRIL		AVG. JULY		AVG. OCT.		RECORD	RECORD
	HIGH	LOW	HIGH	LOW	HIGH	LOW	HIGH	LOW	HIGH	LOW
Barrow	-9	-20	5	-10	43	33	20	10	79	-56
Kobuk N.P.	-2	-20	28	7	66	48	27	15	90	-64
Nome	13	0	27	10	57	45	34	21	86	-54

PRECIPITATION (INCHES)	AVG. JAN.	AVG. APRIL	AVG. JULY	AVG. OCT.	ANNUAL RAIN	ANNUAL SNOW
Barrow	0.2"	0.2"	0.9"	0.5"	5"	28"
Kobuk N.P.	0.7"	0.8"	2.7"	0.9"	16"	60"
Nome	0.9"	0.7"	2.3"	1.3"	16"	56"

■ Food, Lodging, & Tours

RESTAURANT PRICES

Per person, without drinks, tax, or tip

$ = under $15   **$$** = $15–$25   **$$$** = over $25

ROOM RATES

Per room, per night, double occupancy

$ = under $70   **$$** = $70–$100   **$$$** = over $100

AMBLER *map page 272, C-3*

Population: 309
Visitors information: 907-445-2122 (City Office), or try Kobuk River Lodge (below)

◆ LODGING
Kobuk River Lodge. Three cozy, rustic rooms upstairs from store and (in summer) two efficiency cabins. Basic restaurant also. *907-445-2165.* **$$$**

ANAKTUVUK PASS *map page 272, D-3*

Population: 282
Visitors information: 907-661-3520 (National Park Service); www.nps.gov.gaar

◆ TOURS
Warbelow's Air Ventures. Fly-in day tours from Fairbanks, Memorial Day to mid-September. Beautiful flightseeing, and ground tour of the mountain-rimmed and windswept Inupiat Eskimo village of Anaktuvuk Pass. *907-474-0518 or 800-478-0812; www.warbelows.com.*

ARCTIC VILLAGE *map page 272, F-3*

Population: 152
Visitors information and day tours if arranged in advance: 907-587-5328

◆ LODGING
Parish Hall. Bring your own sleeping bag. *Reservations: 907-587-5328.* **$**

BARROW   *map page 272, D-1*

Population: 4,581
Visitors information: 907-852-5211 (City Office); www.kingeider.net/king5.html

◆ RESTAURANTS
Arctic Pizza. Downstairs is family-oriented; upstairs is a dining area with an ocean view. *125 Apayauq Street; 907-852-4222.* **$$$**
Northern Lights Restaurant. Standard fare of decent quality. *5122 Herman Street; 907-852-3300.* **$$–$$$**
Pepe's North of the Border. Enchiladas, tacos, and chiles rellenos in the northernmost Mexican restaurant in the United States. Next door to the Top of the World Hotel, it also serves seafood, chicken, steaks, and hamburgers. *1204 Agvik Street; 907-852-8200.* **$$$**
Teriyaki House. Serves Japanese and Chinese fare; opposite Alaska Airlines. *1906 Pakpuk Street; 907-852-2276.* **$$**

◆ LODGING
Barrow Airport Inn. Modern hotel offering such amenities as cable TV, telephones, full kitchenettes (in nine of the 16 rooms), and complimentary morning coffee served in the lobby. Near the airport. *1815 Momegana Street; 907-852-2525.* **$$$**
Top of the World Hotel. Forty-four rooms in the ultimate polar community, with a restaurant and a stuffed polar bear in the frontier-style lobby. Rooms are comfortable, with baths, TV, and telephones. *1200 Agvik Street; 907-852-3900 or 800-882-8478; www.alaskaone.com/topworld/hotel.* **$$$**

◆ TOURS
Alaskan Arctic Adventures. Wildlife viewing and photography; northern lights tours in season, birding. *6475 North Star Street; 907-852-3800.*

BETTLES   *map page 272, D-3*

Population: 43
Visitors information: 907-692-5191 (City Office)

◆ WILDERNESS LODGE
Bettles Lodge. Fly-in lodge at the Bettles Airport offers six rooms with shared

baths in the main lodge—a historic landmark dating from 1948—plus four with private baths and Jacuzzi (and four with shared bath) in the newer Aurora Lodge. Aircraft fuel, gift house, restaurant, and liquor store also located here. Winter dog sled trips and northern lights viewing a specialty. *Reservations: P.O. Box 27, Bettles, AK 99726; 907-692-5111 or 800-770-5111; www.bettleslodge. com.* $$$

◆ TOURS

Bettles Air Service. Run by Bettles Lodge; tour packages and bush air service. *907-692-5111 or 800-770-5111; www.bettleslodge.com.*

Brooks Range Aviation. Flying service, wheels and skis, to all Brooks Range and Arctic locations, including the Arctic National Wildlife Refuge. *907-692-5444 or 800-692-5443; www.brooksrange.com.*

COLDFOOT *map page 272, D/E-3*

Population: 13

Visitors information: 907-678-5209 (summer only)

Coldfoot Camp. The only visitors facilities in this end-of-the-line, last-of-the-frontier town. At the restaurant ($–$$), frequented mainly by truckers, diners sit side by side at long wooden tables and benches. Motel rooms, 80 in all, are bare-bones but expensive ($$$). Northern lights viewing from September through March. *Mile 175, Dalton Highway; 907-474-3500 or 866-474-3400; www.coldfootcamp. com.* $$$

COUNCIL *map page 272, A-4*

◆ WILDERNESS LODGE

Camp Bendeleben. Originally a 1900s gold-mining post, this is now a year-round, reservation-only camp near Nome featuring fishing for Arctic char, grayling, and salmon. Other activities include ice-fishing, bird-watching, and photography. Three-night minimum; rates include all meals and transportation between the lodge and Nome. *Reservations, October–May: 12110 Woodward Drive, Anchorage, AK 99516; 907-522-6663; no phone at the camp; from June through September, mail contact is: P.O. Box 105, Nome, AK 99762; www. campbendeleben.com.* $$$

Deadhorse (Prudhoe Bay) *map page 272, E-2*

◆ Lodging

Arctic Caribou Inn. Near Deadhorse airport; 45 rooms with private bath, lounge and dining areas. Departure point for tours to the oilfields and the Arctic Ocean. Open late May to early September. *Reservations: P.O. Box 340111, Prudhoe Bay, AK 99734; 907-659-2368 or 866-659-2368; www.arcticcaribouinn.com.* $$$

◆ Tours

Northern Alaska Tour Company. Cross the Arctic Circle, view wildlife on the arctic tundra, tour Prudhoe Bay oilfields, and spend the night in Prudhoe Bay on the three- or four-day Prudhoe Bay Adventure package, which travels between Fairbanks and Prudhoe Bay by air and by van along the Dalton Highway. *907-474-8600 or 800-474-1986; www.northernalaska.com.*

Fort Yukon *map page 272, E/F-4*

Population: 595
Visitors information: 907-662-2479 (City Hall), or try Alaska Yukon tours, below

◆ Tours

Alaska Yukon Tours. Native-run fish-camp tours. *710 Sled Street, Fort Yukon; 907-662-2727 or 888-389-8566.*

Warbelow's Air Ventures. Tours to Fort Yukon leave from Fairbanks Airport each evening at 7 from Memorial Day to mid-September; one-hour flight, one-hour guided tour in bus, and return. *907-474-0518 or 800-478-0812; www.warbelows.com.*

Kaktovik (Barter Island) *map page 272, F-2*

Population: 293
Visitors information: 907-640-6313 (City Hall); www.kaktovik.com
Visitors to the Arctic National Wildlife Refuge often fly into Kaktovik. For flights to Kaktovik, contact Frontier Flying Service (907-450-7200), which flies there from Barrow and Fairbanks.

◆ Lodging

Waldo Arms Hotel. Accommodations—13 rooms—and meals. If you're a guest, meals are included in overnight rate. *907-640-6513.* $$

◆ Tours

Alaska Flyers. Provides drop-off service to the Arctic National Wildlife Refuge; also photo and scenic flights. *907-640-6324.*

KIANA *map page 272, B-3*

Population: 388
Visitors information: 907-475-2136 (City Office), or try 907-475-2138 (Kiana Trading Post)

◆ Tours and Lodging

Kiana Lodge. A rustic, out-of-town lodge on the Kobuk river. Features fishing for the exotic sheefish and trips to the Kobuk Sand Dunes. Food and boat trips included in price. Native operated. *907-475-2149.* $$$
Lee's Sea Air. Air tours and flying service in Kobuk Valley area. *907-475-2101.*

KOTZEBUE *map page 272, B-3*

Population: 3,500
Visitors information: 907-442-3401 (City Hall); www.cityofkotzebue.com

◆ Restaurants

Bayside Restaurant. Local favorite with American standbys like burgers. Views of the Kotzebue Sound. *Shore Avenue; 907-442-3600.* $–$$
Empress Restaurant. Reasonable Chinese-American cooking. *Shore Avenue; 907-442-4304.* $

◆ Lodging

Nullagvik Hotel. Owned by local Native corporation, very busy in peak season. Overlooks Hotham Inlet; it is built on pilings to keep it from melting underlying permafrost. In the center of town—ask for third-floor rooms to reduce occasional late-night noise. *308 Shore Avenue; 907-442-3331; www.nullagvik.com.* $$$

◆ Tours

William Reich. Local Inupiat provides boat transportation and basic guiding to visitors wishing to hike, pick berries, view wildlife, or visit archaeological sites such as Cape Krusenstern. *907-442-3026.*

NOME   *map page 272, A-4*

Population: 3,505
Visitors information: 907-443-6624; www.nomealaska.org/vc

◆ RESTAURANTS

Fat Freddie's. Serves breakfast, lunch, and dinner, including seafood, steaks, and shakes. Overlooking the Bering Sea. *50 Front Street; 907-443-5899.* $–$$

Milano's. Pizza and Italian food, plus Japanese food. In the Old Federal Building. *110 West Front Street; 907-443-2924.* $$

Polar Café. Standard breakfast fare served all day, as well as lunch and dinner entrees. Very friendly waitstaff. *225 Front Street; 907-443-5191.* $–$$

◆ LODGING

Aurora Inn. Newest hotel in Nome, nicely appointed, with 68 rooms and a view of the Bering Sea. *302 East Front Street; 907-443-3838 or 800-354-4606; www.aurorainnome.com.* $$$

Nugget Inn. With 46 rooms, this is one of the larger hotels in Nome; a convenient place to stay pending your departure to the hinterlands. Bar on premises. *135 Front Street; 907-443-2323 or 877-443-2323; www.nomenuggetinn.com.* $$$

◆ TOURS

Circumpolar Expeditions. Cultural tours across the Bering Strait to Siberia, and custom adventures in Alaska including trips to the North Pole. *907-272-9299 or 888-567-7165; www.arctictravel.net.*

■ FESTIVALS AND EVENTS

■ MARCH

Bering Sea Ice Golf Classic, Nome. Only in Alaska—a golf tournament played in mid-March on the pack ice of the Bering Sea. *907-443-6624.*

Iditarod Trail Sled Dog Race, Nome. Dogs and mushers begin the race on the first Saturday in March in Anchorage and cross tundra, rivers, mountains, and the ice-locked sea coast to reach the finish line in Nome nine to 15 days later. Festivities in Nome include arts and crafts shows, a reindeer potluck, the fancy-dress Miners and Mushers Ball, and the Iditarod Awards Banquet. *907-376-5155 (907-443-6624 for Nome events); www.iditarod.com.*

■ **MAY**

Polar Bear Swim, Nome. On Memorial Day, ice permitting, Nomites dip into the 35°F frigid waters of the Bering Sea to test their hardiness (or foolhardiness). *907-443-6624.*

■ **JUNE**

Midnight Sun Festival, Nome. Held the weekend closest to the summer solstice to celebrate the 22 hours of daylight on the longest day of the year. Activities change every year, but have included a street dance, BBQ, mock bank hold-up, and parade. *907-443-6624.*

■ **JULY**

Northwest Native Trade Fair, Kotzebue. Eskimo games, dances, and other activities. *907-442-3401.*

■ **SEPTEMBER**

Rubber Duck Race, Nome. Rotary Club's annual Labor Day fundraiser includes rubber duck race in the river, bathtub race, and parade. *907-443-6624.*

S O U T H W E S T

West of Kodiak and Afognak islands on the Alaska Peninsula is a vast wilderness of marshy tundra and more than 60 smoldering volcanoes. Much of this territory now lies within the boundaries of Katmai National Park and Preserve, Lake Clark National Park and Preserve, Aniakchak National Monument and Preserve, and Wood-Tikchik State Park. The thousand-mile-long Aleutian Island chain, with its wild, barren coasts and colonies of fur seals, walrus, puffins, and murres, begins at the southwestern end of the Alaska Peninsula

Comparatively few travelers make it out to sparsely populated southwestern Alaska, and most of those who do travel by plane; no roads lead from Anchorage into this area. Although prices vary, it's standard for a roundtrip plane flight—from Anchorage to Kodiak and on by bush plane to an isolated park—to cost $1,500 or more per person in round trip transportation fees. And bear in mind that weather can sock in the Kodiak airport for days at a time in the middle of summer. A marine ferry follows the coastline and stops at many of the Aleutian Islands, but travel is time-consuming and dependent on good weather.

Southwestern Alaska's largest town, Dillingham, is a major fishing port, but most people visit the peninsula and its neighboring mountains and islands to visit the McNeil River or Brooks Camp bear viewing platforms, for sport fishing, or for big-game hunting. Regardless, the region evokes superlatives; it also has much to offer river rafters, sea kayakers, hikers, campers, and wildlife photographers.

■ EARTHQUAKES, TIDAL WAVES, AND FISH-FILLED SEAS

Much of southwestern Alaska rests on top of one of the most active tectonic areas in the world. In 1946, for example, a tidal wave generated by seismic activity in the Aleutians completely swept a local U.S. Coast Guard lighthouse out to sea; the reinforced concrete structure had been located on a rocky point 10 stories above the high tide mark. The 14 men inside were never accounted for. Five hours later the same wave struck Hawaii, killing 159 and causing $25 million in damage. It then sped south over the equator to slam into Chile, rebounded, and hit the other side of Hawaii, where it caused more damage. In 1964, southwestern Alaska

Horned puffins are at home in Alaska's Aleutian and Pribilof islands.

THE WORLD'S MOST DANGEROUS JOB

Among the many dangerous professions Alaska has to offer, one is the deadliest of all: tanner (or snow crab) and king crab fishing. Every year men and women lose their lives when the 120-foot crab boats are caught in the ferocious storms that rake the Bering Sea and Gulf of Alaska. Winds of more than 100 miles per hour and seas of 50 feet are not uncommon. Sea spray can freeze so quickly and become so thick on deck that boats capsize from top weight before crews can clear the ice with sledge-hammers and baseball bats.

Iron crab pots weigh 750 pounds and must be maneuvered by hand on deck night and day while the boat pitches and rolls in howling gales and ice storms. Roughly 15 percent of the crabbers are incapacitated each year. But the lure of big money provides ever-fresh recruits for the skippers and canneries of Kodiak Island and Dutch Harbor. In the boom years of the late 1970s and early 1980s each crew member could pocket more than $20,000 after a successful catch lasting six weeks. A precipitous drop in the king crab population between 1981 and 1985 weakened the industry for a few years, but then fishermen began harvesting tanner (snow) crab and opilio crab, and the high-risk employment continues.

endured another seismic calamity when the Good Friday earthquake wrecked salmon canneries on Kodiak and the subsequent tidal wave destroyed the harbor and the city.

The human spirit is tough, though, and resilient, and Kodiak was soon rebuilt into what it is today—a bustling, thriving economic center for the North Pacific fishing industry. The seas are filled with gold in the form of salmon, halibut, pollack, and other edible species. So rich are these resources that other nations—especially those along the Pacific Rim—bring their factory fleets into the area. The Alaskan Congressional delegation is forever petitioning the White House to impose sanctions on those countries (such as Taiwan) that employ rapacious and/or outlawed fishing practices. There is the very real concern that some of these fisheries may soon disappear. The lessons in this respect are recent—the once-thriving king crab industry in Kodiak and Dutch Harbor is now but a shadow of its former self.

A ▼ B ▼ C ▼ D ▼

Norton Sound

Kwikpak
YUKON
DELTA
Pastol
Bay
Saint
Michael
Unalakeet
Kaltag
Galena
Ruby

① Black
Kwikpuk
Grayling
Innoko
National
Wildlife
Rufuge

Yukon Delta
Anvik
Ophir
Tatalina
McGrath
Denali
National
Park
and Preserve

Hooper Bay
National
Pilot Point
Marshall
Holy Cross
Iditarod
Sterling
Landing

Ohogamiut
Wildlife
Kalskag
Stoney
Point
Mt Hesperus
9,828

② NELSON
ISLAND
Refuge
Akiak
Tulusak
Sleetmute
Mt.Gerdine
11,258

Cherfonak
Bethel
Lime Village

Kipnuk

Kwigillingok
Kuskokwim
Bay
Quinhagak
Nuyskuk
Lake
Lake Clark National
Park & Preserve
Ice Field
Redoubt Vol
10,197
Kenai
①

Carter Spit
Carter
Togiak
National
Wildlife
Refuge
Togiak
Lake
Nerka
Wood-Tikchik
State Park
Port Alsworth Visitor Center
Nondalton
Iliamna
Lake
Clark
Iliamna Vol
10,016
Pedro
Bay
Anchor
Point
Homer

③ Platinum
Cape Newenham
Dillingham
Igiugig
Iliamna
Lake
Augustine Vol
4,025
Seldovia

Cape Pierce
Ekuk
McNeil River State
Game Sanctuary
Kvichak
Kamishak
Bay

Naknek
King
Salmon
Brooks
Camp
Katmai National
Park and
Preserve
Mt Douglas
7,064
Port William

Walrus Islands
State Game
Sanctuary
Egegik
Mt Denison
7,620
AFOGNAK
ISLAND
Port Lions

Bristol
Bay
Cape Chichagof
Egegik Bay
Cape Greig
Ugashik Bay
Cape Menshikov
Pilot Point
PENINSULA
Karluk
KODIAK
ISLAND
Kodiak

④ Mekoryuk
Kikmiktalikamiut
NUNAVIK
ISLAND
Cape Mohican
Cape Corwin
Cape Mendenhall
Port
Heiden
Aniakchak National
Monument
and Preserve
Old Harbor
SITKALIDAK
ISLAND

Nelson Lagoon
Port Moller
ALASKA
Mt Veniaminof
8,225
Chignik
SUTWIK ISLAND
TRINITY
ISLANDS

Ivanof Bay
SEMIDI
ISLANDS

UNGA
ISLAND
Sand Point
Ferry
CHIRIKOF ISLAND

NAGAI ISLAND
BIG KONIUJI ISLAND

⑤ LITTLE KONIUJI ISLAND
SIMEONOF I
CHERNABURA I
Gambell
Northwest Cape
Savoonga
West Cape
SAINT
LAWRENCE
ISLAND
Sevak Camp
Northeast
Cape
Southeast Cape

Elevation
in feet
11,670
5,000
4,000
3,000
2,000
1,000
Sea Level

SOUTHWEST

Miles
0   50   100

0   50   100   150
Kilometers

■ KODIAK ISLAND *map page 319, C/D-4*

In 1899 naturalist John Burroughs described Kodiak Island as a "pastoral paradise"; nearly one hundred years later, if you visit Kodiak during the summer you'll probably agree. One hundred miles long and located 252 air miles south of Anchorage and the Kenai Peninsula, Kodiak is strategically set on the edge of the warming Japanese current. Bathed in continual precipitation, it and its sister islands are every bit as green as Ireland, and if you come, as Burroughs did, from icy Prince William Sound or from the dry forests and tundra of the Interior, the sudden wash of green landscape will be quite startling. Someone once referred to Kodiak as the "northernmost Hawaiian Island," and sometimes when you are on Kodiak, hiking in a dense jungle world beside a clear stream, the description does not seem too far off.

Because of its moisture and greenery, Kodiak supports an incredible proliferation of wildlife: brown bears, Sitka black-tailed deer, elk, mountain goats, pink salmon, sockeye salmon, coho salmon, king salmon, chum salmon, arctic char, steelhead, arctic grayling, bald eagles, otters, weasels, foxes, and more than 200 species of birds (from tundra swans to golden plovers). And the wildflowers—fireweed, shooting stars, wild blue iris—are out of this world. The place is like an enormous greenhouse where the humidity and temperature have been carefully controlled by Mother Nature to make conditions perfect for growing flowers. Thankfully, almost all of Kodiak Island—which totals 1,865,000 acres—is forever protected from development as the Kodiak National Wildlife Refuge. Because of the rugged coastline, no place on the island is more than 15 miles from the sea—a favorable geographic situation that fosters three habitats: rain forest, grass meadowland and tundra, and glaciated high country.

You will probably reach Kodiak Island either by air or via the Alaska Marine Ferry. In either case, you will find yourself in the town of Kodiak, which is quite large by Alaskan standards (6,334 souls in the 2000 census). The town was rebuilt after the tidal wave from the 1964 earthquake washed over it, and it is consequently quite modern in appearance. Here are all the amenities—hotels, motels, restaurants, stores, campgrounds, post office. You will notice quite a few boats docked in the harbor, as Kodiak is the third-largest commercial fishing port in the country. Stroll along the harbor, smelling the sea on one side, while the aromas of coffee and cooking food on the other coax you into one of the waterfront cafés.

The island of Kodiak was considered an emerald paradise by sea-weary explorers and traders.

■ In the Town of Kodiak

Visitors Center

There are several worthwhile attractions in the town of Kodiak. Stop first at the **Kodiak Visitor Information Center** (100 Marine Way; 907-486-4782 or 800-789-4782) on the waterfront to learn more about the diverse recreational possibilities on the island. Run by the Kodiak Island Convention and Visitors Bureau, the center is loaded with brochures, pamphlets, and information on tours, air charters, fishing lodges, and so forth.

Baranov Museum

A majority of visitors to Kodiak stop in at this museum across the street from the visitors center. It is housed in the oldest Russian-built structure remaining in Alaska, a three-story log building constructed from 1805 to 1808 by Alexandr Baranov as a warehouse for the Russian-American Company. Later, from 1911 through 1948, it was a private home. The museum displays artifacts from Kodiak's Native and Russian past and has a wonderful collection of archival photos illustrating island history, including the damage wrought by the 1964 earthquake and tidal wave (which this building survived). The photos are in pull-out albums and you can flip right through them. *101 Marine Way; 907-486-5920.*

Holy Resurrection Russian Orthodox Church

Also nearby is the beautiful Holy Resurrection Church, which serves a parish established in 1794 (when the American West had yet to be explored by Lewis and Clark). The church building itself, adorned with twin blue-onion domes, is much younger. The third church on the site, it was built in 1945 and, like the Baranov Museum, survived the 1964 earthquake. The church is generally open for guided tours one hour a day in summer and at other times by appointment. *Corner of Mission and Kashevaroff roads; 907-486-3854.*

Alutiiq Museum and Archaeological Repository

Across the street from the Holy Resurrection Church, this museum opened its doors in 1995 thanks to a $1.5 million grant the Kodiak Area Native Association received from the Exxon Valdez Oil Spill Trustee Council. The grant gave a big boost to KANA's existing culture and heritage program, which had been created to

The Ascension of Our Lord Orthodox Church in Karluk, built in 1888, is a reminder of Kodiak Island's Russian heritage and one of the oldest Russian Orthodox churches in Alaska.

Beautiful Kodiak

For naturalist John Burroughs, who only a few weeks earlier had explored cold and misty Prince William Sound, the transition from the realm of frozen glaciers and granite rock to Kodiak Island, warmed by the Japanese current and drenched in rain, was profound:

Never before had I seen such beauty of greenness, because never before had I seen it from such a vantage ground of blue sea. . . . At one point we passed near a large natural park. It looked as if a landscape gardener might have been employed to grade and shape the ground and plant it with grass and trees in just the right proportion. . . . Our course lay through narrow channels and over open bays sprinkled with green islands, past bold cliffs and headlands, til . . . we reached the village of Kodiak, called by the Russians St. Paul. . . . How welcome the warmth! We swarmed out of the ship, like boys out of school, longing for a taste of grass and of the rural seclusion and sweetness!

—John Burroughs, *The Harriman Expedition,* 1899

---

preserve and promote the language, traditions, and arts of the Alutiiq (Aleut Eskimo) people. The institution now contains more than 100,000 artifacts representing 7,500 years of area history and prehistory, as well as photos, video and audio tapes, books, maps, natural history specimens, and contemporary Native works of art. The museum mounts changing exhibitions from all of this abundance, and also hosts traveling exhibits. *215 Mission Road; 907-486-7004.*

■ **Kodiak Island Excursions**

Buskin River
There is an unusually good road system (for Alaska) around Kodiak, and you can use it to reach some interesting sites. Only 6 miles west of downtown on the Chiniak Road is the **Buskin River,** which has excellent fishing in season—the Buskin River State Recreation Site has camping sites and short nature trails.

Fort Abercrombie State Historical Park
East of town, the state park has hiking trails around an old World War II military installation. Past Fort Abercrombie, there is a trail at the end of the road to Termination Point, which offers a nice view of the surrounding headlands and sea.

More extensive explorations can be undertaken to the south, on the road that passes the Buskin River State Recreation Site to such places as **Womens Bay, Happy Beach, Cape Greville,** and **Pasagshak Bay.** During the deer-hunting season, these roads will be very busy with hunters. (Rifle-hunting seasons for bear are in April and September; for deer and elk, in the autumn.)

Backcountry

Those with an interest in seeing the backcountry can arrange to be transported by boat or air to any one of a number of remote wilderness locations, both in Kodiak National Wildlife Refuge (recreational cabins available for rent) and in nearby Shuyak Island State Park. Afognak Island and Raspberry Island to the north are very popular with sea kayakers, sport fishermen, and big-game hunters. Kodiak also has its share of fishing lodges, many on Native corporation land and some run by the corporations. You can put your car on the ferry at Homer and be driving around Kodiak 12 hours later, watching from your front seat as brown bears feed on sea-run Pacific salmon. That's pretty incredible.

Kodiak Island is perhaps best known for its large brown bear population.

■ LAKE CLARK NATIONAL PARK AND PRESERVE

map page 319, C/D-2/3

The name of Dick Proenneke, a pioneering homesteader, will forever be associated with Lake Clark National Park and Preserve, located across the Cook Inlet from the Kenai Peninsula. Proenneke arrived in 1967, fell in love with the rugged wildness of the place, and eventually found some good land and built a sturdy cabin from hand-felled logs. He became a modern Thoreau, a man who went out and actually did what most only dream of—building a wilderness cabin and living off berries, fish, big game, and the other bounties of the northern land. His experiences inspired the book *One Man's Wilderness: An Alaskan Odyssey:*

> What was I capable of that I didn't know yet? What about my limits?
> Could I truly enjoy my own company for an entire year? Was I equal
> to everything this wild land could throw at me? I had seen its moods
> in late spring, summer and early fall, but what would winter bring?
> Would I love the isolation then with its bone-stabbing cold, its
> brooding ghostly silence, its forced confinement? At age 51, I
> intended to find out.

Today, Proenneke is a legend at Lake Clark (as is former governor Jay Hammond, who also had a log home in the area) and his book is required reading for anyone contemplating a visit to this beautiful park.

Although it is no longer possible to settle at Lake Clark, which is now a national park, you may still visit the place and appreciate the vast solitude and wilderness that is now forever protected from further development. At 3,653,000 acres, the park is approximately 12 times larger than Grand Teton National Park in northwestern Wyoming, with plenty of country to hike, camp, fish, photograph, and boat in. Regular commercial flights from Anchorage to Iliamna, a tiny community 30 miles southwest of the park boundary on 90-mile-long Iliamna Lake, provide one means of access. From this point, employing an air taxi or chartering a boat is necessary, as you are now in the Alaska bush. There are, quite simply, no roads beyond the rather narrow confines of the village, and the park, like most Alaska public lands (federal or state), is also without roads or trails. Another alternative is to fly a charter from Anchorage, Kenai, or Homer west over Cook Inlet into the park.

As you drive the Sterling Highway from Kenai to Homer, the two volcanoes you see across Cook Inlet—Redoubt and Iliamna—are within Lake Clark National

Park. They often steam harmlessly, but have erupted on several occasions in recent years. In 1992, a Boeing 747 flying through the ash cloud of one of these eruptions lost power in all four engines; after restarting one engine, it made an emergency landing in Anchorage. Sometimes, during an eruption, the towns of the Western Kenai are coated with enough acidic ash to destroy the paint finish of a car. Still, the view of these towering, active cones is incredible.

In Lake Clark you will find everything from coastal rain forests to alpine tundra, from active volcanoes to serene fjords, from high mountain lakes to saltwater estuaries. The wildlife is just as diverse, ranging from belugas and killer whales at the mouth of the Tuxedni River on the east to grizzly bears and Dall sheep on the tundra slopes above Port Alsworth on the west. The salt and fresh waters in and around the park offer some of the greatest fishing opportunities in North America—the Newhalen River is as famous for its fantastic runs of red salmon as the Iliamna River is for its trophy rainbow trout (which you can catch and release all day, or until your arm falls off, whichever comes first). Forty-mile-long Lake Clark, the largest of the many lakes within the park, and nearby Iliamna Lake support the world's largest runs of sockeye salmon—fish that eventually go on to live in Bristol Bay (on the northwest side of the Alaska Peninsula) and form the basis for the most productive commercial salmon fishing operations on the planet.

If you are concerned about the crowds on the Kenai Peninsula or in Denali National Park, Lake Clark National Park may be the place for you. Here you will experience much of the same beauty—both of landscape and of wildlife—but with a fraction of the people around you. Because of the additional air travel it will be more expensive, but having come this far, you may decide a little extra is worth it in order to have a truly once-in-a-lifetime experience.

Iliamna, 102 people strong, is located on the north end of Iliamna Lake (the largest in the state), about 225 miles southwest of Anchorage. The town is strategically located—fly north and you are soon in Lake Clark National Park, turn south and within a short time you are flying over Katmai National Park. Some of the largest rainbow trout in the world can be found in the Kvichak River system at the southwest end of the lake, while other drainages of this vast, freshwater inland sea—including the Newhalen River, on the outskirts of Iliamna—also have excellent trout, and the area boasts some of the best salmon fishing in the state. In the autumn berry-picking in the area is excellent, as well as hunting in the national wildlife refuges for black and grizzly bear, moose, and caribou. Accommodations in

In this old postcard, photographer M. Hohner shoots photographer W. A. Hesse taking moving pictures of Katmai Volcano in 1913.

Iliamna are limited to several lodges (very pricey ones) and a couple of bed-and-breakfasts. There are a couple of stores featuring local native crafts, plus several outfitters and guides that can get you into the backcountry.

Port Alsworth, a village of 104 people on Lake Clark itself, is another possible access point for the park. Connected by regular flights from Anchorage, the community has several lodges and a public campground, as well as the park headquarters. Fishing and drop-off services by boat or air may be available. Call the Port Alsworth Visitor Center (907-271-2218) for information, or contact the National Park Service (907-781-3751).

■ KATMAI NATIONAL PARK AND PRESERVE
map page 319, C-3/4

On June 6, 1912, following a week of severe earthquakes, the Novarupta Volcano south of Iliamna Lake suddenly exploded as if it had been hit by a nuclear bomb. The entire top of the mountain was violently blown off, throwing enormous quantities of pumice, ash, and rock across the Alaskan landscape. Scientists estimated the total volume of displaced planetary material in this event was in excess of 7 cubic miles—two times that expelled in the great 1883 Krakatau explosion in Indonesia. A nearby river valley was buried in 700 feet of solid debris. There followed hellish blasts of superhot gas, lava, pumice, and ash. The whole northern hemisphere of the planet was wrapped in a haze for weeks from this single catastrophic eruption: on Kodiak Island, high noon was turned into blackest midnight for two days, while a thousand miles away, in Vancouver, Canada, acid rain from the blast caused drying clothes to fall apart on laundry lines. A year later, sunsets and sunrises were still brilliantly colored from the volcanic particles that had not yet settled out of the atmosphere.

Four years later, exploring the still-smoldering area for the National Geographic Society, Robert Griggs discovered the primary scene of destruction, an area now referred to on maps as the **Valley of Ten Thousand Smokes.** In his book of the same name, Griggs describes "one of the most amazing visions ever beheld by mortal eye":

> The whole valley as far as the eye could reach was full of hundreds, no thousands—literally, tens of thousands—of smokes curling up from its fissured floor. . . . Some were sending up columns of steam which rose a thousand feet before dissolving.

Every summer people drive halfway across the country just to see Yellowstone National Park's famous Old Faithful geothermal geyser, which periodically shoots 100 feet in the air. But imagine hundreds of steam vents that reached 1,000 feet in the air—10 times the height of Old Faithful—plus a thousand ascending to 500 feet, and thousands more the size of the Yellowstone landmark. The sight of these geysers in the remote Katmai Valley must have convinced all who saw them of Mother Nature's ultimate power and authority in this world.

Although the activity of the steam vents has ceased, the valley remains a sight to amaze. Wisps of steam still rise from the volcanoes, some with acidic cauldrons still boiling. Today, the Valley of Ten Thousand Smokes forms the centerpiece of this park, which was first designated a national monument in 1918 and reached its final configuration under the 1980 Alaska Lands bill, with a total of 4,268,000 acres under protection as park or preserve. This makes the park almost twice the size of Yellowstone—the largest national park in the Lower 48. Eight major river systems and 15 volcanoes are within park boundaries. In addition, Katmai protects one of the largest populations of brown bears in the world. These bears, which feed on the spawning salmon, grow to mind-boggling size, with adult males regularly reaching weights in excess of 1,000 pounds.

In Katmai the bears are easily viewed at **Brooks Camp** on Naknek Lake. An alternate bear-viewing site with far less development and human traffic is the **McNeil River State Game Sanctuary.** Both McNeil and Brooks are located on salmon rivers that are heavily used by the bears in the summer months. These are the places where virtually all those "bear catching salmon at a waterfall" pictures are taken. At McNeil River, administered by the state of Alaska and outside Katmai National Park boundaries, there are generally more bears and fewer people than at Brooks, where during peak season crowds of people vie for space on viewing platforms. However, access to McNeil is controlled by a limited entry permit lottery and is difficult to obtain. Both offer bear-viewing opportunities of a lifetime and are worth every penny. (See "Wildlife," page 52, for more information on these sites.)

In either case, because there are no roads into the national park or the sanctuary, access is by flying from Anchorage to **King Salmon,** location of Katmai National Park headquarters (907-246-3305); many visitors then catch local floatplane charters to these specific destinations. Others use Homer or Kodiak as jumping-off places. A variety of air charter services, guides, and tours are available in all three towns, and it's strictly a matter of preference and your personal logistics. In addition

Wildlife viewing is big in Katmai National Park, and here hikers spy something worthwhile.

to the wildlife-viewing opportunities, Katmai offers some of the finest sport fishing for grayling, northern pike, rainbow trout, and sockeye salmon in Alaska. There are also some fantastic opportunities for rafting, kayaking, hiking, and camping in this extraordinary park. All plans for such undertakings, however, should be made as much as six to seven months in advance.

■ ANIAKCHAK NATIONAL MONUMENT AND PRESERVE
map page 319, B-4

Imagine walking through a giant outdoor diorama of the moon and witnessing the same sort of otherworldly scenery that Neil Armstrong and Buzz Aldrin observed on the Sea of Tranquility in 1969. Imagine trekking across a valley of cinders and lava and pumice, with nothing connected to the human race anywhere in sight—a desolate landscape out of the parables of Heraclitus or the mind of Thomas Merino. Imagine that you are walking across the ruins of a volcano so large that its collapsed caldera forms a basin 6 miles across, with a total area of 30 square miles (larger than Manhattan Island). Imagine all this, and you have Aniakchak National

Photographers get a close-up view of brown bears in Katmai National Park.

Monument—bizarre, oddly beautiful, and so remote that until 1922 the caldera was unknown to all but the few Native people who lived in this area.

Aniakchak is literally at the end of the world—400 miles southwest of Anchorage. It is accessed in stages, first by flying commercially from Anchorage to King Salmon, and then from King Salmon to Meshik (Port Heiden), and then in a charter from Meshik into the national monument. This initial journey, just to reach a wilderness launching point, can take anywhere from two to five or six days, depending on the weather (which is notoriously unreliable on the Alaska Peninsula). Visitors normally head for **Surprise Lake,** a short flight from Port Heiden, to go fishing or on a float trip. Surprise Lake, stunning emerald green in color, is fed by geothermal springs and lies just inside the collapsed Aniakchak Caldera—which looks like a circular sand castle with one small notch caved in, through which the Aniakchak River flows.

In the caldera you'll see wildlife, including grizzly bears, caribou, golden and bald eagles, red foxes, and other common peninsular fauna. The volcano last erupted in 1931, and most geologists believe there is currently no danger in visiting the area. Primitive camping and backpacking are permitted. *Monument headquarters is in King Salmon; 907-246-3305.*

■ **DILLINGHAM AND VICINITY**   *map page 319, B-3*

Dillingham is located about 320 miles southwest of Anchorage, on the shores of Bristol Bay. More than 500 boats are based in Dillingham—part of the great fleet that annually fishes for salmon in productive Bristol Bay. Because of its commercial importance, Dillingham has regular commercial airline service from Anchorage, and is thus more accessible than many other parts of Southwestern Alaska. Visitors will find an array of hotels, restaurants, and stores. The town also provides access to two world-class natural sights: Walrus Islands State Game Sanctuary and Wood-Tikchik State Park.

■ **WALRUS ISLANDS STATE GAME SANCTUARY**   *map page 319, B-3*
Walrus Islands State Game Sanctuary, encompassing seven islands and their surrounding waters in northern Bristol Bay, is located about 70 miles southwest of Dillingham and is normally reached by boat charter from Dillingham via the small Eskimo village of Togiak. More than 10,000 walruses summer at the Walrus Islands, as well as up to 1,000 Steller's sea lions and hundreds of thousands of puffins, auklets, gulls, cormorants, kittiwakes, and murres. There is also a small population of red foxes. This place is a mecca for wildlife photographers, and well worth the somewhat difficult journey.

■ **WOOD-TIKCHIK STATE PARK**   *map page 319, B/C-3*
With 1.6 million acres, Wood-Tikchik State Park is the largest state park in the United States. Its vast system of lakes is interconnected with various rivers and streams, and steep snowy peaks tower over the still, clear glacial waters. There is abundant wildlife—moose, black and grizzly bears, wolf, fox, lynx, marten, and beaver—and, as in all Alaska state parks, hunting is permitted. Fishing is the area's primary attraction, though, with Dolly Varden, rainbow trout, northern pike, arctic grayling, and, of course, red salmon all found here. There are quite a few excellent (but *very* expensive) fishing lodges in the area.

■ ALEUTIAN ISLANDS

■ UNALASKA AND DUTCH HARBOR *map page 335*

The city of Unalaska and its associated port, Dutch Harbor, near the base of the Aleutian chain, is one of the most spectacular and neglected destinations in the entire state. A lush volcanic landscape, bathed in ocean mist, makes for brilliant lighting and incredible displays of summer wildflowers. Rich birding and sea mammal–viewing opportunities abound, often right on the local road system. Two fine local museums and a number of monuments pay homage to the area's rich history and cultural heritage. World War II era bunkers still stand in people's front yards and on the heights guarding the harbor, and bomb craters from the 1942 Japanese aerial attack make events of half a century ago seem like yesterday.

Unalaska is also a growing destination for saltwater anglers seeking monster halibut; the world record 459-pounder was caught here in 1996, and 100- to 200-pound fish are taken with regularity. A handful of local tour operators provide everything from birding trips to long-distance kayaking and volcano climbing, and there are restaurants and lodging to fit most budgets and tastes. Dutch Harbor has the added attraction of being the largest commercial fishing port in this hemisphere, and one of the largest in the world. There is an unvarnished honesty to this working town, and people are disarmingly friendly. So why does Dutch Harbor/Unalaska go begging for visitors?

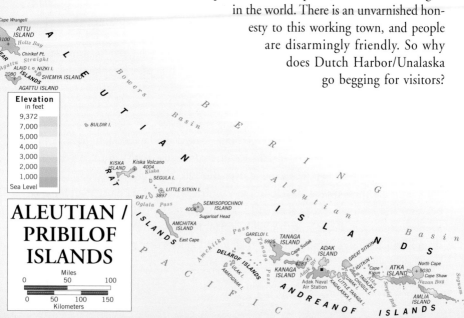

ALEUTIAN / PRIBILOF ISLANDS

It can all be put down to one word: accessibility. The city is, after all, located on an exceedingly remote island. Daily flights are often delayed or canceled due to the notorious Aleutian weather, and the Alaska state ferry, the only other option, runs just once a month, and only in the summer season. However, Unalaska, like the rest of the Aleutian Islands, remain an alluring destination for the intrepid independent traveler.

■ ALASKA MARITIME NATIONAL WILDLIFE REFUGE

The sheer geographic immensity of this preserve is beyond the ability of most of us to comprehend. First of all, the refuge is not in one place but consists of more than 2,400 scattered pieces of real estate. To the arctic north, for example, on Cape Lisburne, there is a parcel at about 70 degrees north latitude. On the south, by contrast, is tiny Forrester Island in the Panhandle, about the same latitude as Prince Rupert, British Columbia (54 degrees north latitude). Forrester Island is at longitude 133 degrees. Attu Island—on the far west and nearly to Russia—is at longitude 174 degrees. Amazing. That is an east-to-west distance as great as that from Jacksonville, Florida to San Diego, California, and a north-to-south distance that would span the entire east coast of the Lower 48.

These islands, headlands, coves, bays, inlets, passages, beaches, estuaries, reefs, rocky islets, cliffs, mountains, lakes,

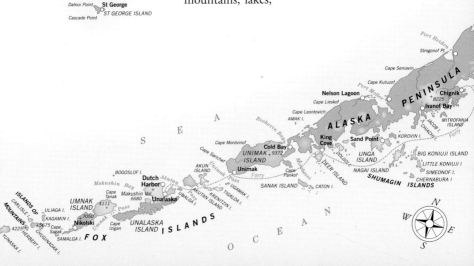

THE HUNT

I am not entirely comfortable on the sea ice butchering walrus like this. The harshness of the landscape, the vulnerability of the boat, and the great size and power of the hunted animal combine to increase my sense of danger. The killing jars me, in spite of my regard for the simple elements of human survival.

No matter what sophistication of mind you bring to such events, no matter what breadth of anthropological understanding, no matter your fondness for the food, your desire to participate, you have still seen an animal killed. You have met the intertwined issues—what is an animal? What is death? . . .

It is easy to develop an affection for the Yup'ik people, especially when you are invited to participate in events still defined largely by their own traditions. The entire event—leaving to hunt, hunting, coming home, the food shared in a family setting—creates a sense of well-being easy to share. . . .

–Barry Lopez, *Arctic Dreams,* 1986

rivers, streams, and volcanoes preserve wildlife—Steller's sea lions, walrus, sea otters, northern fur seals, polar bears, whales, orcas, grizzly bears, wolves, wolverines, deer, caribou, eagles, and most of all, seabirds. It is estimated that the immense refuge supports more than 40 million birds. One of the most popular sites in this respect is also one of the most remote—Attu Island, where the bloodiest Aleutian battle was fought in World War II. Here die-hard birders flock early each summer in the hope of identifying rare Asian species as they migrate north to the Arctic. The visitors center for this refuge is in Homer: **Alaska Islands and Ocean Visitor Center** (95 Sterling Highway; 907-235-6961), where you will find staff happy to outline the many recreational possibilities—birding, hiking, camping, boating, sport fishing, big-game hunting—available in this remote and unusual preserve.

■ PRIBILOF ISLANDS

The Pribilof Islands are an increasingly popular destination for wildlife lovers, with commercial airline access from Anchorage during the summer months. (This "scheduled" service is often subject to weather delays that may last for days, however.) St. Paul Island hosts the world's largest colony of northern fur seals, and both harbor seals and Steller's sea lions are easily seen during the summer season. The islands also support some of the largest seabird colonies on the planet, including puffins, auklets, murres, kittiwakes, cormorants, fulmars, and rare species from the Russian Far East. The constant rains and fog in this area make the tundra wildflower displays, which peak around the summer solstice, particularly magnificent. Virtually every wildlife photographer of note in North America—from Tom Mangelson to Galen Rowell—has made a pilgrimage to this wildlife paradise.

St. Paul Island, by Louis Choris, Otto von Kotzebue's shipboard artist during the voyage of 1815–1817.
(following pages) Unalaska is one of the Aleutian Islands' principal towns.

■ Travel Information

The Southwest comprises the Aleutian Islands and the Pribilof Islands, the Kodiak Island group, and the Alaska Peninsula. Geographically, this vast area is character-ized by windswept grassy tundra and some spruce forests. Most is undeveloped wilderness, without roads. Most visitors travel to the Southwest from Anchorage.

■ Getting There and Getting Around

By Ferry
Travelers can reach Kodiak Island from Homer on the Kenai Peninsula in 10 hours on the ferry *Tustumena* for around $75, from Seward for roughly $90. From Valdez on Prince William Sound the fare is $145. For those wishing to travel out to the Aleutians, this same ferry will make the week-long journey from Kodiak to Dutch Harbor once a month in the summer. *Kodiak Ferry Terminal, 100 Marine Way, Kodiak; 907-486-3800 or 800-526-6731; www.dot.state.ak.us/amhs/index/html.*

By Plane
Air is the most popular way to see the Kodiak National Wildlife Refuge and its neighboring sites. Many floatplane companies provide access to the numerous remote attractions not served by road. A typical fare from Anchorage to Kodiak runs $500–$600 round-trip. From Kodiak, visitors typically hire small floatplanes that carry them to remote destinations in the refuge, or across Shelikof Straits to Katmai National Park and Preserve. Bear viewing is the big attraction.

Traveling from Anchorage to Kodiak and on to the Alaska Peninsula by bush plane varies in cost depending on what part of the peninsula you visit. One-day round-trip flightseeing tours for bear viewing are also available in Kodiak and begin around $500 per person.

Island Air Service. Based in Kodiak, provides air service to villages in the Kodiak area, plus charter services. *1420 Airport Way, Kodiak; 907-487-4596 or 800-478-6196; www.kodiakislandair.com.*

PenAir. Service to southwestern Alaska, including Unalaska/Dutch Harbor and the Pribilof Islands. *800-448-4226; www.penair.com.*

Sea Hawk Air. Kodiak floatplane service. *907-486-8282 or 800-770-4295; www.seahawkair.com.*

■ CLIMATE

This region encompasses the enormous, barely populated interior region of Alaska's southwestern quadrant, lined by busy coastal fishing ports and canneries along the Bering Sea. However, it is the Aleutian Island chain and the great national parks of Lake Clark and Katmai that most people know best. The moderating influence of the Japanese current keeps the climate of most Aleutian Islands mild and rainy, as represented by Adak (midway along the island chain) in the chart below. The isolated Pribilof Islands, in the middle of the Bering Sea, are fog-shrouded and chilly year-round. Kodiak Island has a climate similar to the Aleutian Islands and fog and storms may ground air transport for several days on end. Lake Clark National Park has a climate more closely associated with interior Alaska, with harsher winters but warmer summers.

SUNLIGHT

SUMMER MAXIMUM	SUNRISE	SUNSET	# OF HOURS
Adak	6:27 AM	11:10 PM	16:43
WINTER MINIMUM	SUNRISE	SUNSET	# OF HOURS
Adak	10:52 AM	6:38 PM	7:46

TEMPS (F°)	AVG. JAN. HIGH	LOW	AVG. APRIL HIGH	LOW	AVG. JULY HIGH	LOW	AVG. OCT. HIGH	LOW	RECORD HIGH	RECORD LOW
Adak	41	30	46	40	52	48	48	43	80	8
Kodiak	38	23	48	39	60	52	50	39	85	-12
Lake Clark	24	3	41	22	67	45	41	25	90	-50
Pribilofs	33	22	41	35	47	43	42	34	64	-26

PRECIPITATION (INCHES)	AVG. JAN.	AVG. APRIL	AVG. JULY	AVG. OCT.	ANNUAL RAIN	ANNUAL SNOW
Adak	6.5"	5.2"	5.5"	7.7"	70"	102"
Kodiak	4.7"	3.9"	3.6"	7.6"	61"	40"
Lake Clark	2.1"	2.4"	2.2"	3.1"	29"	100"
Pribilofs	2.3"	1.4"	2.7"	3.3"	28"	56"

■ Food, Lodging, & Tours

RESTAURANT PRICES

Per person, without drinks, tax, or tip

$ = under $15   **$$** = $15–$25   **$$$** = over $25

ROOM RATES

Per room, per night, double occupancy

$ = under $70   **$$** = $70–$100   **$$$** = over $100

BETHEL *map page 319, A/B-2*

Population: 5,471
Visitors information: 907-543-2047; www.bethelak.com

◆ RESTAURANT
VIP Restaurant. Caused a stir with its sushi bar when it opened in 2006. *1220 Hoffman Highway; 907-543-4777.* **$$–$$$**

◆ LODGING
Allanivik Hotel. For quiet elegance in the bush, stay in a Queen Anne–style suite or a standard room. Exercise room, meeting room, and travel services. *1220 Hoffman Highway; 907-543-4305.* **$$$**
Bethel Longhouse Hotel. 39 rooms, standard amenities. *751 Third Avenue; 907-543-4612 or 866-543-4613; www.longhousebethelinn.com.*   **$$-$$$**

DILLINGHAM *map page 319, B-3*

Population: 2,466

◆ RESTAURANTS
Muddy Rudder. Popular restaurant for locals; open for breakfast, lunch, and dinner. *100 Main Street; 907-842-2634.* **$$-$$$**
Murphy's. Restaurant and bar. Formerly named Ricardo's; the old sign is still up. *Wildmill Hill; 907-842-1205.* **$–$$**

◆ LODGING

Beaver Creek Bed & Breakfast. Comfortable home, nice folks. Rooms and cottages. *Aleknagtik Road; 907-842-7335 or 866-252-7335; www.dillinghamalaska. com.* $$

Bristol Inn. Popular, in-town lodge. *104 Main Street; 907-842-2240 or 800-764-9704; www.alaskaoutdoors.com/bristolinn.* $$

KATMAI NATIONAL PARK & PRESERVE *map page 319, C-3*

Visitors information: 907-246-3305; www.nps.gov/katm

◆ WILDERNESS LODGES

Brooks Lodge. Modern cabins circle the rustic main lodge. Activities include fly fishing, brown bear viewing, and tours of the Valley of Ten Thousand Smokes. Packages range from one-day standard to four-day deluxe. A two-night air and lodging package is about $1,200 per person, double occupancy (meals not included). Open June to mid-September. *Reservations: Katmailand, 4125 Aircraft Drive, Anchorage, AK 99502; 907-243-5448 or 800-544-0551; www.katmailand.com.* $$$

Grosvenor Lodge. This lodge, accessible by floatplane, is surrounded by streams and rivers that are a sports-fisherman's paradise. Accommodations are in three cabins with electricity and shared baths. Exclusive and expensive. Open June through September. *Reservations: Katmailand, 4125 Aircraft Drive, Anchorage, AK 99502; 907-243-5448 or 800-544-0551; www.katmailand.com.* $$$

Kulik Lodge. Accessible by floatplane and especially popular with fly fishermen, these two-person cabins are equipped with electricity and baths. Open June to mid-October. *Reservations: Katmailand, 4125 Aircraft Drive, Anchorage, AK 99502; 907-243-5448 or 800-544-0551; www.katmailand.com.* $$$

◆ CAMPGROUND

Brooks Camp Campground. An inexpensive alternative ($8 per night) for camping and bear viewing at Brooks Camp, run by the National Park Service. Well-organized and safe. Reservations necessary. *Reservations: 800-365-2267; reservations.nps.gov.*

◆ TOURS

Coastal Outfitters. Fly-in brown bear photography excursions based from a luxury yacht on the Shelikof Coast of Katmai National Park; also customized fishing tours. Highly recommended. *907-286-2290; www.xyz.net/~bear.*

Katmai Air Service. Daily flightseeing tours from Brooks Camp in Katmai National Park, air charters to and from King Salmon and Katmai National Park wilderness lodges. *P.O. Box 278, King Salmon, AK 99613; 907-246-3079; or 4125 Aircraft Drive, Anchorage, AK 99502; 907-243-5448 or 800-544-0551; www. katmailand.com.*

KING SALMON *map page 319, C-3/4*

Population: 442
Visitors information: 907-246-4250

◆ LODGING
King Ko Inn. Newly remodeled. Cabins with kitchenettes; central lodge with café. *907-246-3377 or 866-234-3474; www.kingko.com.* $–$$$

◆ TOURS
Branch River Air Service. Floatplane service for bear viewing, sightseeing, fishing, and hunting trips on the Alaska Peninsula, including Katmai National Park. *4540 Edinburgh Drive, Anchorage, AK 99515; 907-248-3539 (winter) or P.O. Box 545, King Salmon, AK 99613; 907-246-3437 (summer); www.branchriverair.com.*

KODIAK (KODIAK ISLAND) *map page 319, D-4*

Population: 6,344 (Kodiak city)
Visitors information: 907-486-4782 or 800-789-4782; www.kodiak.org

◆ RESTAURANTS
Eagle's Nest Restaurant. Fine dining, specializing in innovative seafood recipes and steaks; extensive wine list. In the Buskin River Inn. *1395 Airport Way; 907-487-2700; www.kodiakadventure.com.* $$–$$$

El Chicano. Surprisingly authentic Mexican favorites, such as homemade tamales, chiles rellenos, and menudo. *103 Center Street, in the Old Bakery Mall; 907-486-6116.* $

Henry's Great Alaskan Restaurant. A big, boisterous, popular place, with a big menu that includes burgers, sandwiches, pastas, steak, seafood, and desserts. *512 Marine Way; 907-486-8844.* $

King's Diner. Locals come for standard American fare, especially hamburgers. *1941 Mill Bay Road, beside Lilly Lake; 907-486-4100.* $

◆ LODGING

Best Western Kodiak Inn. Comfortable lodging, with a restaurant. *236 Rezanof Drive; 907-486-5712 or 888-563-4254; www.kodiakinn.com.* $$–$$$

Buskin River Inn. Located by the airport, about 4 miles from downtown, with a restaurant on the premises known for its good seafood. Guests can fish for salmon in the river that runs past the hotel. *1395 Airport Way; 907-487-2700 or 800-544-2202; www.kodiakadventure.com.* $$$

Shelikof Lodge. Modern hotel in downtown Kodiak with lounge, restaurant, 38 rooms, and airport shuttle. *211 Thorsheim Avenue; 907-486-4141; www.ptialaska. net/~kyle.* $$

◆ WILDERNESS LODGES

Afognak Wilderness Lodge. Rustic, fully equipped, remote cabins offer nearby hiking, fishing, and photography. *Reservations: Afognak Wilderness Lodge, Seal Bay, AK 99697; 907-486-6442 or 800-478-6442; www.afognaklodge.com.*

Alaska State Parks Cabins. Four public-use cabins (sleeping up to eight people) are available on Shuyak Island for $65 per night. Two cabins on Afognak Island sleep a maximum of six people for $35. Reservations can be made in writing up to six months in advance. *Reservations: 1400 Abercrombie Drive, Kodiak AK 99615; 907-486-6339; www.alaskastateparks.org.* $

Kodiak National Wildlife Refuge Cabins. Seven rustic public-use cabins sleeping four. Maximum seven-day stay; assigned by a lottery; write for application and return it by January 2 for April–June dates, or by April 1 to stay July–September. *Reservations: 1390 Buskin River Road, Kodiak, AK 99615; 907-487-2600 or 888-408-3514; kodiak.fws.gov.* $

◆ TOURS

Dig Afognak. Hands-on participation in an archaeological excavation; five-day programs at remote, comfortable sites on Afognak Island. *Native Village of Afognak. 907-486-6357; www.afognak.org.*

Kodiak Island Charters. Ocean fishing and sightseeing for up to 16 passengers; giant halibut and king salmon are the specialties. *907-486-5380 or 800-575-5380; www.gofishingkodiak.net.*

Kodiak Tours. Daily full- and half-day tours of the city of Kodiak. Also arranges bear-viewing and fishing trips. *907-486-3920; www.kodiaktours.com.*

Kodiak Treks. Hiking and wilderness adventures, bear viewing at a remote lodge on Uyak Bay. *907-487-2122; www.kodiaktreks.com.*

Munsey's Bear Camp. Five-day fishing and photo excursions on the Kodiak Island coastline. Expect spectacular views of brown bears, whales, bald eagles, and puffins. *907-847-2203; www.munseysbearcamp.com.*

Mythos Expeditions. Charter boat for wildlife viewing, kayak trips, and custom adventures. *907-486-5536; www.ptialaska.net/~mythosdk/mythos.*

ST. PAUL (PRIBILOF ISLANDS) *map page 335*

Population: 532 (St. Paul city)
Visitors information: 907-546-2331; www.alaskabirding.com/home.html.

◆ RESTAURANT

Trident Seafoods Galley. Cafeteria-style dining. Seafood and American dishes. Has the advantage of being the only game in town. *Downtown St. Paul; 907-546-2377.*

◆ LODGING

King Eider Hotel. Dating back to the 1880s, this simply decorated but comfortable hotel caters mostly to tour groups who come to the remote island to see the fur-seal rookeries and seabirds. The 25 rooms all have shared baths. *Downtown St. Paul; 907-546-2477.* $$$

◆ TOURS

St. Paul Island Tours. Birding and seal-viewing tours catering to both amateur and professional photographers. View rare species. Highly recommended for serious birders. *877-424-5637; www.alaskabirding. com.*

UNALASKA/DUTCH HARBOR (UNALASKA ISLAND) *map page 335*

Population: 4,283 (Unalaska city)
Visitors information: 907-581-2612 or 877-581-2612; www.unalaska.info

◆ RESTAURANTS

Amelia's. Serves a range of American and Mexican food. Popular breakfast spot. *Off Airport Beach Road, Dutch Harbor; 907-581-2800.* $$

The Chart Room. Fine dining in the Grand Aleutian Hotel. The Wednesday night all-you-can-eat seafood buffet is a local favorite. *498 Salmon Way, Dutch Harbor; 907-581-3844.* $$-$$$

◆ **LODGING**

Grand Aleutian Hotel. This luxury hotel has 106 rooms, six suites, two restaurants, and a three-story atrium lobby with a stone fireplace. *498 Salmon Way, Dutch Harbor; 907-581-3844 or 866-581-3844; www.grandaleutian.com.* $$$

Unisea Inn. Less-expensive sister property to the Grand Aleutian. 20 rooms above the small boat harbor. *907-581-3844 or 866-581-3844; www.grandaleutian.com.* $$

◆ **SPORT FISHING**

F/V Lucille. Captain Dave Magone specializes in halibut and salmon charters. *907-581-5949 ; www.unalaskahalibutfishing.com.*

■ FESTIVALS AND EVENTS

■ JANUARY

Russian New Year and Masquerade Ball, Kodiak. A mid-January celebration of Alaska's colonial heritage. *907-486-3524.*

■ MAY

Kodiak Crab Festival. Held on Memorial Day weekend, the event includes a parade, survival-suit races, a blessing-of-the-fleet ceremony, and musical performances. *907-486-5557.*

■ SEPTEMBER

Kodiak State Fair and Rodeo. For three days ending on Labor Day, Alaskan-style cowboys compete; also features stock car races, watermelon seed–spitting and pie-eating contests, and a crafts fair. *907-486-6380 or 800-789-4782.*

S T A T E W I D E
T R A V E L   I N F O R M A T I O N

NOTE: Much of Alaska is a wilderness and travelers proceed at their own risk. Compass American Guides cannot ensure the safety of any tour or mode of transportation listed in this book for the readers' convenience. We recommend that readers contact the local visitors bureaus for the most up-to-date information (see "Official Tourism Information" in this chapter), as conditions and prices change frequently.

■ AREA CODE AND TIME ZONES

The area code for the entire state of Alaska is 907, except for the town of Hyder, on the Canadian border, which is 604.

Alaska has two time zones. Southeast to the western tip of the mainland is on Alaska time, one hour earlier than Pacific time. The western Aleutians are two hours earlier than Pacific time, in the same time zone as Hawaii. British Columbia and Yukon are on Pacific time.

■ METRIC CONVERSIONS

1 foot = .305 meters   1 mile = 1.6 kilometers   1 pound = .45 kilograms
Centigrade = Fahrenheit temperature minus 32, divided by 1.8

■ CLIMATE AND CLOTHING

Alaska has just about everything in the way of weather—from deep freezes of 80 below zero to heat waves of 90 degrees Fahrenheit, from torrential downpours to blizzards, from gale-force winds to perfect calm. During the summer, rain is frequent, and a rain suit and rubber knee boots are recommended. The main thing, whenever taking a hike or venturing forth into the wilderness, is to dress in layers that can be easily removed or added as conditions dictate. It's not unusual in Alaska to experience temperature swings of 20 to 30 degrees in a matter of an hour or two, and under-dressing is one of the most frequent mistakes visitors make. In late spring through early autumn, clothing made of modern windproof and water-

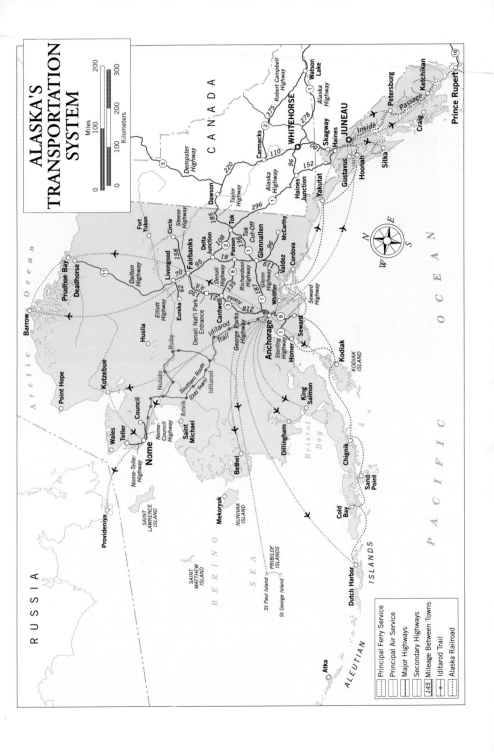

These sled dogs are being transported to Anchorage to take part in the famous Iditarod race, run over one thousand miles from Anchorage to Nome.

proof synthetics—polypropylene fleece and Gore tex–type fabrics—is warm, comfortable, tough, and adaptable; do not rely on cotton garments in damp or wet conditions. Remember that it is always colder on water—streams, rivers, lakes, bays, the ocean—than on land, and prepare appropriately. Binoculars, a folding umbrella, insect repellent, and sunscreen are good to have on hand. Mosquito-net hats or lightweight mesh bug jackets are recommended in marshy areas and many parts of the Interior, where summer infestations can approach biblical proportions.

In the winter, the same layering method applies. Your gear should include a hooded parka of good quality, a wool scarf, a ski mask or balaclava, mittens with liners, and boots with liners. In the winter be certain to drink a lot of water, as frostbite and other effects of cold often occur when tissue has become dehydrated. Cover your cheeks and nose with a scarf or face-mask to prevent frostbite (even a slight wind dramatically lowers the air temperature).

■ GETTING THERE AND GETTING AROUND

■ BY PLANE

Several **major air carriers** serve Anchorage and Fairbanks with daily flights.
Alaska Airlines. *800-426-0333; www.alaskaair.com.*
Delta. *800-221-1212; www.delta.com.*
Northwest. *800-225-2525; www.nwa.com.*
United. *800-241-6522; www.ual.com.*

Juneau is served only by Alaska Airlines. Smaller airlines serve the smaller towns scattered about the state, and light planes can be chartered to virtually any point in the state.

Bush planes offer Alaska travelers the chance to leave the road system behind and see the state's wild corners. They are used by sports fishermen, big-game hunters, wildlife photographers, river rafters, and other passionate nature lovers. The rates can be quite high—several hundred dollars per hour and up, with the rate computed both ways for each trip, because the pilot has to return to the original point. Flying in bush Alaska is generally quite safe; reduce the risks to a minimum by choosing reputable, established flying services.

■ BY FERRY

The **Alaska Marine Highway System**—an excellent ferry system from Bellingham, Washington, to Skagway, Alaska, and points in between in the Inside Passage, as well as to destinations along the western coast as far north as Kodiak—offers another option, for those with more time. Reservations are required year-round, and summer travel should be booked six months in advance. *6858 Glacier Highway, Juneau, AK 99801; 907-465-3941 or 800-642-0066; www.dot.state.ak. us/amhs.*

■ BY CAR

Another option is to drive to Alaska along the **Alaska Highway,** also known as the Alcan, which extends more than 1,500 miles from Dawson Creek, British Columbia (itself hundreds of miles north of the U.S. border), to Fairbanks. This is a major undertaking for both car and driver. The road is no longer the gravel washboard it once was—it's virtually all paved and well-engineered—but it's still hardly a high-speed thruway. Pavement breaks, frost heaves, or potholes are present in certain stretches. Allow a week to 10 days for a leisurely trip. For a mile-by-mile, detailed guide, order a copy of *The Milepost. 800-726-4707; www.themilepost.com.*

■ BY TRAIN

The **Alaska Railroad** provides service between Anchorage and Fairbanks, with stops in such interesting places as Denali National Park. This can be a comfortable and relaxing means of reaching the park. *P.O. Box 107500, Anchorage, AK 99510; 907-265-2494 or 800-544-0552; www.akrr.com.*

■ BY BUS

Various cruise ship lines and sightseeing companies operate guided bus tours of the state. Information about these tours—which are especially popular with seniors and international travelers for whom language poses difficulties—can be had by calling your local travel agent.

Cruise ships and floatplanes line the waterfront of Juneau.

■ ABOUT ACCOMMODATIONS AND WILDERNESS LODGES

(See travel information following each chapter for listings of places to stay throughout the state.) Modern hotels and motels, small lodges, and B&Bs are plentiful in Alaska. Make reservations as early as possible. Wilderness lodges provide rustic but comfortable accommodations (ranging from primitive cabins to very nice guest rooms in a main lodge) and good, occasionally excellent, cuisine. Most are used for sport-fishing and/or big-game hunting trips, but they are also a great place for a leisurely vacation far from the madding crowd. Some lodges—such as the Kantishna Roadhouse, Camp Denali, or the North Face Lodge in Denali National Park—are relatively close to civilization. Others are in the most obscure locations you can imagine—the Unalakleet River in northwestern Alaska, the headwaters of the Wood River in the Alaska Range, the far reaches of the Alaska Peninsula. Wilderness lodges statewide are listed along with other accommodations in the *Alaska: Official State Vacation Planner,* obtainable from the **Alaska Travel Industry Association:** *2600 Cordova Street, Suite 201, Anchorage, AK 99503; 907-929-2200; www.travelalaska.com.*

■ RESERVATION SERVICES

Alaska Private Lodgings. Reservation service for statewide B&Bs and other private accommodations and cabins, and adventure activities. *P.O. Box 200047, Anchorage, AK 99520; 907-235-2148; www.alaskabandb.com.*

Anchorage Alaska Bed & Breakfast Association. Excellent online directory of member properties, with links to let users contact them directly. Toll-free reservation hotline has information on current availability. *P.O. Box 242623, Anchorage, AK 99524; 907-272-5909 or 888-584-5147; www.anchorage-bnb.com.*

Bed and Breakfast Association of Alaska. Provides a online directory and links to properties statewide, many of which offer online reservations. *P.O. Box 202663, Anchorage, AK 99520; www.alaskabba.com.*

■ HOTEL AND MOTEL CHAINS

Best Western. *800-528-1234; www.bestwestern.com.*
Comfort Inn. *800-228-5150; www.comfortinn.com.*
Days Inn. *800-325-2525; www.daysinn.com.*
Econo Lodge. *800-446-6900; www.econolodge.com.*
Hilton. *800-445-8667; www.hilton.com.*
Holiday Inn. *800-465-4329; www.holiday-inn.com.*
Ramada Inns. *800-272-6232; www.ramada.com.*
Westmark Hotels. *800-544-0970; www.westmarkhotels.com.*

■ CABINS, CAMPGROUNDS, HOSTELS

Recreational cabins on public land are scattered throughout Alaska and are among the state's best buys, usually costing from $25 to $45 a night. The greatest number are on **U.S. Forest Service** land—approximately 150 cabins in the Tongass National Forest and about 40 in the Chugach National Forest. For information, contact: *U.S.F.S., 8465 Old Dairy Road, Juneau, AK 99801; 907-586-8800 (Tongass) or 3301 C Street, Anchorage, AK 99503; 907-743-9500 (Chugach); www. fs.fed.us/r10.*

Reservations for all U.S. Forest Service cabins, however, must be made either by phone or online through the **National Recreation Reservation Service:** *877-444-6777; www.reserveusa.com.*

About 40 cabins are available in 15 of the approximately 130 **Alaska State Parks.** They range from $25 to $65 per night and can be reserved by mail (or fax) or in person at state parks area offices or the public information centers run by the Department of Natural Resources, Division of Parks and Outdoor Recreation, in Anchorage and Fairbanks: *550 West Seventh Avenue, Suite 1260, Anchorage, AK 99501; 907-269-8400. 3700 Airport Way, Fairbanks, AK 99709; 907-451-2705. www.dnr.state.ak.us/parks.*

Public campgrounds are operated by the U.S. Forest Service, the National Park Service, the Bureau of Land Management, and Alaska State Parks. The **Alaska Public Lands Information Centers,** one-stop sources of information on all public lands, state or federal, can provide information on all campgrounds, as well as on cabins run by the Forest Service, Alaska State Parks, and other agencies. There are four centers: *605 West Fourth Avenue, Anchorage, AK 99501; 907-271-2737. 250*

Cushman Street, Suite 1A, Fairbanks, AK 99701; 907-456-0527. (Southeast Alaska Discovery Center), 50 Main Street, Ketchikan, AK 99901; 907-228-6220. P.O. Box 359, Tok, AK 99780; 907-883-5667. www.nps.gov/aplic.

Alaska has numerous hostels, but only three (Ketchikan, Ninilchik, and Sitka) are affiliated with Hostelling International (HI). For information on the HI hostels: **Hostelling International–USA,** *8401 Colesville Road, Suite 600, Silver Spring, MD 20910; 301-495-1240; www.hiayh.org.*

For information on all hostels in the state: *www.hostels.com.*

■ FISHING

Probably no other place in North America offers the diversity or quality of fishing as Alaska, whether it is salt water or fresh water, fly or lure or even bait. Most fishermen practice catch and release, especially in trophy waters, but there is also the opportunity for you to ship home (on dry ice) large quantities of halibut, salmon, or pike.

Use a guide if you can possibly afford it—it will be the smartest money you ever spent. (See listings of tour outfits at the end of individual chapters or call the information number listed under the name of each town for advice about local operators.) Guides provide you with the appropriate fishing rod (who among us owns a rod strong enough for a 90-pound salmon or a 250-pound halibut?), the correct lures or legal bait, the safe drift boat or ocean-going craft, and, most important, the expert guidance that will put you into the best areas at the best times.

■ HUNTING

Imagine a place where a state resident license enables the holder to kill three black bears, a grizzly bear, a bull moose, a Dall sheep ram, five caribou per day, three wolves, and so forth. Imagine a herd of 135,000 caribou (the Central Arctic herd) pursued by only 400 sport hunters per year, a ratio of 337 animals per hunter. In Alaska you can hunt for 30 days and never hear another rifle shot or spot the smoke from another campfire—and see game every day.

There are laws regulating what type of game you can hunt. Nonresidents without a guide (but with a license) can hunt black bear, caribou, or moose. With a guide, nonresidents can hunt Dall sheep or grizzly bear. Hiring a guide, however, is costly: a guided 10-day hunt may cost as much as a new car.

If you decide on a non-guided hunting expedition, I suggest you be flown into an area like the Mulchatna River west of Anchorage. You and your buddies (don't even think of hunting alone in the Alaskan outback) will find excellent hunting there, and some of the finest fishing in the state on the river and its tributaries. Get set up in a drop-camp, where someone flies in every couple of days to check on you and transport the meat and antlers out. (It costs a lot to ship the meat out, and if you don't salvage all the meat you will be seeing the inside of an Alaskan jail, not to mention paying fines that will shock you.)

One of the best places for bow-hunting is the road corridor along the Dalton Highway, which begins north of Fairbanks and runs more than 400 miles north to Prudhoe Bay. North of the Yukon River, only bow-and arrow hunting is allowed within a five-mile corridor on either side of the highway. Beyond five miles, rifle hunters may partake, but five miles over tundra is too far to pack out anything, even a Boone and Crockett record-book moose—best to fly into an area where you can float a river or hunt from a well-positioned base camp.

Hunting and trapping licenses are required for all nonresidents (and for residents between the ages of 16 and 60). Licenses may be obtained from any designated issuing agent (such as most sporting goods stores) or by mail or online from the **Alaska Department of Fish and Game:** *Licensing Section, P.O. Box 25525, Juneau, AK 99802; 907-465-2376; www.adfg.state.ak.us.*

■ RIVER RAFTING

Alaska offers some of the finest river rafting in the world, with pristine waters, abundant wildlife, and rivers protected along their entire length, from remote wilderness headwaters to terminal confluences. Some of the best adventures can be had on rivers administered by the Bureau of Land Management (BLM).

■ BEAVER CREEK NATIONAL WILD RIVER

Beaver Creek is popular with the Fairbanks crowd. The river is located in the White Mountains north of town. You put in off the Nome Creek Road on the Steese Highway (Mile 57) and take out near Victoria Creek (accessed only by airplane for the return trip), or—if feeling adventurous—you can float all the way to the Yukon River bridge on the Dalton Highway. Total distance in the first case is 127 miles and, in the latter, 268 miles. There is good fishing for northern pike and arctic grayling along Beaver Creek, and excellent moose and black bear hunting in the fall. This is considered Class I water (a few riffles and small waves). Further information is available from: *BLM, Northern Field Office, 1150 University Avenue, Fairbanks, AK 99709; 907-474-2350; aurora.ak.blm.gov.*

■ BIRCH CREEK NATIONAL WILD RIVER
Birch Creek is another waterway easily accessed from Fairbanks. Rafters put in at Mile 94.5 on the Steese Highway and take out at Mile 147. This trip offers wilderness aficionados a pleasant 126-mile float through the Interior backcountry. Fishing for northern pike and arctic grayling can be quite good. Waters are considered Class I and Class II, with several Class III rapids (long difficult waters for experienced rafters or kayakers only). Travelers often report seeing moose, barren-ground caribou, and black and grizzly bears along Birch Creek, which is popular during the fall hunting season. Further information is available from: *BLM, Northern Field Office, 1150 University Avenue, Fairbanks, AK 99709; 907-474-2350; aurora.ak.blm.gov.*

■ DELTA NATIONAL WILD AND SCENIC RIVER
You'll find the put-in for the Delta River float near the Tangle Lakes on the Denali Highway (Mile 22). This is a 35-mile float, with some turbulent water—Class III rapids—which makes it popular with experienced kayakers. The take-out point is on the Richardson Highway (Mile 212.5). There is good fishing for lake trout in Tangle Lakes. Further information is available from: *BLM, Glennallen Field Office, P.O. Box 147, Glennallen, AK 99588; 907-822-3217; www.ak.blm.gov/gdo/delta1.*

■ FORTYMILE NATIONAL WILD AND SCENIC RIVER
The Fortymile River flows north into the Yukon River from the highlands in east-central Alaska. Access is from the Taylor Highway (Mile 49 or 75). The take-out point is 92 river miles distant at Eagle. There is excellent fishing for arctic grayling and burbot along the Fortymile, as well as good hunting for moose and black bear during the fall hunting season. There is some Class IV (very dangerous) water on this stretch. Further information is available from: *BLM, Northern Field Office, 1150 University Avenue, Fairbanks, AK 99709; 907-474-2350; aurora.ak.blm.gov.*

■ GULKANA NATIONAL WILD RIVER

Gulkana River floats are very popular with Alaskans during the summer. The most common three- to five-day excursion leads down the Main Fork, which is heavily forested, with opportunities to observe moose, eagles, and black and grizzly bears. There is also a king salmon run on the Gulkana that peaks around the summer solstice in late June, which makes it attractive with local fishermen. The trip down the Main Fork is accessed at the Paxon Lake Campground on the Richardson Highway (Mile 161). The take-out is at Sourdough Campground on the Richardson Highway (Mile 147.5). The stretch has one Class III rapid, which at times can be a very tricky proposition. You will see more people on this route than on others in this section, which is a mixed blessing: The higher traffic can mean greater safety, but if you want solitude, the crowds can be a distraction. Further information is available from: *BLM, Glennallen Field Office, P.O. Box 147, Glennallen, AK 99588; 907-822-3217; www.ak.blm.gov/gdo/gulkana1.*

■ UNALAKLEET NATIONAL WILD RIVER

If the crowds on the Gulkana are not for you, then the Unalakleet will be the place. Because it is in an extremely remote corner of northwestern Alaska, the river is seldom visited by summer travelers. Fishing for arctic grayling, arctic char, and salmon (chinook, coho, chum, and pink) is outstanding. You will probably see moose, bears, and eagles along this river. The Unalakleet is accessible only from the air, with the trip typically beginning at Tenmile Creek and continuing 76 miles to the village of Unalakleet. It is normally a Class I (easiest) float. To reach the area you would fly commercial aircraft from Anchorage to Nome or Kotzebue, and then charter an aircraft inland to Tenmile Creek. Further information is available from: *BLM, Anchorage Field Office, 6881 Abbot Loop Road, Anchorage, AK 99507; 907-267-1293; www.anchorage.ak.blm.gov/unkriver.*

■ OFFICIAL TOURISM INFORMATION

Alaska Travel Industry Association. *907-929-2200; www.travelalaska.com.*
Anchorage Convention and Visitors Bureau. *907-276-4118; www.anchorage.net.*
Fairbanks Convention and Visitors Bureau. *907-456-5774 or 800-327-5774; www.explorefairbanks.com.*
Homer Chamber of Commerce. *907-235-7740; www.homeralaska.org.*

Juneau Convention and Visitors Bureau. *907-586-2201 or 888-581-2201; www.traveljuneau.com.*

Kenai Convention and Visitors Bureau. *907-283-1991; www.visitkenai.com.*

Ketchikan Visitors Bureau. *907-225-6166 or 800-770-3300; www.visit-ketchikan.com.*

Kodiak Island Convention and Visitors Bureau. *907-486-4782 or 800-789-4782; www.kodiak.org.*

Mat-Su Convention and Visitors Bureau. *907-746-5000; www.alaskavisit.com.*

Nome Convention and Visitors Bureau. *907-443-6624 or 800-478-1901; www.nomealaska.org/vc.*

Sitka Convention and Visitors Bureau. *907-747-5940; www.sitka.org.*

Valdez Convention and Visitors Bureau. *907-835-4636 or 907-835-2984; www.valdezalaska.org.*

Wrangell Convention and Visitor Bureau. *907-874-2381, 907-874-3901, or 800-367-9745; www.wrangell.com.*

■ FEDERAL AND STATE PARKS, FORESTS, AND REFUGES

Alaska Department of Fish and Game. Information on fishing, hunting, trapping, and recreational activities in state wildlife refuges and sanctuaries, and on the licenses and permits required. *Public Communication Section, P.O. Box 25526, Juneau, AK 99802; 907-465-6166; www.adfg.state.ak.us.*

Alaska Public Lands Information Centers. These inter-agency centers are a superb source of information on state or federal public lands, on everything from bear-viewing areas to cabin reservations. There are four locations. *605 West Fourth Avenue, Anchorage, AK 99501; 907-271-2737. 250 Cushman Street, Suite 1A, Fairbanks, AK 99701; 907-456-0527. (Southeast Alaska Discovery Center), 50 Main Street, Ketchikan, AK 99901; 907-228-6220. P.O. Box 359, Tok, AK 99780; 907-883-5667. www.nps.gov/aplic.*

Alaska State Parks. Public information centers run by the Department of Natural Resources, Division of Parks and Outdoor Recreation, provide info on facilities in Alaska's more than 130 state parks. *550 West Seventh Avenue, Suite 1260, Anchorage, AK 99501; 907-269-8400. 3700 Airport Way, Fairbanks, AK 99709; 907-451-2705. www.dnr.state.ak.us/parks.*

A New Yorker in Alaska

I was celebrating my tenth year as a literary agent in New York when my husband asked if I would like to move to Alaska, much in the same way he would inquire if I would like to split that last bagel. We were sitting in our Hoboken, New Jersey, apartment—seven minutes from the heart of Times Square. Like most denizens of the vast New York metropolitan area, I harbored a love-hate relationship with the city, a relationship that recognized the problems of the place but still considered it the center of the universe. A move out of its orbit, we thought, could easily leave us emotionally and culturally deprived, but by the time my husband received a job offer from the Nature Conservancy of Alaska one month later, my mind was made up. "Let's go," I declared. The deciding factor: I was due to give birth to my first child in the spring. I would soon be obliged to reinvent myself as a mother. How much easier that would be, I reasoned, if I also shed the habits of my child-free self, which had been shaped for so long by one environment.

And so, as I clutched a pile of letters from disbelieving well-wishers wryly wondering "if I could continue my career from an igloo," we boarded an airplane and began a series of flights that would take us north and west to Anchorage. During the long trip, I reflected on the magnitude of the changes ahead. I realized how much we had been looking forward to introducing our child to Hoboken, the birthplace of Frank Sinatra and organized baseball and home of the finest mozzarella and cannolis this side of Naples. I knew he would have been stimulated by the riches of Manhattan— the dinosaurs of the Museum of Natural History, the peregrine falcons in Central Park. What would we do in Anchorage?

We planted our feet on the Anchorage Airport tarmac in the middle of the driest January on record and quickly learned that Alaskans are similar to New Yorkers in that small talk often consists of soliloquies on why they love or hate the place. The first Anchoragite I encountered was the nurse practitioner in the office of my new doctor, who said, "I've put in five years here in Alaska, and I'm getting the heck out next week."

After our son was born I came to learn that one of the greatest joys of motherhood is seeing the world anew from a child's wonder-filled eyes. So much of the world that my son sees for the first time is truly new to me, too: the moose loping down our suburban street, a family of bald eagles standing guard over the post office, the brightly painted Yup'ik masks at the Anchorage Museum of History and Art. I read to him from Cindy Shake's *Alaskan Animal Alphabet*:

N: A NARWALL WATCHES THE NORTHERN LIGHTS OVER NOME
Q: THE QIVIUT QUIVERS WHEN THE MUSK OX SHIVERS.

Images come to both of us from the same lens of inexperience and wonder. As we discover together the abundant attractions of Alaska, so we will encounter its dangers: grizzly and black bears, the sudden, often drastic changes of weather, and winding, one-lane mountain roads. And this city woman–cum–Alaska mother who was once fearless on Manhattan's streets will have to learn a new kind of bravery in order to bring comfort to her son.

–Anne Dubuisson

■ Useful Web Sites

Alaska! Official state site. *www.state.ak.us.*

Alaska Historical Collections. Part of the Alaska State Library's Web site—the Online Collections section is a goldmine of old photos. *www.library.state.ak.us/hist.*

Alaska Historical Society. A brief history of the state, with links to local historical societies. *www.alaskahistoricalsociety.org.*

Alaska Legislature. Click on "Students" and then "The State Capitol" for a video tour of the building. *www.legis.state.ak.us.*

Alaska Magazine. Online version of the magazine that explores "life on the last frontier" 10 times yearly. *www.alaskamagazine.com.*

Alaska Native Heritage Center. The Web site of this Anchorage attraction provides info about Native cultures and links to Native organizations. *www.alaskanative.net.*

Anchorage Daily News. The state's primary daily newspaper. *www.adn.com.*

Exxon Valdez Oil Spill Trustee Council. Facts about the spill and its aftermath. *www.evostc.state.ak.us.*

Fairbanks Daily News-Miner. Daily newspaper with regional coverage. *www.newsminer.com.*

Juneau Empire. Daily news from the state's capital. *www.juneauempire.com.*

The Milepost. All about the state's roads—the Driving Distance Calculator alone is invaluable. *www.themilepost.com.*

Museums Alaska. A rundown of what's happening at museums statewide. *www.museumsalaska.org.*

■ WORDS OF CAUTION

■ BEARS

Never approach an unattended cub, as the sow is always nearby. Never cook in or around your campsite. Walk at least 50 to 100 feet away from camp to cook, so that at night any bear in the vicinity will follow the scent to that spot, not to your camp. Never take food into your tent. Hang it in trees if possible, or store it in a box with clean pots and pans stacked on top of it as an alarm. Dispose of fish entrails as far from your campsite as possible and thoroughly wash your hands. Travel in groups whenever possible. Never hike after dark. Make sounds on the trail that definitely identify you as human. Leave your dogs at home. Carry bear-repellent spray and rehearse its use. If a bear knocks you down or seizes you, and you are unable to deploy the repellent, assume a fetal or cannonball position, with your fingers interlocked behind your neck and elbows bent to knees, so you can protect your head. If the attack persists, fight back vigorously. Sleep with a flashlight, loaded rifle, and repellent very handy. Attacks are very rare.

■ GETTING LOST

If you find yourself lost, do not panic. It is important to relax and stay calm. Sit down, study your surroundings and maps, and listen for sounds that may give you a clue as to your whereabouts. Look for a familiar peak, saddle, or ridge. Remember that the sun and moon rise and set from east to west. If you do not have a compass, examine the foliage to determine the north-to-south orientation of vegetation patterns. Remember that north slopes are generally more heavily forested. If you must spend an unplanned night in the wilderness, take advantage of natural shelters such as caves, rock overhangs, fallen trees, and the bases of large coniferous trees. Look around for edible berries, such as raspberries, blueberries, salmonberries, and rose hips. Always carry emergency gear in your day pack, particularly when you are exploring or scouting from your base camp, which is when people often become lost or disoriented. A day pack should include matches, a candle, lighter fluid, a flashlight, a compass, a poncho, water, food, heavier clothing (hat, gloves, parka, sweater), a map, fishhooks and line, a whistle, a reflecting mirror, and a good knife. Some hikers in Alaska carry sophisticated emergency radios, satellite signaling devices, or GPS especially when traveling in remote wilderness areas.

■ Giardia Lamblia

Giardia is an intestinal parasite that is common in Alaskan water and causes serious gastrointestinal distress. Symptoms include painful intestinal cramps, severe diarrhea, gas, dehydration, dizziness, and extreme listlessness and fatigue. To avoid giardia, boil, filter, or chemically treat all water.

■ Hypothermia

The cold is a real killer in Alaska, and it can pose a threat on a sunny July day as easily as on a dark night in January. Each year, people die after falling in the water while fishing or boating—Alaska's water, much of it glacially fed, is extremely cold. People also die of exposure when they are hiking and suddenly find themselves in a rain, sleet, or snowstorm. Whatever the case, the symptoms are as follows: uncontrollable shivering, cold extremities, and a confused and eventually indifferent mental state. Treatment should never include alcohol, which dilates the blood vessels and accelerates heat loss. It should include wrapping the victim in dry warm clothing, placing him or her in a sleeping bag, or warming him with the body heat of another. To avoid frostbite dress warmly, keep your nose, cheeks, ears, and hands covered, avoid prolonged exposure to the cold, and keep your body fully hydrated.

■ Mosquitoes

Bring plenty of bug spray and avoid low-lying areas, especially when there is little wind. Try to stay near windy ridgetops or as near the breezy shoreline as you can. In parts of Alaska, a head net, long-sleeved shirt, and gloves are a necessity for up to a month every summer. The worst I ever encountered was at Wonder Lake in Denali National Park. The mosquitoes were so bad around the lake that I ran up a 2,000 foot ridge, trailing a cloud of them, to finally reach a point where there was a strong breeze. I stayed up there, shooting pictures of Denali, until after one in the morning, at which time it was safe to descend.

■ Road Travel

In Alaska, wild animals often venture onto the road and create deadly traffic hazards. Always be alert, particularly at dusk, during the night, and at dawn, when animals are especially active.

Alaska embraces several habitat zones. The rain forest here is within walking distance of downtown Sitka, in the Sitka National Historical Park, which is known for its totem poles.

RECOMMENDED READING

Abbey, Edward. *Beyond the Wall, Essays from the Outside* (1984). This book contains a great essay about a river-rafting trip that Abbey took in the Arctic National Wildlife Refuge.

Barker, James H. *Always Getting Ready: Upterrlainarluta: Yup'ik Eskimo Subsistence in Southwest Alaska* (1993). A beautifully photographed portrait of the Native people of the Southwest delta.

Blackman, Margaret B. *Sadie Brower Neakok: An Iñupiaq Woman* (1989). A biography of a fascinating Alaskan figure, the magistrate of Barrow for almost 20 years, as well as an exploration of the unique modern culture of the Arctic.

Brower, Kenneth. *Earth and the Great Weather: The Brooks Range* (1973). Brower's large-format book is now considered a classic of Arctic literature; the photographs are truly outstanding.

Caras, Roger. *Monarch of Deadman Bay: The Life and Death of a Kodiak Bear* (1969). Caras is perhaps our best writer of animal stories, and this is a must-read for anyone visiting the Pacific Coast islands of Alaska.

Carrighar, Sally. *Icebound Summer* (1953). Carrighar's wonderful book details her stay one summer in the Arctic.

Crisler, Lois. *Arctic Wild* (1958). This book documents the stay of a husband and wife in a remote Alaskan wilderness—essential reading for all potential cabin builders.

Goetzmann, William H., and Kay Sloan. *Looking Far North: The Harriman Expedition to Alaska, 1899* (1982). Both John Muir and John Burroughs were part of this historic expedition and this account is an exciting read, illustrated with lovely photographs by Edward Curtis.

Haines, John. *The Stars, the Snow, the Fire: Twenty-Five Years in the Alaska Wilderness* (1989). If you can only afford one book, buy this one. Haines shows you the real Alaska—he lived in the bush for nearly 40 years. Other notable works include *Living off the Country: Essays on Poetry and Place* (1981) and *Fables and Distances* (1996).

Higginson, Ella. *Alaska, the Great Country* (1908). Some fine passages about the Inner Passage. Author Ella Higginson was the Annie Dillard of her day.

Holthaus, Gary, and Robert Hedin. *Alaska: Reflections on Land and Spirit* (1989). This is one of the better literary anthologies, with essays by John Haines, Richard Nelson, and others.

Hopkins, D., J. Matthews, C. Schweger, and S. Young, eds. *Paleoecology of Beringia* (1982). A fascinating if highly scientific read about the land bridge between Asia and North America.

Jans, Nick. *The Last Light Breaking*. Compelling tales of life in the far, far north. Also *The Grizzly Maze: Timothy Treadwell's Fatal Obsession with Alaska Bears* (Dutton, 2005).

London, Jack. *The Call of the Wild* (1904). A timeless story about a dog and all that a dog symbolizes of man's atavism.

Lopez, Barry. *Arctic Dreams* (1986). A scholarly look at life in the far north, by one of our great contemporary naturalists.

Keith, Sam, and Richard Proenneke. *One Man's Wilderness: An Alaskan Odyssey* (1973). In his fifties, Richard Proenneke traveled to Lake Clark, built a cabin, and loved it so much he stayed nearly 30 years. This classic, written by Sam Keith from Proenneke's journals, chronicles the first 16 months.

Marshall, Robert. *Arctic Village: A 1930s Portrait of Wiseman, Alaska* (1933). A detailed look at life in an Eskimo village in the Brooks Range. *Arctic Wilderness* (1956) is a memoir (published posthumously) of Marshall's pioneering explorations in what is today, thanks to him, Gates of the Arctic National Park.

McPhee, John. *Coming into the Country* (1976). McPhee is one of our best travel writers, and this is an excellent read.

Merton, Thomas. *Thomas Merton in Alaska: The Alaskan Conferences, Journals, and Letters* (1989). Thomas Merton, a Trappist monk and one of the seminal minds of the 20th century, chronicles his 1968 visit to Alaska.

Milton, John. *Nameless Valleys, Shining Mountains* (1970). John Milton and Ken Brower crossed the Brooks Range on foot from south to north in the late 1960s; this book is a journal of that incredible adventure.

THE SPIRIT OF AN ADVENTURER

"Now don't," I said, shouting to make myself heard in the storm, "now don't, Stickeen. What has got into your queer noodle now? You must be daft. This wild day has nothing for you. There is no game abroad, nothing but weather. Go back to camp and keep warm, get a good breakfast with your master, and be sensible for once. I can't carry you all day or feed you, and this storm will kill you."

But Nature, it seems, was at the bottom of the affair, and she gains her ends with dogs as well as with men, making us do as she likes, shoving and pulling us along her ways, however rough, all but killing us at times in getting her lessons driven hard home. After I stopped again and again, shouting good warning advice, I saw that he was not to be shaken off. . . . The pitiful wanderer just stood there in the wind, drenched and blinking, saying doggedly, "Where thou goest I will go." So at last I told him to come on if he must, and gave him a piece of the bread I had in my pocket; then we struggled on together, and thus began the most memorable of all my wild days.

–John Muir, *Stickeen: The Story of a Dog*, 1909

Muir, John. *Travels in Alaska* (1915). Muir's prose is strong and vibrant, especially when he writes of Glacier Bay. This should be read by all those visiting the Southeast. Another Muir classic is *Stickeen: The Story of a Dog* (1909), a delightful book about his journey through Alaska with his half-wild companion, Stickeen.

Murie, Adolph. *A Naturalist in Alaska* (1961). Award-winning collection of informal essays on the wildlife of interior Alaska, with drawings by the author's brother, biologist Olaus Murie. Also recommended for those visiting Denali is *The Wolves of Mount McKinley* (1944).

Murie, Margaret. *Two in the Far North* (1962). Murie tells the story of her marriage to the biologist Olaus Murie, and of their incredible adventure in the Alaskan bush before Alaska became a state.

Murray, John A., ed. *A Republic of Rivers: Three Centuries of Nature Writing from Alaska and the Yukon* (1990). An anthology ranging from a chronicle of a journey to the Bering Sea in 1741 to contemporary writings. Other works on

Alaskan wildlife edited by Murray include *The Great Bear: Contemporary Writings on the Grizzly Bear* (1992) and *Out Among the Wolves: Contemporary Writings on the Wolf* (1993). Murray has also written *Grizzly Bears: An Illustrated Field Guide* (1995).

Naske, Claus-M., and Herman Slotnick. *Alaska: A History of the 49th State* (1987). Full of archival photographs from the marvelous collection at the University of Alaska, Fairbanks.

Nelson, Richard. *Hunters of the Northern Forest* (1973). *Hunters of the Northern Ice* (1969). *Make Prayers to the Raven: A Koyukon View of the Northern Forest* (1983). *The Island Within* (1989). A cultural anthropologist, Nelson writes eloquently of native ethnography.

Roberts, David. *The Mountain of My Fear* (1968). An extremely well-written and moving account of Roberts' journey to Denali. Also, *Deborah: A Wilderness Narrative* (1970).

Sheldon, Charles. *The Wilderness of the Upper Yukon* (1911). Written by one of the first literary naturalist-hunters to visit the northland. Another excellent book, especially in preparation for a trip to Kodiak, is *The Wilderness of the North Pacific Coast Islands* (1912). Also *The Wilderness of Denali* (1930), in which Sheldon, who is considered the father of the national park, writes of his first trip to Denali.

Sherwonit, Bill. *Iditarod: The Great Race to Nome* (1991). Everything you ever wanted to know about this spectacular sports event, with stunning color photographs by Jeff Schultz.

Stuck, Hudson. *The Ascent of Denali (Mount McKinley)* (1914). Reverend Stuck's legendary ascent of Denali is a great read—he was an accomplished writer as well as an indefatigable climber of mountains. His *Ten Thousand Miles with a Dog Sled* (1914) is a fascinating account of his tour of the interior of Alaska, during which he visited remote bush villages and spread his faith—back in the days before trains, planes, and automobiles had made their way to the frosty northland.

I N D E X

COMPASS AMERICAN GUIDES

Critics, booksellers, and travelers all agree: you're lost without a Compass.

"This splendid series provides exactly the sort of historical and cultural detail about North American destinations that curious-minded travelers need."
—*Washington Post*

"This is a series that constantly stuns us...no guide with photos this good should have writing this good. But it does." —*New York Daily News*

"Of the many guidebooks on the market, few are as visually stimulating, as thoroughly researched, or as lively written as the Compass American Guide series."
—*Chicago Tribune*

"Good to read ahead of time, then take along so you don't miss anything."
—*San Diego Magazine*

"Magnificent photography. First rate."—*Money*

"Written by longtime residents of each destination...these handsome and literate guides are strong on history and culture, and illustrated with gorgeous photos."
—*San Francisco Chronicle*

"The color photographs sparkle, the archival illustrations illuminate windows to the past, and the writing is usually of the utmost caliber." —*Michigan Tribune*

"Class acts, worth reading and shelving for keeps even if you're not a traveler. "
—*New Orleans Times-Picayune*

"Beautiful photographs and literate writing are the hallmarks of the Compass guides." —*Nashville Tennessean*

"History, geography, and wanderlust converge in these well-conceived books."
—*Raleigh News & Observer*

"Oh, my goodness! What a gorgeous series this is."—*Booklist*

COMPASS AMERICAN GUIDES

Alaska	Kentucky	Pennsylvania
American Southwest	Las Vegas	Santa Fe
Arizona	Maine	South Carolina
Boston	Manhattan	South Dakota
California Wine Country	Massachusetts	Tennessee
Cape Cod	Michigan	Texas
Chicago	Minnesota	Utah
Coastal California	Montana	Vermont
Colorado	New Hampshire	Virginia
Connecticut & Rhode Island	New Mexico	Washington
Florida	New Orleans	Washington Wine Country
Georgia	North Carolina	Wisconsin
Gulf South	Oregon	Wyoming
Hawaii	Oregon Wine Country	
Idaho	Pacific Northwest	

Compass American Guides are available at special discounts for bulk purchases for sales promotions or premiums. Special editions, including personalized covers, excerpts of existing books, and corporate imprints, can be created in large quantities for special needs. For more information, write to Special Markets/Premium Sales, 1745 Broadway, MD 6-2, New York, NY 10019 or e-mail specialmarkets@randomhouse.com.

ACKNOWLEDGMENTS

■ FROM THE AUTHOR

From John Murray for the original edition: I have many thanks to give. First a word of appreciation to my good friend Jeff Gnasse, who put me in touch with Kit Duane at Compass. Also, much gratitude to the many individuals who helped me in Denali National Park—Rick McIntyre, Fred Dean, Ken Kehrer, Russ Berry, Bill McDonald, Michio Hoshino, and Ralph Cunningham. Two fishing guides were most helpful during my annual trips to the Kenai River—Robert Johnson of Ken's Bait and Tackle Shop in Soldotna and Eric Painter of American Wildland Adventures in Cooper's Landing. A special thanks to former colleagues in the English Department at the University of Alaska, Fairbanks: Eric Heyne, Roy Bird, Joe Dupras, Burns Cooper, Lillian Corti, Mark Box, Dave Stark, Mike Schuldiner, Joan Worley. All offered good company and cheer. And finally, deepest thanks to four outstanding Alaskans—Joe Firmin, Lynn Castle, Billy Campbell, and Michio Hoshino.

■ FROM THE PUBLISHER

Compass American Guides would like to thank Jamie Bollenbach for "Art and Culture in Anchorage" and "Alaska Politics"; Nick Jans for "Arctic Seasons" and "Wolves Are Listening," both excerpts from his book *A Place Beyond*, and for his essay, "Bush Etiquette"; Mina Jacobs and Walter Van Horn of the Anchorage Museum of History and Art and Amy Bollenbach of Homer for their contributions to the original edition of this book; and Rachel Elson for copyediting the manuscript of this edition, Ellen Klages for proofreading it, and Joan Stout for indexing it.

All photographs in this book are by Don Pitcher unless noted below. Compass American Guides would like to thank the following individuals and institutions for the use of their photographs or illustrations:

HISTORY:
Page 19, Anchorage Museum of History and Art ▪ Pages 20–21, Bancroft Library, University of California, Berkeley ▪ Page 22, Anchorage Museum of History and Art ▪ Page 23, Anchorage Museum of History and Art ▪ Page 24, Bancroft Library Page 26, Jean-Michel Addor ▪ Page 27, Anchorage Museum of History and Art ▪

Page 32, Library of Congress Geography and Map Division ▪ Page 34, U.S. National Archives & Records Administration ▪ Page 35, Anchorage Museum of History and Art

PEOPLE
Page 41, Anchorage Museum of History and Art ▪ Page 43, Anchorage Museum of History and Art ▪ Pages 44–45, Beinecke Rare Book and Manuscript Library, Yale University ▪ Page 46, Edward S. Curtis Gallery ▪ Page 47, Anchorage Museum of History and Art ▪ Page 48, Beinecke Rare Book and Manuscript Library ▪ Pages 50–51, Anchorage Museum of History and Art

WILDLIFE
Page 58, Nick Jans ▪ Page 77, Nick Jans

SOUTHEAST AND THE INSIDE PASSAGE
Page 86, Anchorage Museum of History and Art ▪ Page 94, Bancroft Library, University of California, Berkeley ▪ Page 105, Alaska Historical Collections, Alaska State Library ▪ Page 112, Bancroft Library, U.C. Berkeley ▪ Page 113, Alaska Historical Collections ▪ Page 116, Bancroft Library, U.C. Berkeley

SOUTH-CENTRAL
Page 145, Anchorage Museum of History and Art ▪ Pages 152–153, Anchorage Museum of History and Art

INTERIOR
Page 248, Alaska Aviation Heritage Museum, Anchorage ▪ Page 254, R.D. Caughron ▪ Page 256, R.D. Caughron

THE ARCTIC:
Page 274, Nick Jans ▪ Page 279, Nick Jans ▪ Page 280, Nick Jans ▪ Page 283, Nick Jans ▪ Page 284, Nick Jans ▪ Page 285, Nick Jans ▪ Page 288, Nick Jans ▪ Page 291, Nick Jans ▪ Page 300, University of Washington Libraries, Special Collections Division, Eric A. Hegg Photograph Collection, PH Coll 274 ▪ Page 302, Nick Jans ▪ Page 303, Nick Jans

SOUTHWEST:
Page 328, Anchorage Museum of History and Art ▪ Page 337, Beinecke Rare Book and Manuscript Library, Yale University

■ ABOUT THE AUTHOR

John Murray worked as an English professor at the University of Alaska, Fairbanks from 1988 through 1994. He has published more than 40 books, including *A Republic of Rivers, Grizzly Bears,* and *Out Among the Wolves.* He is currently the editor of Fulcrum Books' annual *American Nature Writing* anthology of works by known and emerging writers. His reviews, interviews, essays, and articles have appeared in such periodicals as the *Washington Post,* the *Bloomsbury Review,* and *Publishers' Weekly.*

■ CONTRIBUTOR

Nick Jans, who revised this edition of *Compass Alaska,* is a full-time writer and photographer who has lived in Alaska for 26 years, 24 of them in remote Native villages. He is a contributing editor to *Alaska Magazine* and a member of *USA Today*'s board of editorial contributors. He has published essays in magazines and periodicals ranging from *Readers Digest* to the Japanese language arts monthly *Switch.* His fifth book, *The Grizzly Maze,* was published in 2005. Jans currently lives in Juneau with his wife, Sherrie, two dogs, two parrots, and an orphan mink.

■ ABOUT THE PHOTOGRAPHER

After receiving a master's degree in fire ecology from the University of California at Berkeley, Don Pitcher spent 15 summers in the wilds of Alaska and Wyoming, doing work that encompassed everything from mapping grizzly habitat to operating salmon weirs. He is now a photographer and travel writer, basing his travels from Homer, Alaska, where he lives with his wife, Karen Shemet, and their children, Aziza and Rio. Don photographed Compass American Guides' *Wyoming* and is the author of other guides to Alaska, Wyoming, Washington, Yellowstone, and the San Juan Islands. His images have appeared in a multitude of other publications, and his prints are available in Alaskan galleries.

Unleash the Possibilities of Travel With Fodor's

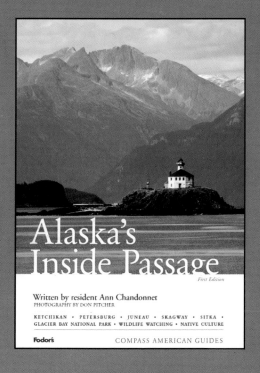

Created by local writers and photographers, our unique Compass Guide brings to life the history, character, and culture of Alaska's Inside Passage.

- Stunning images by one of Alaska's top photographers

- Tips on packing, wildlife watching, and crafts shopping

- The best attractions of the incredible waterway, from Glacier Bay National Park to Haines' bald eagles

Fodor's

For Choice Travel Experiences